Concert Sound

Tours, Techniques & Technology

From the editors of *Mix* magazine

Edited by David (Rudy) Trubitt

Hal Leonard Publishing Corporation

Library of Congress Card Number: 92-075169

These articles were previously published in a somewhat different form in *Mix* magazine.

Book design by Michael Zipkin.

Production staff: David Schwartz, series editor; Brad Smith, general manager; Georgia George, production director; Todd Souvignier, editorial manager; Andy Jewett, editorial assistant.

Cover photos: Steve Jennings (lower right), Jay Blakesberg (upper left) and Susana Millman (background shot).

Photographer credits: Steve Jennings [pp. 3, 5, 8, 9, 11, 17, 21, 33, 34, 46, 77, 78, 79, 80, 81, 85 (top), 87, 88, 91, 92, 93, 95, 96, 97, 99, 100 (top), 102, 103, 109, 119, 120, 121, 123, 124, 127, 128, 129, 132, 133, 135, 137, 141]; Jay Blakesberg [pp. 7, 20, 49, 53, 55, 83, 84, 85 (bottom), 100 (bottom), 105, 107, 113, 114 (bottom), 116, 117, 131]; Tim Benko [p. 149]; Joe Giron [pp. 159, 160, 161]; Lewis Lee [p. 106]; Susanna Millman [p. vii (bottom)]; Henry Diltz [p. 89]; Rudy Arias [p. 114 (top)]; Elizabeth Annas [p. 70]; Ron Delany [p. 139]; Stan Studio [pp. 143, 145].

Graphics by Chuck Dahmer.

Special thanks to Deanne Franklin and Ralph Jones, whose suggestions helped make the book more useful.

MIXBOOKS
6400 Hollis St., Suite 12
Emeryville, CA 94608
(510) 653-3307

Also from MixBooks
Sound For Picture
Music Producers
Hal Blaine and the Wrecking Crew

MixBooks is a division of Act III Publishing.

Printed in Winona, Minnesota, USA

ISBN 0-7935-1991-8

Table of Contents

Clubs and Theaters

Festivals

Introduction

THE PATH TO KNOWLEDGE IS NOT ALWAYS AN EASY ONE. THIS IS ESPECIALLY TRUE IN THE live sound field, where many are self-taught, learning by their mistakes and from observing the techniques of others. Most of us would benefit from a detailed conversation with an experienced professional, but these valuable encounters are rare.

That's why we've assembled this book. In these pages, you'll find advice from dozens of pros in the sound reinforcement field. In their own words, you'll hear how they do their jobs night after night, working behind the scenes with the world's top performers. (Please note that this book is not an introductory text. If you're starting fresh, you should also get a book on the basics, such as Yamaha's *Sound Reinforcement Handbook.*)

Concert Sound is divided into two basic sections. The first contains chapters which tackle specific live sound topics—everything from miking drums to finding a job to saving your hearing. You'll find a broad selection of information you won't find in any other book.

The second section profiles individual tours, ranging from club gigs to massive stadium shows. In these chapters, you'll hear top engineers describe their own special tips and techniques. Because there are quite a few tours covered, we've included a special topic finder on pages 74-75 to help you locate advice on the subjects that interest you most.

I've always learned by asking, and I'm especially grateful to all those who have taken the time to answer. I hope this book will encourage some questions and answers of your own.

David (Rudy) Trubitt

Foreword

WHEN I STARTED OUT, SOUND SYSTEMS WERE CALLED PUBLIC ADDRESS (P.A.) SYSTEMS. There were just two- and four-channel microphone mixers. Speakers were made of metal and sounded accordingly. Mix booths with consoles were something you found in a studio. Whether it was a musical event or the governor was in town to speak, the system was the same.

In 1966, I was working as a recording engineer and electronics designer in a studio owned by a man named Lloyd Pratt, a well-known '50s cabaret bass player who gave me my start. One night I went to see the Grateful Dead at the Fillmore Auditorium. The sound system was one little speaker on each side of the stage—Pigpen was singing, but there was just a gurgle coming out. Being accustomed to hearing music over high-quality monitors—and being somehow blown away with what I thought was the Dead's (and the entire San Francisco music scene's) musical direction—I immediately flashed on a sound system scaled proportionally to what the band was doing. That meant the system would have to grow in quality and quantity by a factor of about a trillion. When I described this vision to the band, they seemed to agree, and in fact encouraged it. That's what I love about the Dead; they're willing to experiment, and the fact that they give a damn about playing music and know what that means made it possible for us to create and achieve what is now many chapters in the book of rock and roll sound.

I began developing my version of this model of concert sound and at the same time began producing and engineering records in the San Francisco music scene, which by 1967 was thriving. One of the basic concepts in this model was to create, if possible, what I called the "studio listening environment" live for an entire audience. To do it, I had to break a number of sacred precedents. The first real shock to the promoter vultures was our then-ridiculous request to mix from the center of the audience instead of the traditional backstage "wings" or side position. Since this "killed" profitable seating, they thought it was extravagantly absurd. Another of my sins was having the nerve to replace the hopelessly inadequate little mic mixers with large studio mix boards with many inputs, patch bays, and effects bus capabilities. This one offended the old-school studio engineers as well. It's a story of change that we all take for granted today, but at one time, we shed blood for it.

We have always been experimenters, designing and building a lot of equipment from scratch. We started in the '60s hopping up guitar amps, creating hybrid guitars and electronics, and eventually wound up involved in every facet of sound development.

By the beginning of the '70s, a consortium of pretty bright thinkers were experimenting with substances including sound-oriented electronics, speaker design, amplifiers, microphones, etc. That was the crux of what was known as the "Wall of Sound," a sound system sponsored and owned by the Grateful Dead and created by this consortium to conduct experiments. We were asking questions that hadn't been answered, at least to

BY

DAN

HEALY

The Wall of Sound in 1974; Healy

our satisfaction. The "Wall" was an "Erector set" that could be configured in virtually limitless ways. As much as possible, we tried to do it differently each time we played. We experimented not only with different configurations, but different components.

Ultimately, we designed and built most of the electronics involved, because no one except us was questioning the fundamentals, such as what different filters sounded like, what capacitors of different composition sounded like, even what distortion was inherently found in wires, switches and connectors. The audio electronics community in the '60s scoffed when we proposed non-inductive speaker wire and oxygen-free copper wire. Today this is commonly considered important.

Until the Wall, large-scale sound reinforcement stemmed from principles mostly developed by Bell Labs and Western Electric, beginning with the telephone and then with P.A. development for the motion picture industry (talkies), which began in 1927. Between then and 1960, very little more was done to research speaker or electronics design. The transistor was the first real news in years, but it was really when NASA funded the development of the integrated circuit that high-density technology began to get into gear. The early-generation crossovers and signal processors, which would have been prohibitively large with tube technology, weren't compact or reliable enough even with transistors. If the microprocessors we use in our system today were made with tubes, they would fill Madison Square Garden and heat half of Manhattan.

During the Wall period, we would sometimes go back to the shop and stay up three days in a row preparing a new idea for the next weekend's show. One of the places we played at a lot was Winterland, and if nothing else were going on, we would con the management into letting us in days early. We'd spend long hours experimenting, conducting tests and then tearing it down and rebuilding it. By the mid '70s the economy succumbed to inflation, and it was no longer possible to support the Wall. It was very large, very heavy, took a long time to set up and was very expensive to transport. However, we gained immensely in experience and knowledge. It had served its purpose.

Between 1976 and 1981 the Dead toured with rental systems. During this time John Meyer, one of the original members of the "consortium," took what we learned from the Wall, along with his own research, and developed the forerunner of what we have today.

Efficiency on all levels was the operative term: high-level electronics, computerization, complete speaker, horn and cabinet redesigns, rigging and transport considerations—a whole new system from the ground up. It sounded better, had greater sound output, was much more compact, took fewer people less time to set up and tear down, and had the flexibility to be configured for all applications.

Ultrasound is who we have today. They own and maintain our entire system, which began as a Meyer but is now a "Grateful Hybrid." While they do work for other people, they are the sound of the Grateful Dead. Ultra's Don Pearson has been an instigator, cohort and true friend, without whom we would be in the Dark Ages. For example, he devised the use of computer mapping of our venues, scanning in architectural drawings alongside scale models of our speaker systems. We can then "set up" the system and know what the place will sound like before we get there. Don was also the first to use fast Fourier analysis combined with equalization modification and image correcting in real time. With it, we can turn a sports arena into a concert hall. It's light-years ahead of anything else.

When it's all working as planned, I can "erase" the sound of the room and the sound of the system, leaving just the band, the audience and the music. It's truly the experience of a lifetime. By the gift of the Great Spirit and phenomenal luck I have had the opportunity to work and learn and be helped by the best of the best, and for this I'm eternally thankful. They're the ones who deserve the real credit. I'm just the mixer.

Dan Healy, 1993

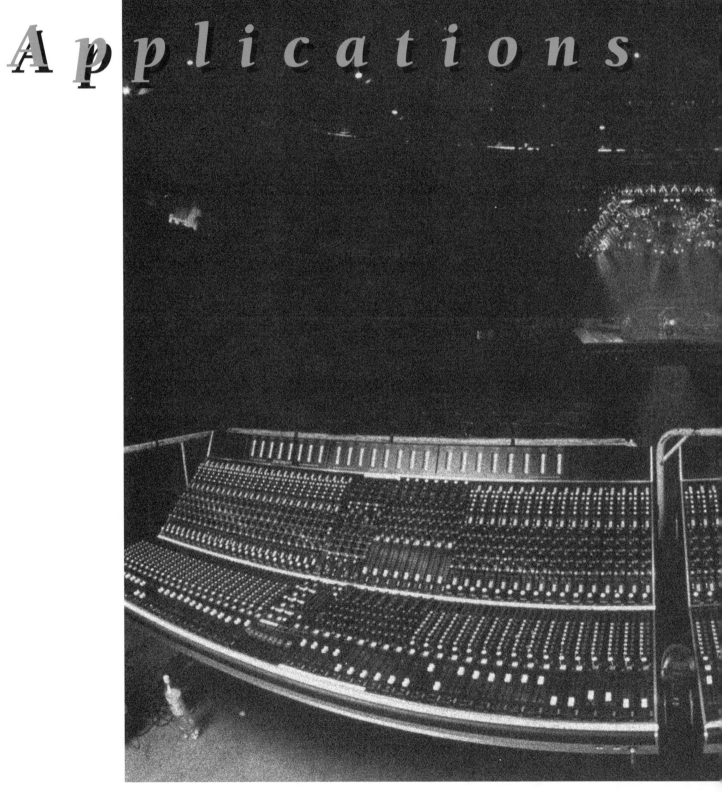

Applications

The Psychology of Monitor Mixing

T HE MONITOR MIXER HAS ONE OF THE hottest seats in sound reinforcement. He or she can make a good show great, by helping the band play at its peak. However, a difficult venue, poor equipment or an inadequate mix can have the opposite effect. There are endless stories about angry musicians taking out their frustrations on monitor engineers. So the ultimate goal is communication with the players—how to build it and when to use it. But first, let's meet some of the engineers who've got it.

In The Beginning

Geep Parker started like many who entered the live sound field in the late '60s: He hooked up with a local band during his college days. The band was signed, their label was bought, and Parker followed them from the Midwest to California in 1970. When the band split, Parker wound up at an early management company of Jackson Browne's, doing sound for Browne and Bonnie Raitt. In '74 Parker moved to Nashville to work with Carlo Sound, Browne's contracted sound company. "I was involved with the early Eagles, the late Allman Brothers, the Bay City Rollers and a lot of Southern rock bands like Wet Willie," Parker says.

Parker describes the trend towards specialization during that period. "It became more difficult to do several different jobs. What used to be an 18-foot truck filled with lights, sound and band equipment became a 48-foot truck filled with nothing but sound. At Carlo, the monitor mixer

progressed to front-of-house—that's the way it was with a lot of early sound companies. But more people were specializing, because if you were actually doing your job to take care of the monitors and plug in the stage, you didn't have time to get out and survey the house and figure out what was going on there." In 1978 Parker joined Maryland Sound Industries (MSI), and has been there ever since.

Paul Sontheimer began his travels as a musician and woodworker. After a move to Dallas in the late '70s, he landed a job in Showco's woodshop building cabinets. He began mixing monitors for Showco in 1981. "My first monitor gig was a trial by fire, with people yelling at me and this and that," says Sontheimer. "I just tried to maintain my composure through it all. Right after that I mixed the opening acts for a Chaka Khan tour. I learned how to run the monitor board, learned some of the tricks of EQ'ing vocal mics. I spent three years with Rick James. It was a lot of work, but I learned how to mix big 12-piece bands. In the early '80s, Showco did a lot of R&B bands, so I did The Barclays, Cameo and people like that." Following that, Sontheimer worked with James Taylor in the mid-'80s. "That was good," he says, "because it gave me a different perspective on sound. Before that it didn't matter how it sounded, as long as you could get it loud enough."

Trust

"Doctor" Dave Staub was with MSI from '79 to '88. During that stint, he worked

BY DAVID
(RUDY)
TRUBITT

Eric Clapton, Paul Simon

with acts such as Harry Chapin, Juice Newton, Frankie Valli and Whitney Houston. Next came Paul Simon's "Graceland" tour in 1987. After a break from the road, Staub was called back for Simon's "Rhythm of the Saints" world tour with Clair Brothers. "Doing monitors for a band is more of a sociological or psychological thing," Staub says. "Anybody can come out here and be a good technician and get the monitors loud, but the bottom line is to get the band to trust you. If they're comfortable working with you, and you with them, you get trust. I find, especially at this point [during the tour], that I have very few conversations with the band during the show. There are some incidental things, but I don't change anything much during the show. I try to get the band thinking that if it doesn't sound right, maybe it's something that someone on stage is doing. Otherwise, I have 18 people looking at me constantly through the whole show."

But how is trust built? "It was hard to get it with Paul," Staub admits. "It took me all of '87, which is why I'm back out with him now. It took a little while to get [drummer] Steve Gadd around, too. I don't think he'd ever done a tour like this before, and he was uncomfortable at first. I had to say, 'Here's what's going on, here's what I can and can't do about it, and together we can try things and make it work.' Honesty is always the best policy. You go out and tell people what you can and can't do and you hope that they'll respond to that. Also, everybody [on the Simon tour] understands how complicated this is—it's definitely one of the most complex systems on the road."

Parker describes another reason why trust is essential. "The great catch-22 of any musician's career is that they can't hear themselves play [from the audience's perspective]. No matter how many videotapes you make, the musicians can't sit in the audience and hear it exactly as they do," continues Parker, "so the band has to build a trust with the people they're working with. The artist has to be confident that you know what you're talking about, and they have to inspire trust in you that what they're saying has some validity. But of course, this is a service industry and the customer is always right."

The Relationship

The most delicate part of a monitor engineer's job may be building a working relationship with the artist. Paul Sontheimer comments on his longest gig to date—Showco client Eric Clapton. "He's a great guy. I worked with him for six years, up until last year. I learned a lot about the psychology of monitors—when to say things and when not to say things. You know by the end of three songs what it's going to be like and how you're going to act for the rest of the show. Either you'll keep a low profile or laugh and joke with people—it's just one of those things you pick up on. There were a few times working for Eric when I might have pressed a point too much by asking him too many questions. That's how I learned when to back off and leave a musician, who has a lot more on his mind than just technical things, alone."

"In a long-term relationship," Parker says, "you learn their interests. They don't want to know which power amps produce what, they want to know the result and if you can get it. In a short-term situation, you have to suss it out, and that's where experience comes in. You have to trust your instincts."

Another useful skill is the ability to keep a cool head in tense situations. "There are horror stories about the artist who is unable to be pleased, no matter what," Parker continues. "You hear about artists who will throw things at the monitor mixer, or stalk off the stage and blame it on the technician. Well, it happens. We've all been fired from a gig, whether in the middle of a tour or after it's over. It's

unavoidable, because sometimes the personality mix just isn't there."

"An interesting experience came up when Phil Collins joined the Clapton tour," Sontheimer volunteers. "I had a few technical problems one night, and Phil gave me a look like, 'Hey, what's going on here?' You could see that the man was upset. I was called into the dressing room after the show and he tells me, 'No matter what happens out there, when the show's over, that was out there. In the heat of the moment I'm going to get mad, but don't take it literally.'"

One point was mentioned more than once: "If the artist doesn't say anything, you assume there isn't a problem," Parker says. Sontheimer concurs: "If nobody said anything bad, then you assume it's good. Don't go looking for trouble or fishing for answers or trying to find out what the vibe was. If you don't hear anything, you're doing fine."

Dealing With Requests

"When working with musicians," Parker says, "you need to interpret their language. There are musicians who are also studio technicians who can know as much about audio as you do. Others are people who have a vision, but they don't tell you in terms like '3 dB at 400 cycles.' They tell you in colors, terms like 'boxy,' all different types of sound idioms that you have to interpret. If you're only working with an artist once, you have to guess. But if you are fortunate enough to discover an artist who is having a successful career, who likes and trusts you and carries you along, over time you learn to interpret what it means when they say 'it sounds a little woolly.'"

Sontheimer elaborates: "There are two categories of requests: reasonable and unreasonable. Let's talk about reasonable. Obviously, level changes are fine. I'd say 50% of level changes are up and 50% are down. One thing I learned a long time ago was that people always ask for more, and you get to a point when something's going to blow up. Psychology starts here! Let's turn all that down to give the impression of turning this up. It always seemed to work, and does to this day."

And an unreasonable request? "Let's say you have a kick drum with one channel of equalization, but you send it to 16 different places," Sontheimer says. "It's going to go all over the stage, but you start to work on the sound at the drum kit. Now, you get it to sound good there, but what's it going to sound like when you put it through another type of speaker cabinet? People standing in front of wedges without sub-bass say, 'This doesn't sound like it does back there!' All of a sudden, everyone wants the kick to have separate EQ for every send on the board." Fortunately, there is another alternative. "If you know people are going to be complaining, EQ the drum around the wedges. Then boost 80 or 90Hz narrow band and cut 200-400 Hz on the channel, and fix the drummer's monitor with the graphic or the crossover."

A little diplomacy goes a long way when dealing with difficult requests. Parker explains: "You don't say, 'No, you can't do that.' You say, 'Well, there are obstacles.' Your attitude has to inspire communication, because if there's an adversarial relationship, there's no way two people are going to be able to work together optimally on the stage. Of course, we're talking specifics, like if there's one leader. But there are also individuals in that band, and each one wants something different. It's a juggle, because someone will say, 'He's playing too loud, so I need more of this.' If you give the first person more, it becomes too loud on stage, and then the house mixer is coming to you saying, 'There's an awful lot of bass coming off the stage,' and the bass player says, 'I'm way down, it's not me.' It's a constant juggle. You try not to volunteer your own opinions—you just try to give people what they ask for."

While creating a consistent sound-field regardless of venue is the ideal, the reality is another matter. "If it's a difficult room, you can only do so much," Staub explains. "In arenas, the room is going to swamp you. What happens [at the soundcheck] is that some people will play four measures and freak out. I'll get them to play a little bit more, and tell them, 'This is going to be a weird room. I'll do what I can to help you, and you do what you can to help me.' It all goes back to having that trust."

Finally, requests born from inexperience create a whole new set of problems. A typical question might be, "Why doesn't it sound like the album?" Describing his tour experience with a new artist fresh from the studio, Sontheimer says, "I was always changing monitor configurations to make it better. The entire tour ended up being an experiment, which taught the artist a lot about sound, but it was also bad because there was no consistent reference point to go by."

Listening To The Music

Although it's certainly not a prerequisite, many live sound engineers are musicians themselves. It's a fair bet that every mixer who succeeds has a keen ear for music and for the interaction that takes place between players. How, then, do monitor mixers respond to the intangibles of musical interplay?

Dave Bryson has mixed monitors for Tom Petty & the Heartbreakers since 1978.

Tom Petty

APPLICATIONS: SOUND TECHNIQUES

George Benson

A little diplomacy goes a long way when dealing with difficult requests.

"Because I've been with them that long," explains Bryson, "I hear little things and see when someone's playing off of someone else, and I mix them up for each other. They don't even notice it, because that's what they're into. I know them well enough that they'll give me a free hand; I don't stand there waiting for instructions. I'll get instructions if something's not right, but if it's a good night I'm the invisible man. I have fun mixing—just enjoy yourself and get into it."

Jim Yakabuski was out as the monitor mixer for Van Halen's 1991 tour. He offers some general comments: "If singers have a difficult night," explains Yakabuski, "you try and give them everything you can psychologically. A lot of times it's almost opposite to what they want. They'll want to be tucked down in the mix a little more so they don't hear themselves as well and don't hear if they're straining or whatever. That's one of the psych lessons you learn."

"In essence," Parker says, "a monitor mixer creates an onstage atmosphere that the artist can be comfortable in. If you do 120 shows with an artist over a year, you can tell within the first song and a half whether it's going to be a good night or not. Now, you can't account for the fact that it sounds great but the audience just sits there—you can see it drain away. There's nothing you can do about that. But if the artist starts feeling pressured and looks over to you to do things, you don't cop an attitude. You do everything you

can to help them feel comfortable. And it's a fragile balance. The most inane thing can throw it off—it'll still be a great show, but it won't be *the* great show."

"I think this job is at least 50 percent psychology," says Sontheimer. "You have to know what you're doing technically, but at the same time you have to have a feel for it. Being a musician myself helps me." Sontheimer has trained a number of people during his time with Showco and offers some advice. "I tell them to be low-key and not get too involved with the musicians until the band becomes comfortable with you. The main thing is to make everything as consistent as possible. That's why people have rehearsals. After a week or two on the road, you should be able to make the mix as consistent as possible."

"Psychology is more important than technology," concludes Staub. "You have to get along with people. Successful monitor engineers can go out with any band and fit in and build trust. Great gear certainly helps, but without it you still have to do the show. That's where the people who know all the little head secrets make it happen."

Monitor Case Study: George Benson

UNDERSTANDING AN ARTIST'S NEEDS IS THE first step towards a successful monitoring experience. Here, George Benson and his house engineer/production manager Bruce Galloway explain how Benson's personal requirements are met.

"That stage sound is extra, extra important," Benson says. "I like to have those monitors up close so they really become monitors—not just an addition to the sound, but something I can depend on before it gets out there."

Guitarist/vocalist Benson doesn't mind spending time at the soundcheck so he can feel comfortable. "There's nothing like being there and checking it out for myself and getting the right balance between what's bouncing off the wall and what's actually coming at me from the front monitors and the sidefills. The sidefills give me the environment that I'm used to, a normal environment independent of what's going out in the theater, because that's too late [delayed]. That won't help you."

"George works so much of the stage that he actually uses the sidefills for the majority of his sound," engineer Galloway says. "He uses two wedges in the front to fill in a little dead area in the middle of the stage. He can really go anywhere he wants without it fluctuating much."

"Perhaps I should have them put a little guitar in the front monitor," Benson says. "In the past that hasn't proven to be good because they always give me a direct sound. The amplifier seems to round out the sound. With the monitor in front, I hear the pick too much. I don't like that 'ping' sound."

"I try to adapt to any situation in the house. But we really work on the stage sound in great detail," Galloway says. "We want it this way only. If his voice isn't reproduced the way he's used to hearing it, it's almost like using a different amplifier to play his guitar through. He wants it to sound natural. The guy has done a lot of shows, so he knows what his voice sounds like. That's why we strive hard to keep all the monitoring together for him.

"Even when it looks like it's going to cut me short on time, I'll let the monitor engineer get his whole thing together without even listening to the house system. A lot of times he needs an extra half-hour of peace and quiet to do what he's going to do. By giving him that time, everything's set and things aren't going to be changing on me. Then it's up to me to do what I've got to do. I think mixing monitors is much more difficult than mixing house. You've got eight, nine or ten small P.A. systems scattered around the stage, within a foot or two of the microphones."

Benson knows what he wants to hear in his monitors. "I get the bass drum and keyboards and the vocals. The other guitar player doubles as a singer, and we have a female vocalist who plays light percussion, so we put a little of that in and try to get a balance," Benson says. "I like to hear the bass drum to get the real timing, because he's so far back, and that split-second makes a difference. A tune can really go downhill because of that misconception of time. I've found that if I get that click of the bass drum it really helps us stay in sync. And the keyboards are in there for inspiration. They make me want to sing, and they give me ideas. I bounce off their harmonies and rhythm concepts." —Robin Tolleson

In the hot seat: Monitor engineer Ricardo Caltagirone of Sound on Stage mixes The Jefferson Starship at San Francisco's Warfield Theater

APPLICATIONS: SOUND TECHNIQUES

Guitar Reinforcement: Three Top Mixers Share Their Techniques

BY DAVID (RUDY) TRUBITT

Robert Scovill

Robert Scovill is best known for his tours with Rush and Def Leppard. His work was recognized by Mix *readers when they voted him sound reinforcement engineer of the year in the 1992 Technical Excellence and Creativity (TEC) Awards. Here, he shares his thoughts on general advice for working with a variety of guitars, styles and players.*

Mix: Generally speaking, how would you approach an electric guitarist in each of three styles: modern hard rock—very high distortion with a lot of bite; a slightly cleaner blues/rock tone; and a completely clean player in a jazz, pop or country setting?

Scovill: This scenario applies to all three situations: The first question I will ask the player is, "Were you happy with the sound you got on the record?" If the answer is yes, then I will want to know, "What mic(s)/amp/speaker combination did you use during the recording process to get the sound you used on the record?" If he knows the particulars, then I try the setup used in the recording process. I believe the techniques used there are just as valid out here; I mean, come on, a good sound is a good sound. Nine times out of ten the [modern hard rock] sound you have described is recorded with an SM57. So, because I know the mic so well, I will start from there, but nothing is written in stone. I also like the Sennheiser 421s.

[For a blues type tone,] the same questions as above and then...find something that has a smooth top end and a warm bottom—typically a high quality condenser or even tube mic.

[And a clean player,] again, I would ask the same questions as above. This time though, I would probably try a composite of a dynamic and a condenser. Typically a SM57 or N-Dym 408 and a AKG 460 or

Eric Clapton, Rush's Alex Lifeson and U2's The Edge

even an EV CS15—there's a very pristine top end on that mic.

At this point, I would like to add that with the programmable preamps and sophisticated switching systems available, in all likelihood you could get all of the sounds mentioned above coming at you during a given show. So tailoring a mic to a given sound becomes a lot of trial and error and a bit of a compromise, if not totally impractical. With that in mind, I would suggest trying a speaker simulator. There are some excellent ones on the market today. I have used them with outstanding success with Rush and now with Def Leppard.

Mix: If you did choose to mic a speaker, how might you choose the one to use in a multi-speaker cabinet?

Scovill: Generally, in a 4x12 cabinet I will mic one of the top speakers to try to keep some of the floor reflections out of the microphone.

Mix: Anything to add regarding mic placement relative to the cone, and how that placement might vary in an isolation box/doghouse situation?

Scovill: Now in my opinion, this is a critical procedure once you get the desired sound. I will work with this consistently throughout the rehearsal stages of a tour. I have had guys look at me as if I were

crazy, but I have been down this road in the studio. I can hear differences in the response when the mic is moved fractions of inches, so I will work with it until I am satisfied with the result. Since I have started using isolation boxes with most of the players I tour with, this can result in a very stable guitar sound, because once you find the sweet spot of the speaker you can secure all the components [i.e., cabinet and microphone] so they do not shift around during travel. Another advantage of this way of miking speakers is, if you have separate amplifiers or preamplifiers driving them, you can do a bit of your own EQ before it hits the mic. The reason for trying to get your own EQ on the miked source is that guitar speakers are very directional and very rarely is the player in the direct listening field of the cabinet (the speaker is rarely, if ever, at ear level). Therefore, he has a tendency to over-brighten it or overly boost the low end, so with your own front end [ahead of the miked speaker], you can compensate for it.

Mix: Do you have a favorite mic for acoustic guitar? What trade-offs would you make in mic positioning and EQ when rejection on a noisy stage, feedback control and optimum tone are all competing factors?

Scovill: You have to take into consideration the genre of music you are talking about. For instance, if it's a very intimate setting, say for country music or a soloist situation, and the required monitor level is not out of hand, I will certainly consider miking the guitar with stand-alone microphones. I like the AKG 460s anywhere around the bridge, or even a Neumann KM84. Now if the artist needs to be a bit mobile in the same setting, I will try to get him to use a clip-on condenser mic around the F-hole [sound hole]. Maybe a Ramsa or Sony low-profile mic, or bridge-type pickup. Now the other scenario is in a high-SPL environment where the player wants to be mobile all night, typically a rock or pop setup. Here, you are almost bound to use some sort of transducer in the bridge. There are some good ones out—I particularly like the one that is in the Takamine guitars, and I heard that Paul Gilbert of Mr. Big used one that was a Hamer guitar, but I don't know the origin or type of pickup used in either of those guitars. The Ovation Collector Series guitars also sound really good. One other note with bridge transducers: Depending on the sound you are going for, have the player try different string gauges on the guitar. You can decrease a lot of your low end and top end EQ by going to a lighter string gauge.

Kind of an interesting turnaround to this line of thinking would be what the guitar player for The Alarm used extensively for a while. He had a regular acoustic guitar with an electric guitar pickup in the F-hole that he played through his normal amp setup. It looked and sounded fantastic.

Mix: What's your preference for getting effects from a guitarist with his/her own rack? Effects direct with a dry mic on their amp? Wet and dry mixed by the player, through the amp and miked off a speaker?

Scovill: I definitely prefer to get the effects mixed and miked from the player's amp or from an isolated version of the player's setup. There are a number of reasons for this. The most important is that the effects will affect how the guitar player plays. If you add delays or even chorusing and the player cannot hear them, it is unlikely that you will get it to sit the way you want it to. A footnote to this is if you have isolation boxes for the system and your miked source includes delays, etc., as the delays die out, the ratio of delays to stage noise or room ambience coming into the mic is very high. Another reason would be to take some of the pressure off me to perform all the guitar effects as well as the rest of the show. In effect then, the guitar player or his technician—whoever is doing the program changes—is like having a second set of hands on the console, and that can be very welcome.

Mix: Because so many players use programmable effect systems, might you work with them to fine-tune any presets that might be problematic in the house?

Scovill: Absolutely, because the guitar player is not listening to his effects in the context of the mix. A common problem here is with two guitar players: Sometimes both will use a lot of chorusing, when in fact with two players you are going to get some natural chorusing anyway if they are playing unison parts, so you have to be a bit selective. But it is very important to get actively involved in it, and it takes a fair amount of time to get tweaked in.

Mix: Any anecdotes that might be interesting? For instance, the most effective way to ask a guitarist to turn his amp down?

Scovill: If you have a guitar player that is out-of-bounds on the volume side of things, it is something you kind of need to get on as soon as possible if it looks like it is going to be a big problem. Once he works at a certain volume, even for a short time, it is virtually impossible to get him to turn down without seriously denting his ego as well as his vibe. I am usually pretty flexible on it, and I will feel out the player for any signs of common sense. Usually, something along the lines of, "The more I hear coming off the stage, the less I am likely to have in the P.A." tends to work pretty well. Now, one of two things will generally happen next: We will find a happy medium, or I will be asked to look for other work. So far, so good.

Mike Ponczek

Mike Ponczek has mixed Eric Clapton since 1984, except for a two-year gap while he was out with Paul McCartney (Rob Collins took over the reins during the interim). Ponczek was also system engineer/audio project coordinator for Rock in Rio II and was named sound reinforcement engineer of the year by Mix *readers in the 1991 TEC Awards. I spoke with him during Clapton's fall '92 tour.*

Mix: Do you use isolation boxes with Eric Clapton's guitar sound?
Ponczek: From about 1984 to 1986 we used an amp backstage. When Eric went to the four-piece group—Clapton, Collins, Phillinganes and East, we stopped using it. All his sounds, the tones that he gets, are through his guitar and his fingers—that's it. There's only two effects—the wah-wah pedal and the chorus.
Mix: So now you're just miking his onstage amps?
Ponczek: That's right. There are two mics—a Shure SM57 and an Electro-Voice RE27. They're both placed in the same position, approximately a fist away from the grille cloth, as a rule of thumb. Not too close, not too far away.
Mix: Which mic is doing what?
Ponczek: They're two separate tones, and

one serves as a backup for the other. The 57 is used exclusively in the monitors. I usually use the RE27 [in the house mix]. It's a much smoother tone, and the tone that it gives me is much more workable to EQ. You also have to look at what's placed next to it—in this band, there's a bass amp next to it. There's some shows where [bassist Nathan] East will play to the P.A. and turn his bass amp off. But sometimes [the bass amp is] quite loud, and there's good rejection with the RE27.
Mix: Any other stage conditions that you have to compensate for?
Ponczek: Eric sings quite a bit off-mic. With this setup here today (a shed show), 40% of the guitar is coming in though his vocal mic. If it was just his guitar, it'd be great, but I have to compromise. If you were to go into a studio and mix down a live tape, you'd just have the vocal mic come up when he's singing, [otherwise] it'd be off. Here I have to roll a lot of the high end off the guitar mic to get a natural sound out here.
Mix: Do you ever add effects to his guitar sound?
Ponczek: In the more classic songs like "Badge" or even "Layla," I try to keep the sound of his guitar and the band [true to the original recording]. On the more modern sounds, I might add some effects, especially DDL, as he uses no delay onstage.

Joe O'Herlihy

Joe O'Herlihy has mixed U2 since the late '70s. In this interview, conducted at one of the

Zoo TV outdoor shows late in 1992, he tells us how he presents the sound of one of today's most recognizable guitarists to audiences all over the world.

Mix: What's your approach to Edge's guitar setup for this tour?

O'Herlihy: Basically, this tour is an identical process to what we've done through the years. In this case, Edge has got four vintage Vox AC30s and two Randall amplifiers. The structure of his guitar sound is based upon various different combinations of these amps at any one given time. There are various different [effects] treatments sent to different amplifiers, and it's a combination of those that is the Edge sound.

The difference from tour to tour is the character and quality of sounds—that has changed dramatically. For instance, the guitar processing on *Achtung Baby* is fairly unique. It's something that we have tried to reproduce as much as we can. We're using a Bob Bradshaw switching system that makes a very complicated studio-type setup practical in a live context. It's a massive computer-based switching system that sends different processed signals to various destinations, and it also does level changes so that when it gets there it's at the right level for that treatment.

Mix: Does everything from that system ultimately feed an onstage guitar amp, or do you take any of it direct?

O'Herlihy: The only direct signal in the process is an acoustic guitar DI, and it's a combination—I use the clean [DI] acoustic sound as the main ingredient for the blend, and it's filled in with Vox #1 or Vox #4 or something like that. Otherwise, there isn't any clean, clinical guitar DI as such. Everything has a treatment of some description on it.

Mix: During the arena leg, Edge was playing a Strat-style guitar on "Angel of Harlem" that had a great acoustic sound.

What kind of pickup system was involved there?

O'Herlihy: That was a guitar Yamaha and Edge had been working on—it was a couple of different piezo-type pickups that they had under the bridge. It was an experimental guitar, and he grew to like it quite a bit. But we had a bit of difficulty in a couple of buildings with the wireless setup for it because the technology was a prototype. So, we ended up going back to the natural acoustic for the outdoor leg, because he liked the wood sound and all that sort of feeling. But that electric had an incredible sparkle—it was a really, really good acoustic guitar sound. It was incredible to look at him with this thing that looked like a Stratocaster strapped on to him and making it sound like an acoustic.

Mix: What kind of microphones do you favor for his amps?

O'Herlihy: I tried at the start of the tour to get as much studio quality and dynamics through the whole thing as I could. I used AKG C-414s, and they were *too* good, to be perfectly honest. They were too clean; they were fabulous. But, unfortunately, for this application it gave us too much of an almost clinical type of sound, so we went back to the old reliable SM57s. We've also got a couple of SM56s up there because they are shock-mounted, just in case. Everything is on rolling risers, and I didn't want any resonance or anything like that. He likes it nitty and gritty, and there were certain things that the studio microphones were taking away from that—it's a different context on record, as you can well imagine. So we went back to the old reliable 57s and 56s.

Mix: What about mic position?

O'Herlihy: We go for center cone placement as much as I possibly can—right on the dust cap. But some of the Voxes, because of the vintage they are, have this wooden baffle cross blocking that center point. That's where the 56s come in, because you can pivot and point them real well. And it is a vital part of the whole thing—you're off-center or off your measurement by a few inches and it does sound quite different.

Mix: How many of the original speakers are left in these amps?

O'Herlihy: Original speakers—that's another crusade. We've gone and collected as much as we can. We've been very lucky—it's all genuine original vintage speakers. There's a combination in one amp—an old blue Vox-Jensen speaker and a Jensen silver. [The other amps] are predominantly the blues.

Mix: What's the difference in tone between the blue and the silver speakers?

O'Herlihy: My impression is that the silver's got kind of a softer tonality. It's a really minute texture thing. They have their little, little differences. Technically, you could put them on the scope and it would tell you they're the same. It's a texture thing. We do have a fairly substantial stock of each, and we've been good so far, touch wood, and haven't blown stuff up.

When you get it re-coned, it's different because of the tightness. You don't get the wonderful warmth in the sustain with a new cone kit. It's quite precise—it doesn't have the flexibility from years of movement. I think something quite unique about the Vox sound is the speaker system.

Mix: You're so in touch with the details of his setup…

O'Herlihy: When you work with an artist, I think it's vital to know everything about where he's at and what he's doing. He's a virtuoso, and he understands the technical side of things as well. It's fairly unique, in the sense that a lot of people are very good players but might not get the optimum out of their treatments.

Mix: While he's made it such an inseparable part of his style…

O'Herlihy: Oh, absolutely—it's definitely the Edge sound, or the "Edge orchestra," as I affectionately christened it many moons ago. From the old [Electro Harmonix] Memory Man days right up to where we are now, it's been an incredible natural progression. It's great to be part of it.

The Effects of Mic Splitting

BY DAVID
(RUDY)
TRUBITT

EVERY ENGINEER PAYS ATTENTION TO MIC selection and placement. However, one often overlooked area of mic performance comes from the electrical connections downstream of the mic itself. "It's really important to see what the ultimate load is on all those microphones," says engineer Bruce Jackson, known in live sound circles for his long tenure mixing Bruce Springsteen and as co-founder of A/D converter manufacturer Apogee Electronics.

"Say you've got a main monitor mix on stage right and a smaller monitor mix for specific players on stage left," Jackson says in regards to stage layout and its effect on mics. "There might even be another little submixer for the drummer. It also goes out over a couple hundred feet of snake to the house console. All those loads sitting across the microphones [if hard-wired in parallel] make the mics sound different. This shows up first with condenser or electret mics. Condensers are more sensitive to loading than dynamics." The result? "The highs don't sound as open and clear. The mic just sounds squished and held down."

"A console," Jackson continues, "is usually designed to operate happily in its own little world, but not necessarily in conjunction with other consoles. The situation gets even worse when the recording truck comes along. Often, they won't even know what they're loading you with. Even if there's a transformer split box, they may try to tap off the microphone on the direct side but let you believe you've still got your normal setup. Then when the show starts, everyone goes crazy because the monitor and house levels are weird, some mics are hotter than others and so on. You have to have a close working relationship with everyone in that situation."

You also need to know what you're loading the mics with, and this calculation starts at the input of each console. "When you just have one console with a bridging input," Jackson says, "it's probably got an input impedance over 1k ohms. But with three of them in parallel it comes down to just a few hundred ohms. A 300-ohm load will definitely compromise the sound of condenser microphones."

The obvious way to reduce load impedance (without eliminating consoles, of course) is to use transformers. "Although they're very expensive, there are advantages to having a transformer splitter," says Jackson. "Deane Jensen originally designed these three-way split transformers, so you come in with the mic and go out to three isolated outputs. The other big advantage with transformers is the control over grounding issues. With the 1988 Springsteen tour, I got fed up with the interconnection problems, which were even worse because we were carrying a big recording console that we only used on some nights. I wanted a very controlled situation, and I had the luxury of making a great big transformer split box. So we had a known situation every day and didn't have to chase our tails when someone plugged or didn't plug something in. But a great big split box costs tens of thousands of dollars, which is a luxury most companies can't afford. Generally, they're just using hard-wired splits and you end up tying all the grounds together. It gets complicated deciding which becomes the master ground reference and which the slave off that reference."

Of course, transformers have long been used at the console input to address grounding concerns. "Even though active inputs offer a lot of advantages, transformer-isolated inputs really help you out from a grounding point of view," Jackson says. But as you've probably guessed, you don't get something for nothing. "The trouble with transformer [isolated inputs]," adds Jackson, "is that it's hard to get high bridging impedance with them, which results in increased mic loading."

Another alternative is the use of active mic splitters, which present their own pros and cons. "The positive," says Jackson, "is that an active splitter loads the microphone correctly and distributes a buffered signal to the other consoles. The negative is 'How do you control the gain?' Usually, you like to be able to tweak your gain to put it in the optimum position, but

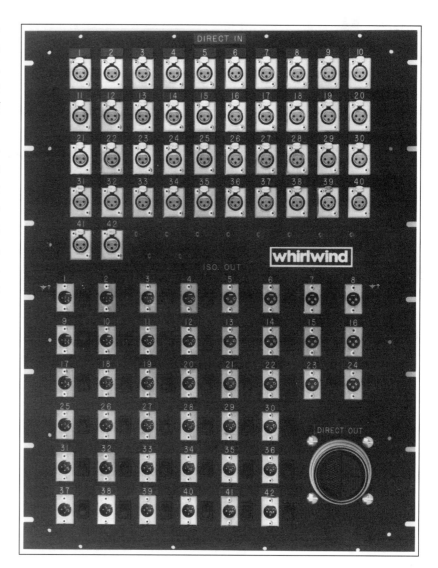

with an active split you have to optimize the sensitivity of the mic preamp at the split box, which is not located at the house position. Even though the monitor guy will probably be controlling the input gain of the splitter, the output level that works for one console is probably different for another console. You have to make sure you're not compromising your dynamic range or raising the noise floor. You also need to consider the grounding for the splitter."

There's no one solution, just as there's no "best" microphone—it all depends on

the situation. But next time you're wondering why a mic isn't delivering what you expected, consider that it might not be the mic or its placement. "Before you even get into the selection of microphones, you need to have a solid accounting of what's happening," Jackson concludes. "Try unplugging the monitor board and listening to what the mic sounds like in the house. Then listen to the level drop and the sound change when you plug it back in. See what happens, and remember that microphones usually sound better when they're lightly loaded."

Whirlwind's passive transformer splitter; BSS's MSR-604 active mic distribution system

"A console is usually designed to operate happily in its own little world, but not necessarily in conjunction with other consoles."
—Bruce Jackson

Drum Miking Techniques

BY DAVID (RUDY) TRUBITT

"THE DRUM NEEDS TO BE TUNED PROPERLY before a microphone ever gets near it," says veteran engineer Robert Scovill, known for his work mixing house for Rush and Def Leppard. "Once it's tuned, choosing the right microphone becomes easy, because you're tailoring the sound with the microphone rather than trying to cover up a deficiency in the drum. If you have a great microphone on a poorly tuned drum, miking it only provides a better or worse representation of that badly tuned drum. The sound has to be sorted out before it ever hits the microphone. [Rush's] Neil Peart is superb at tuning his drums and keeping them under control."

As is evident in the photo, Peart's is no small drum kit. The sizes of the individual drums, however, are modest. "A bigger drum does not necessarily constitute a bigger drum sound," says Scovill. "How many times have you heard about people coming into the studio with their huge drum kits, trying to get this big sound and failing miserably? Then they go into the corner and pull out a little Camco kit with shallow drums that's been used on every other session, and they end up sounding huge on the record.

"The same thing applies with live work: Try tight miking patterns to pick up specific areas around the drum. Don't use extremely ambient or wide-open sounding microphones, because much of that ambience is destructive. In the studio, [mic interaction] supports the ambience of the room it's recorded in. When it's live, you have to pick specific, precise slices of drums and re-create the ambience of the record electronically."

On Scovill's second tour with Rush, he did a few things differently. "The Ramsa mics [see photos] are obviously the biggest change," he says. "They're a little wider than cardioid, and their off-axis response is really good. It keeps everything out of the back of the microphone, which is important since we have monitor speakers blasting up into the microphones. In a situation like this, the off-axis response pattern is probably just as important as the on-axis. You're trying to keep out as much sound as you're trying to pick up."

But how tight is tight enough? "It's a compromise—you could go to a supercardioid on every mic and end up with a very one-dimensional sound on a tom or a snare drum. That's why the Electro-Voice N-Dym Series work so well: they're tight off-axis, yet still have an open, defined sound. That's why you'll see those mics on probably 70 percent of the kits out there. You don't get a lot of bleed; consequently, it's very easy to gate the mic. You don't have to worry about a lot of cross-triggering or the monitors opening up the gate." Drawmer gates are used throughout.

Another major change for this tour was in the kit itself. Previously, Peart had used two kick drums. "But he wanted it to sound like one drum," says Scovill, "and we tried to do that. Finally, common sense caught up with us and we realized that if we wanted it to sound like one kick, we should just use one drum. The dual kick-pedal

technology has come around enough for him to feel comfortable with two beaters on one drum."

Sometimes finding the right mic for the job contains an element of chance. "I was looking through Rush's mic stash for a good, high-quality condenser to put on chimes and snare bottom—things like that," Scovill explains. "I just happened to pull out a Calrec CB20C with a CT50 capsule, and it was excellent—I swear by it now for snare bottom. It's pointed a little off-axis from the drum head so that it doesn't get so much body out of the drum. It's a light blend [with the top mic] and gated tightly so you don't hear that much of it, but it's really a good-sounding microphone." The snare top? A Shure SM57. "Some things never change," notes Scovill.

Though proper miking is essential, the point where all these mic signals end up is

Neil Peart's drum kit is covered with a variety of mics, including Ramsa WM-S series clip-on mics (see detail at left), Ramsa and Beyer M88 on kick, EV N/D408As on rack toms, EV RE20s on floor toms, Countryman Isomax on chimes, AKG 451 on hats and AKG 414 for overheads.

The AKG D112 (left) and Sennheiser MD421 are other popular drum mics, most often used on kick and toms, respectively.

"If the drum's tuned correctly and you have the right match of microphone and diaphragm size to the drum's size, you won't have to do any drastic tone shaping. Use EQ to enhance the fundamentals— the player's attack and the intensity you're trying to create."
—Robert Scovill

an equally important link in the chain. "If you don't have a good-sounding console with good-sounding EQ, it's a hopeless task," says Scovill. "That's why I choose the consoles I do [Rush uses two Gamble EX56s]. They have an excellent preamp section and excellent EQ. As much as I hate to say it, it all comes back to basics. I'll take a console any day that has three things: great metering, great preamps and great EQ. A console can have all the bells and whistles in the world, but if it can't do those three, I don't want to have anything to do with it. The Gamble is a simple console that is very effective."

How does Scovill see EQ fitting into the process? "If the drum is tuned correctly and you have the right match of microphone—particularly the diaphragm size related to the drum's size—you won't have to do any drastic tone shaping. Then

you're using EQ to enhance fundamental things, like the player's attack on the drum and the intensity you're trying to create. Especially with Neil, I try to be true to what he's trying to accomplish. I feel self-conscious about smearing what he's doing up there. It's like looking into a blurred mirror—it would be a very false portrayal of what's happening. It's a good philosophy to have with drums: If you try to force a sound on the drum, you're going to fail nine times out of ten. Let the drum come through like it sounds up there and just amplify the vision of that drum."

In the end, it comes down to bringing all of the performance to the audience. "It really bugs me if I go to a show and see some guy up there playing something that I can't hear," Scovill says. "That's probably why I got into this business."

Mix Position and Room Acoustics

BY DAVID (RUDY) TRUBITT

*I*T GOES WITHOUT SAYING THAT YOUR MIX *position has an effect on how you mix a show. But how does one go about making this crucial choice? The subject was covered at Synergetic Audio Concepts (Syn-Aud-Con) 1993 Live Sound Reinforcement Workshop. Following is a distillation of the workshop staff's advice on this important topic.*

Ideally, you should be able to choose the location of your house mix position. In this case, common sense dictates choosing a spot representative of a large part of your audience. Although a point directly between the left and right speaker arrays maximizes one's stereo imaging, it is often not a wise choice.

"With all conventional sound systems," says Showco's M.L. Procise, "There is an aberration we all live with. When you have two sources in the room, they have to sum somewhere. In the center of the room, you get an additional 3-5dB peak in the low bass of the system."

"You have this thing that we call 'Power Alley,'" explains Audio Analysts' Albert Leccese. "When you have wavefronts coming from each side of the stage, at low frequencies you're going to have a peak right down the middle."

"When you have this 5dB peak in the low bass," explains Procise, "it's difficult to make sure everybody else in the room is getting good bass response, since you're being inundated with bass. What we try to do instead is move the console slightly off the center line or in front of one speaker stack, so that we won't have to be subject to that summation in the center."

Note that where there's a peak, a null will also be lurking nearby. "Off to either side of the center line," warns Leccese, "you're going to have a narrow area that's going to have no bass in it. That's a null at which certain frequencies are going to cancel. If you happen to choose that spot for your mix position, then you're going to be mixing bass-heavy, as opposed to bass-light."

Besides anomalies in frequency response at various points in the room, one should also be aware of strong reflections. "Sometimes," continues Leccese, "you may end up putting the mix position where the first reflection from the ceiling or the side wall is [focused]." In some cases, these reflections can be anticipated by visually scanning the surfaces of a room. Imagining walls as mirrors can help, as sound and light reflect in similar ways. However, a simple visual inspection is often inadequate in more complicated spaces. Leccese suggests another approach: "Early in the morning, there's a bunch of activity at the stage end of the room. There's boxes rolling around, there's people banging and clanging, rigging is going up—all kinds of noise is originating from the stage area. [While this is happening,] I like to walk around the hall and listen. If I'm in a certain place and, my eyes tell me there's a forklift over *here*, but my ears tell me it's over *there*, [where I'm standing is] not where I'm going to put my mix position, because at that particular spot there is a nasty reflection coming from the

The Grateful Dead and Ultrasound at the Oakland Coliseum before a New Year's Eve show. Early in their career, the Dead and mixer Dan Healy (see foreword) had to lobby hard for the right to place their mix position in the audience area, rather than being pushed off to the side by promoters coveting the valuable center seats.

approximate location of where the P.A.'s going to be."

Of course, this selection process assumes that you have a say in the matter. "Sometimes you don't have a choice where you have to set up the console," warns Randy Stiegmiester of Maryland Sound Industries. "You might go into a theater and end up in the back row, too close [to the P.A.], or clear off to one side." What then? "We live in a world of compromise in audio," says Procise. "You have to do the best you can from wherever you have to sit. You might be sitting in the back, but you should walk the room and know what it sounds like everywhere else—then you can live with the compromise."

"You basically have to do a mental correction factor," adds Leccese. "This is what a particular instrument sounds like when I'm over here. When I go over there, it sounds like that. Therefore, there's a correction factor that you can apply for each and every single instrument. After you've

worked with a band in a particular place for a while, you get a pretty good idea of what it should sound like [in different parts of the room]."

Even if you have a free hand in choosing your mix position, audience members will be spread throughout the acoustical anomalies of the room. Therefore, "it's your duty to walk the room during the day and check out the system," urges Stiegmiester. "Don't sit on your butt and let somebody else tell you what's happening."

Remember that your mix station itself can color your perceptions. If you're mixing from a riser, your ear level obviously will be well above the audience around you. Furthermore, the space under a riser can create a resonant cavity, creating low-end anomalies. And, adds Stiegmeister, "You might have some bass-trapping created by the little pit you create with your console and racks. Maybe if you move your racks a little bit you'll eliminate some

reflections that are only coming to you and nobody else. So there's lots of little physical things that can affect your space."

Finally, the ability to mentally project yourself into the sound-space of other parts of the room is equally important for mixing monitors, according to freelance monitor engineer Randy Wietzel (who was recently out with Michael Jackson). "Don't just stand behind the console. It's real important to walk the stage, stand in everybody's area and listen to what they're hearing. You have to [remember] the sounds in each stage area and correct for

those problems, not for what you're hearing [from behind the console]. It's really important that you memorize what the stage sounds like, so that when you make your adjustments, you can 'hear' what's happening on stage."

So bear this in mind next time you set up your mix position. Whether you have a choice of location or just the option to shift a rack or two, remember that hearing what's going on, as well as being able to imagine the sound in various parts of the audience, is the first step towards a successful mix.

Mix position for Gloria Estefan (sound by Maryland Sound Industries)

Emergency Acoustical Treatments

BY RICHARD ZWIEBEL

MANY LIVE PERFORMANCES TAKE PLACE IN venues that were designed without much attention to acoustics. Each auditorium, gymnasium, convention center, church or club has different acoustical characteristics that affect how well the audience hears the performance. It is difficult to provide quick, portable acoustical solutions for problematic venues when constrained by a small budget. Usually, only low-cost materials or materials that can be rented can be considered for temporary use. Though no two rooms are the same, we can consider some common acoustical problems, look at remedies that have been applied in the field and suggest a few possible solutions.

A show that takes place in a gymnasium, convention center or other large multipurpose venue presents the most common problems. These rooms, especially the older ones, were typically designed with minimal acoustical treatment and are often highly reverberant. To make them acceptable for musical performances on a permanent basis would require adding absorptive material to the room surfaces. This can often be costly, and most facilities will not spend the money to correct such problems.

How can you deal with these issues on a temporary basis? The first thing you should do is decide whether the overall reverberance is the problem or if specific reflections are responsible. If faced with the latter, determine which reflections are the most offensive. Look the room over and listen to it. From where do you hear large echoes returning? In most large rectangular spaces that are constructed of block, the rear wall of the room is the worst offender. Usually, a large, distinct reflection can be heard off of this wall. Since sound travels at approximately 1,180 feet per second, if the wall is 100 feet away from the stage, a clearly audible discrete echo will return to the stage in about 236 milliseconds. Of course, music is not a single discrete sound, but a constant source of varying sounds. As all of these echoes blur with the sound emanating from the stage, it becomes more difficult to hear clearly. The sound quality can be inferior, compromising the audience's enjoyment of the show.

Tom Rose, an acoustical consultant with The Joiner Consulting Group in Arlington, Texas, says that for popular amplified music in multipurpose concert venues, "deader is better." He points out that filling as many seats as possible is not only beneficial in terms of income and crowd excitement, but also adds acoustical absorption to the room in the form of human bodies. In spaces where a finished ceiling exists and trusses are not exposed, he suggests renting pipeframe (typically used for display booths at conventions) from display products suppliers and hanging standard velour theatrical curtains (available from theatrical supply houses).

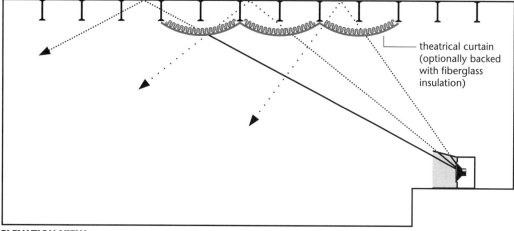

ELEVATION VIEW

theatrical curtain
(optionally backed
with fiberglass
insulation)

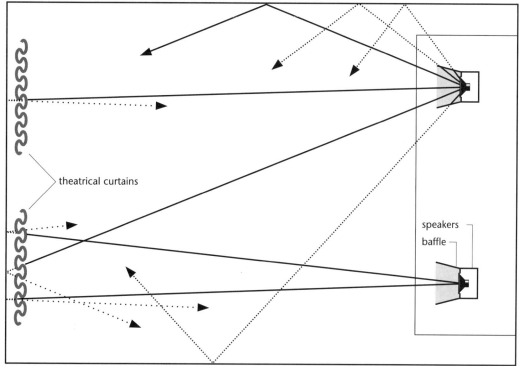

theatrical curtains

speakers
baffle

OVERHEAD VIEW

Theatrical curtains can significantly reduce reflections when deployed over fairly large areas, while smaller baffles around loudspeakers minimize unwanted reflections at the source.

These can be placed across the back of the room. The standard curtain base usually will place the curtains about two feet from the wall. This air space behind the curtain is desirable, as it will improve low-frequency absorption. Adding additional absorptive material behind the curtain can further improve the sound of the room. Rick Talaske, of the Talaske Group in Oak Park, Ill., agrees that using floor stands and acoustical drapery across the back of the room yields a significant improvement with a reasonable amount of effort.

Rose adds that in a gymnasium or convention center where the roof trusses are exposed, the ceiling reflection can contribute significantly to the reverberant field. This also can be treated. Start by laying an absorptive fabric such as theatrical curtains on the floor. Heavier curtains are preferred, though he cautions against the use of a heavy industrial tarpaulin canvas, plastic-coated or tent-type fabric.

Next, attach ropes to the trusses every 20 to 30 feet, and then hoist the fabric up so that the sound emanating from the stage will have a reduced reflection off of the ceiling. The sound can be improved further by attaching standard R-13 unfaced fiberglass thermal building insulation to the top of the cloth before it is hoisted up. The insulation should be attached to prevent it from bunching up once it is suspended from the ceiling. Covering 50% of the ceiling in this manner can make a significant improvement. Choose areas that would block a reflection from the stage and prevent its arrival in the audience. You can distinguish these areas by imagining a mirrored ceiling. If you were in the audience and you looked into an area of the mirrored ceiling, would you see either the stage or speaker systems? If so, then this area of the ceiling could be a desirable location to add absorption. If you would not see the stage or speakers, then the absorption could be put to better use elsewhere.

Other materials can be used to provide ceiling absorption as well. To deaden a room that was used as both a rehearsal space and an echo chamber at Bearsville Studios, Michael Guthrie (of Telex Communications in Wykoff, N.J.) used hair and jute carpet padding. He reinforced it with gaffer's tape and metal grommets, then suspended it from the ceiling. By adjusting the height, he was able to adjust the bandwidth of absorption. Guthrie points out that though this material was quite inexpensive, it also was very fragile.

Dave Andrews of Andrews Audio Consultants in New York City used theatrical curtains (Duvetyne) to improve the sound quality of shows in theaters such as the Showboat in Atlantic City and The Winter Garden Atrium, a large, highly reverberant room in Battery Park City, N.Y. He hung a series of battens off of eye hooks attached to the roof trusses or pipes with draperies hung off of these, which broke up the paths of reflection from the ceiling.

When using theatrical curtains for amplified music, a simple rule of thumb is "the more the better." Side walls and ceilings also may produce unwanted echoes and can add to the reverberance of the room. Obviously, you cannot cover all of the walls and ceiling with acoustical drapery. In fact, these lateral reflections may sometimes be desirable. But when they aren't, there are more feasible strategies you can employ to control them.

By hanging the drapery close to the speakers, you can reduce the level of sound hitting the walls and ceiling. To do this, stand at the speaker and move the frames with the curtains so that you cannot see the surface that you believe to be an "offender." Since the curtain is located adjacent to the speaker, a much smaller quantity of curtain is required than would be needed to cover the entire wall. While theatrical curtains are far from an ideal product for the problem, they do offer the most "bang for the buck," while remaining easy to set up and transport. Adding a second layer of curtain on a separate frame behind the first can improve the performance. As you add curtains, listen to what effect they have; one single curtain will not make a lot of difference, but the sum total of all of the curtains may result in the desired improvement. Use your ears to determine what works best for the room. If available, an instrument such as the Techron TEF 20 analyzer allows you to accurately see and measure the existing acoustical problems and evaluate each change you make. Materials other than curtains also can be used. For example, sheets of plywood covered with fiberglass batting are a possibility, although they are much more difficult to handle.

Rather than using curtains to absorb sound, Peter D'Antonio, president of RPG Diffusor Systems in Upper Marlboro, Md., fabricates panels out of laminated paper honeycomb which are stiff, yet lightweight. The surfaces are treated with one to four inches of semi-rigid fiberglass and fabric upholstery. These baffles form "barn doors" around the cluster and are angled toward the ceiling, floor and side walls. While these panels are not as readily available or as easy to install as curtains, they offer significantly better performance by essentially flush-mounting the cluster, as is typically seen in recording studio control rooms.

The baffles offer three advantages: They place portions of the side walls, ceiling and stage in the acoustic shadow of the cluster, thereby minimizing reflections from these surfaces; they improve the low-frequency directivity of the cluster; and they offer appreciable low-frequency gain to the sound system. These baffles should be as large as possible for maximum effect.

D'Antonio also feels that it's important to improve the acoustics onstage. He uses Biffusors™, a product that provides absorption on one side and diffusion on the other, as onstage gobos. First, a "curtain" is placed around the drummer, with the absorptive side facing in and the diffusive side facing the rest of the band. Then more Biffusors are placed around the stage, typically with the absorption facing amplifiers and the diffusion facing acoustic performers, such as vocalists and horns. By properly locating the gobos, a performer using an acoustical instrument can hear the natural sound of his or her instrument more clearly, because the energy is returned, rather than lost in an absorber. The sound level of other instruments at his or her location is not reduced.

This setup has been used successfully on many of the DMP and Telarc live-to-2-track recordings and by Greg Hockman at the Stardust. In a room where excess reverberance is not a problem, diffusors placed at the rear of the room can improve the sound quality by returning energy to the room without the undesirable slap typical of an untreated wall. Because the sound is not absorbed as it is with curtains, audience members at the rear of the room (where the sound level is the lowest) benefit from the added level of sound returning from the diffusors. Diffusion essentially improves the coverage of the sound system. Although church sanctuaries often are designed with acoustical considerations in mind, the particular requirements of musical performances are rarely the sorts of considerations the designer anticipated. Many churches are too reverberant for amplified music and can be treated in a similar manner.

Gary Harris, of Gary and Timmy Harris in New York City, provides sound reinforcement services for operatic performances. He tells of a situation at the Wolf Trap Amphitheatre (before it was rebuilt following the 1982 fire) in the Washington, D.C. area where he added natural reverberance. Wolf Trap is an amphitheater with a covered seating area open to the outdoors at the entire rear and sides. Since opera requires a reverberant space, Harris chose to place microphones in the pit and hang speakers in a walkway about 30 feet in front of the proscenium (over the audience), aimed at the proscenium arch. Because the arch was diffusive and the speakers were 30 feet away, he was able to combine an electronic system with natural characteristics to create an initial delay (caused by the distance from the speakers to the proscenium to the audience) and a diffuse field for the orchestra in combination with Farrel Becker's superb direct sound system for vocals. This system was used quite successfully in the '70s for performances such as *Aida*, *The Flying Dutchman*, *War and Peace* and *Madame Butterfly*. Harris also has used a temporary installation of RPG Diffusors on the pit rail at the Opera House in Boston to improve the pit acoustics during performances conducted by Sarah Caldwell.

Andrews also uses electronic solutions for acoustical problems. Sometimes the facility's or promoter's concern for appearance precludes the use of physical treatments. By using a distributed approach to the sound system, it is possible to place many speakers in the hall at a much closer proximity to the audience. Because the speakers are closer, they can be turned down in level, thereby exciting the room to a lesser degree and improving the ratio of direct sound to reverberant sound.

Use your eyes and ears and some common sense to improve the acoustics on a temporary basis. The cumulative effect of many "little things" can make the difference between a mediocre show and a successful one.

At the Winter Garden show mentioned earlier, Andrews combined acoustical and electronic solutions to provide high-quality sound in a large reverberant space filled with glass and marble, which most people would consider unacceptable for live musical performances. To make matters worse, performances took place from both ends of the room. He was unable to use acoustical draperies due to aesthetic concerns by venue management, so he used two separate sound systems, one for each direction, fed from the left and right channel of the mixing console. This system had 30 distributed speakers in and around the audience, located in palm trees, stage left and right, all delayed and equalized with the SIM® equalization process. No listener was more than 20 feet from a speaker.

Noisy mechanical systems also can affect a room's sound quality. These sorts of problems cannot be easily corrected, except by the facility. In some cases, acts or sound companies have requested that the systems be run right up until the performance and then shut off. Obviously, the facility management must consider health and comfort issues in making this type of decision, but it may be worth the request. If enough people bring the problem to the facility's attention, it may be fixed in time for your next performance there.

The best solution to acoustical problems is for a qualified acoustical consultant to properly design the facility or correct existing problems. Unfortunately, budgetary constraints often prevent this ideal situation. In these cases, it is necessary to use your eyes and ears and some common sense to improve the acoustics on a temporary basis. The cumulative effect of many "little things" can make the difference between a mediocre show and a successful one.

Wireless Mics in Sound Reinforcement

W

BY
GEORGE
PETERSEN

HETHER IN A SMALL CLUB OR A TELEVISED mega-festival in a packed stadium, wireless systems are almost certainly in use somewhere onstage. Once available only to the top touring acts, advancements in RF (radio frequency) technology, along with the miniaturization of transmitter circuits, have helped to make pro-quality wireless systems affordable to just about any sound reinforcement company, large or small.

But one thing hasn't changed: the need for reliability, especially in live performance situations, where the concept of a "second take" is mere fantasy. Besides top-quality audio performance, a wireless rig used in sound reinforcement has to be rugged enough to stand up to the abuses of the road, as well as provide protection from interference on the ever-crowded airwaves. We talked to a number of sound reinforcement companies and asked for some of their solutions to problems concerning life in the wireless lane.

BURNS AUDIO
Sun Valley, California

Located in the small town of Sun Valley, Calif., Burns Audio has carved out a niche for itself by specializing in sound reinforcement for live television events. Past clients have included the Grammy Awards, Academy Awards, People's Choice Awards, Golden Globe Awards and Country Music Awards, to name a few. According to company representative Dave Bellamy, Burns Audio also maintains a healthy rental business, supplying audio equipment to all the major TV networks, and their wireless complement includes Sennheiser 2003 UHF and Vega R-42 VHF systems.

What's the most important consideration when renting a wireless system?

The main thing we focus on is making sure that our equipment is working as well as it possibly can before it leaves here, and we have an extensive diagnostic and maintenance program to make sure that is the case. If you're in a position to rent RF, be sure you rent from a company that really takes care of the units, so you'll know that they'll work well. Dealing with RF has really become a specialty in this business.

I'm heavily involved with frequency coordination: A unit won't work if it's on the wrong frequency or conflicting with another unit. For example, I'm sending a unit out today that's going to Boston and then to Miami. I have to know what television stations are in those areas, plus I have to know if there are any other radio frequencies being used in those individual venues. A lot of what I do is investigation—finding out what's going on to avoid any possible problems downstream. I have a book listing everybody's frequencies everywhere, and I keep it constantly updated, along with what frequency preferences people have.

How do you feel about UHF vs. VHF systems?

There are few UHF transmitters out there, and you're going to have less potential for interference because there's so little traffic in UHF. For that reason alone, you're going to have fewer problems.

Shure L Series wireless
system

changed it to use a replaceable battery. I don't think we'll ever see rechargeable or reusable batteries in this business. It's certainly not a cost factor, especially in terms of a show's budget and what's at stake.

dB SOUND
Des Plaines, Illinois

While this 20-year old firm specializes in national and international tours, dB Sound also handles industrial shows for clients such as Mitsubishi Motors and Nintendo. As a leading sound company in the Midwest, dB has worked closely with Electro-Voice in the design of products such as EV's Manifold Technology and DeltaMax loudspeaker lines. A few of dB's past and current clients include Aerosmith, AC/DC, Prince and UB40, according to dB representative Todd Johnson.

How important are batteries?
Batteries are a very important issue. We use Duracells. They're excellent batteries, with a good battery life and consistent performance, but they also fit well into the battery compartments of the Vega transmitters. Occasionally, a client may try using an old battery that checks out fine on a static voltage test with a voltmeter, but the voltage may drop way down when the transmitter is turned on. Generally, battery problems are minimal. Just put in fresh batteries after the rehearsal, before you go to tape or go on the air.

Some time ago, there was some talk about rechargeable batteries making some headway into the wireless mic business. Any progress in this area?
Nobody uses rechargeable batteries, since you never know if it's up to full charge. No one wants to take the risk of putting in a battery that might go dead during a performance. And every time you recharge a battery, it becomes weaker. Everybody is afraid to use rechargeables. A couple of years ago, Vega came out with a system that had rechargeable batteries, but they

What kind of wireless systems are you using at dB?
For most of the touring we use Cetec Vegas—the R-42s or the R-32s. We try to stick with the R-42 units, which are pretty consistent and can take a lot of abuse. I have the new Shure diversity systems out on the Nintendo shows—they're pretty reliable. We also have some older Nady units that I'll send out if the job only requires one or two channels in a limited area for a night.

How do you feel about UHF systems?
UHF systems are a little trickier to use. You have to be more adept at being able to tune them—squelching them out and finding frequencies that are between local TV stations. Once you get the knack of using UHF, they're not so bad—they're just not as user-friendly as VHF systems. Antenna placement is more crucial with UHF, and they are more affected by metal things like lighting trusses. However, UHF does offer a greater selection of frequencies, which is a big factor. It's like anything else—you just have to get used to them. I just finished using the latest model of Sony UHFs, and I was impressed with

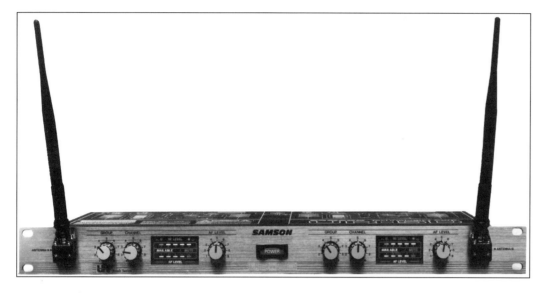

Samson UHF Synth Series
wireless system receiver

their performance. They were really good compared to the older, rackmount Sony UHFs. I've also used some of the Sennheiser UHF stuff. They don't play around—it's the best stuff I've ever used, although they're expensive.

What trends have you noticed in the wireless industry?

An artist may have a preference for a certain mic capsule on a wireless, and two years ago you didn't have much of a choice. Today, you can call up Vega and get an EV 757 or just about anything you want, and it's about time that they did that. You wouldn't think that this was so much of a big deal—unless you're dealing with a condenser mic—but for a long time, capsule selection was pretty limited. Other manufacturers are also offering wider selections. Samson has come out with an interchangeable capsule thing, and Beyer is working on one, because with their system, you have to unscrew the capsule to change the battery. The big Beyer rig is good-sounding and quite clean.

How do you deal with RF problems?

In downtown Chicago here, we've got one of the heaviest RF fields in the world. It's a fact, because before I worked here I did the extended run of the play *Hair*, and we had 12 channels of wireless there in this big theater right next to the El [elevated streetcar] tracks. We went through quite a few systems with that, trying to get it just right. One time I had an interference problem, which turned out to be caused by a guitar player's cheap wireless in a club next door. Their first set started at 10 p.m., and we'd start having problems every night at that time. With wireless systems, you always have to think about what's around you.

Frequency selection can be pretty touchy. I keep in contact with the different people who own wireless systems in this area, and I know what everybody else has. For example, the people at On Stage Audio (Elk Grove Village, Ill.) have a list of what I have—everybody helps each other, so you don't have a problem.

Any general advice about placing antennas?

I like to keep antennas within line of sight, as close to the receivers as possible, and try to keep antennas away from metal. The whole antenna thing is a trial and error process—it doesn't work the same way in every place. We had some problems on a Nintendo show in a convention center in Cleveland. There was a lot of metal in the structure, and moving the antennas five feet cleared up the problem. With our Shure system, we've got a distributed antenna system that's real clean and nice, with six units mounted in a rack. A lot of the time it's best to use a distributed antenna system in hotels and things, so instead of having 6 million antennas we use a pair of antennas with a splitter.

Anything else?

Dealing with wireless is a pretty touchy

Vega Pro Plus T-89
wireless transmitter

issue, but making sure that everything is well-maintained and keeping fresh batteries is the key to success. When I was doing *Hair*, I tried just about every battery in the world, looking for something that lasts longer, and Duracell seemed to do it. I probably went through about 15,000 batteries with that show. I start a show with fresh batteries and change them at the intermission. I'm not one for taking chances with batteries. If you get to a crucial point where you should have changed that battery and you didn't, then you'll pay for it. At that point you're being penny-wise and pound-foolish.

ELECTROTEC PRODUCTIONS
Canoga Park, California
Founded in 1982, Electrotec keeps headquarters in Southern California and subsidiary facilities in Nashville and London. According to engineer Jeff Forbes, some of Electrotec's recent clients included Alabama, Elvis Costello, Jefferson Airplane, Randy Travis, The Eurythmics, Barry Manilow, Tesla and Tom Petty.

What kind of wireless systems does Electrotec use?
We own some Nady equipment—the 700 Series, 701 Series and down. We've just started checking out the Samson series, which has the ten-channel receiver that allows you to change channels if you have any RF problems—and our first indication is that it's quite good. That's all we own. A lot of times we rent Vega or HME systems. We don't maintain a large stock of wireless here, because it seems that more and more of the artists have their own wireless systems.

What are your major concerns about wireless performance?
A lot of engineers talk about different capsules or types of lavaliers to use, but our main concern with wireless systems is reliability and how well the transmitter locks to the receiver, because the best-sounding mic capsule in the world won't do any-

thing for you if the signal is drifting all over. This can depend on a lot of things—where the performer is onstage in relation to the receiver, the venue itself and local communications in the air. We always do RF checks after rehearsals, by taking a mic out onstage and listening for any spots that are "dead." If that occurs, you can move the antennas or receivers, but if that doesn't help, then you need to notify the performer that the mic is less effective in those areas.

Often, everything works fine during the rehearsal, and problems come up at night, when security people, the police or remote television crews show up. These people weren't there during the rehearsal, and now you've got a bunch of walkie-talkies and wireless communications. Suddenly the air is full of all kinds of transmitted signals, and the ability of your mic to lock to its receiver [can be compromised in] these situations. If someone keys a 5-watt walkie-talkie while standing in the monitor area next to a receiver that is looking for a 1/2-watt output from a hand transmitter, it can pop them real good. So you need to keep these away from the receivers and make sure the staff is aware of the problem.

How do you deal with common wireless problems?
You generally have one main mic for the lead singer and a backup mic. With Barry [Manilow], we'd also have multiple handheld mics transmitting on the same frequency. Usually, if you have a problem with your wireless, it's a problem with the transmitter being dropped or hit. Then you can just grab the damaged one and provide another operating on the same frequency, which saves the engineer from having to repatch or set up another input channel. We also usually carry a spare wireless setup, because you'll find that some cities or areas are notorious when it comes to RF problems. There's a place in Jacksonville, Florida, that's next to a big transmitting antenna. During the day you

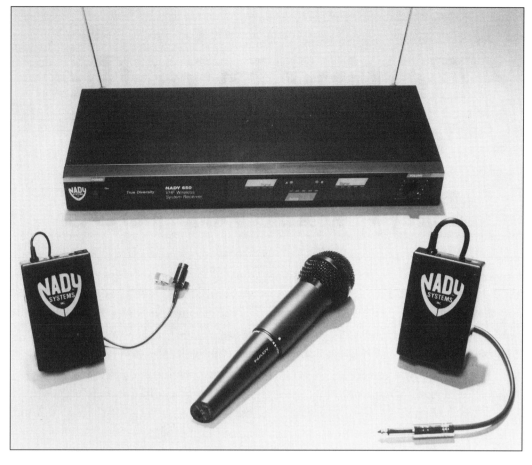

Nady 650 wireless system

usually have problems, but at night the transmitter goes to half-power and everything's okay.

When we did Barry on Broadway we had occasional problems—with all the taxis, police and other theaters in the area, you have a lot of RF. Consequently, you try to maximize your chances of keeping the signal as clean as possible between the transmitter and the receiver. With Barry, we just put his receiver onstage in front of him, so at any given time, it wasn't more than about five or six feet away. Yet even with the receiver that close, we'd still have problems on some nights, which gives you an indication of just how bad that area can be in terms of RF problems. It's almost an unspoken rule that whenever you're using wireless onstage, you also have a wired mic as a backup. There isn't a performer in the world who won't be seen performing

with a cable, if it's the difference between being heard and not being heard.

Anything else?

Wireless can be very helpful, especially when you're working in bad weather, because the performer is not really tied to anything you could get a shock from. We did a show with the Go-Go's where the lead singer was running around in the rain, and we didn't have to worry about her getting shocked, since there wasn't any physical connection to the audio system. We had a situation with Barry, where he was out singing in the rain during this mini-hurricane in Memphis, Tennessee. The management came running to us, wondering if he could get shocked while onstage, but he couldn't get shocked because he wasn't plugged into anything, so they left him out there and he had a ball doing the show.

"There isn't a performer in the world who won't be seen performing with a cable, if it's the difference between being heard and not being heard."
—Electrotec's Jeff Forbes

Getting In at the Ground Floor: Entry-Level Jobs

BY DAVID (RUDY) TRUBITT

WHILE SEVERAL OF THESE CHAPTERS provide some insight into the sound business from an owner's perspective, this section offers guidance for those looking to get their foot in the door. What do local, regional and national sound companies look for in new hires?

The bottom line is attitude (or lack thereof). In other words, don't apply if you're not a team player. "One of the things I tell people when they come in," says Bruce Burns of Burns Audio, "is that there are two sides to the sound business. Fifty percent is knowing how to do proper sound, and fifty percent is getting along with the people you work with." This sentiment was echoed by Stephen Zelenka, formerly of Maryland Sound's West Coast touring division: "What MSI stresses is attitude, willingness to learn and [a desire] to be part of a team. On the road, you might know everything about audio, but if you've got no personality, you're going to have a *lot* of trouble surviving."

Besides a winning attitude, most companies prefer some prior experience, including basic electronics and/or physics, previous live sound work and possibly some related college education. Also, a good driving record and willingness to drive a truck is a plus. Keith Holmlund of Swanson Sound Service Co., a regional company based in Oakland, Calif., points out that other skills are important, too. "We also look for someone with mechanical skills; when you get a product, it doesn't come packaged in the box and ready to go—the rack rail might not be on the right side, the casters won't always fit. You have to be good with your hands. That's a problem in this area, because high schools are cutting all their wood and metal shop programs."

Many sound companies voice concern that recording-oriented trade schools might not provide graduates with strong skills for sound reinforcement work. "The discipline, etiquette and work ethic required in our business is such a hands-on learning process that it's difficult to develop a program for it," says Mark Friedman of See Factor (Long Island City, N.Y.). Rick Baynard of Total Concert Productions (St. Petersburg, Fla.) agrees. They've hired graduates from audio schools, but first put them through an additional 250-hour internship to complete their live sound background.

"I find that putting them in with an engineer who's done a thousand shows gives them a lot more real-world experience," Baynard notes, "and the most recent intern we hired seemed to enjoy that setting more, too." Bruce Burns also expressed caution. "The resumes I get from people out of these recording schools are people that want to do recording, and we just don't do that. I say, 'This is not what you're looking for. We go out and load trucks and lift speakers.' It's a lot different

environment from the recording studio."

Rocky Norton of Sound Reinforcement Services (Athens, Ga.) views the issue in broader terms. "I think it's a great start that there are these schools cropping up. But I'm not sure how well they prepare students for the real world. I think that's true of school in general, not just the audio schools."

As always, there are more people looking than there are entry-level jobs. "I've gotten more resumes this year from people who are better qualified than ever before," See Factor's Friedman says. So what makes one prospective applicant stand out? "An intelligence factor, I guess," Rocky Norton says. "We look for a spark, an enthusiasm, an intelligence, an ability to learn. Not

people who would just be like robots and do exactly what you say, but who think for themselves as well."

"I look for character," MSI's Zelenka concludes. "They could call me 40 or 50 times, and I never tell them to stop. The ones that drop off quick I know aren't particularly interested. All sorts of people call for all sorts of reasons. It's the people who are the most passionate about it who interest me."

From Clubs to Arenas— One Engineer's Story

MANY ENTER THE LIVE SOUND FIELD WITH hopes of mixing arena shows on a state-of-the-art sound system, but it's generally better to have more realistic career expectations. Nevertheless, while the myth of

Most entry-level positions have little to do with mixing music. Here a crew readies a system fielded by UK sound companies Concert Sound and Britannia Row for a Dire Straits show.

Engineer Bruce Gasber

the overnight success is just that, there are people who work their way up from clubs into some of the highest-profile venues in the country.

One example is Akron, Ohio's Bruce Gasber. How did he do it? "I worked with a club act that played six nights a week, every week," says Gasber. "It was all one-nighters, carrying a full production. I took that P.A. in and out, maintained it, put it up and trouble-shot it." Longer tours at home and in Europe helped, too.

He also credits a stint as house engineer and assistant production manager as a great learning experience. "I worked in a Las Vegas-style show house in Akron. We would do acts like Bob Hope, Tom Jones and David Copperfield—a cabaret sort of thing." There he had the chance to work with visiting sound companies. "As I started to work with the majors," he adds, "I realized that it's not any different—the concepts remain the same. In fact, it's easier, because the gear is better." This kind of exposure works both ways: If you make an impression on a visiting crew, good or bad, word gets around.

Remember that opportunity can knock with unfamiliar gear in hand. "Over the course of my career," he says, "I've dealt with everything from a Peavey Mark III or a little Studiomaster club board, up to a Gamble." In such situations, getting up to speed quickly inspires confidence—floundering doesn't.

Eventually, Gasber landed a steady gig with rock guitar instrumentalist Vinnie Moore, based on a recommendation by Moore's previous soundman. This kind of close association with an artist can be the best ticket up: If the artist gets a shot and chooses to bring you along, you get to ride their coattails. In Gasber's case, this opportunity came when Moore landed an opening shot with Rush, who were touring arenas with major sound company Electrotec.

Gasber's first arena show turned out to be Madison Square Garden. Did someone say pressure? "It wasn't any different," Gasber insists. "I had a console. I had processing. I had the band. I had the front end. Just make it go—the same as any other day. Some guy came up to me and [Rush mixer] Robert Scovill after the show and said 'How do you get to this?' Robert passed the question to me. I told him 'I've done years and years of clubs, with every system imaginable, hauling it in and out, mixing in every situation—I've done my homework. I came in here and just kind of banged it out.'"

Being a Road Manager

BY
ROBYN
GATELY

"*H*ELLO." *HER VOICE WAS SOFT, YET STILL bright and cheerful. I opened the door and there she was…radiant. She took my arm and we whisked out the door. Fifty feet down the hallway, she stopped and said, "Have a good show!" and she was off—off to show 10,000 people a good time.*

In my business, that's the peak of the perfect day: delivering the artist to the stage in a great mood, ready to give it all to the audience. Me? I'm a soundman/road manager. It's an impossible job, and that's why I love it.

Some tours enjoy the luxury of everyone having only one job. However, economic considerations don't always make this possible. Experienced sound engineers who are very organized can greatly increase the value of their services by becoming sound engineer/road managers.

People who do both are very well paid for the service. The greatest part of the cost of taking a person on the road is usually not the salary, but the road expenses. Therefore, it's not uncommon for the road manager/sound engineer to be paid 50% to 100% more than a sound engineer who travels with a separate road manager.

A road manager (often referred to as an RM) is responsible for everything that goes on—or goes wrong—on the road. Generally, an RM does not make travel and hotel arrangements; that's what the tour manager (or the office) is for. But the RM does deal with any problems on the road, so if the hotel or venue screws up, it becomes their job to make things right.

The biggest challenge facing the novice RM is learning how to think fast. Artists are not known for their patience, so it's crucial that you quickly alleviate any worries.

One of the acts I work with is Judy Collins, who is well-known for having accomplished the impossible several times in her life. In the first five minutes I spent with her, I realized that any answer containing the word "no" would result in chaos. Nothing is impossible, so if she is told "no," she must then prove it *can* be done. Therefore, impossible requests require answers like, "I'll see what I can do," "I'll do the best I can," or "I'll take care of it."

Road management is an extremely stressful occupation. You are required to have all of the answers *now*. For instance, at the end of the show, the promoter and concessions want to pay you, the band wants to know their pickup times for the next day, the stage crew wants to get your stuff packed, the record company has 45 people coming backstage, and the star wants to know if the limo driver is waiting—all at the same time. Remember that the order in which you handle these requests may determine whether you have a job tomorrow!

Organization Is Essential

The most important part of being a good soundman/road manager is advancing the gig. At least a month (preferably four to six weeks) before the show, you should obtain a *work* or *gig sheet* (see p. 37) from

Once you arrive at the venue, the first ten minutes are crucial. During this time, everyone formulates their opinion of you and decides whether they're going to work with you or against you.

the management, including the following:

- Date of show
- Travel arrangements, including plane flight number and time, and car and van pickups at the airport
- Hotel name with address, phone number and room service hours
- Distance from airport to show
- Distance from airport to hotel
- Distance from hotel to show
- Venue name, address and phone number
- Promoter's name and phone number
- Sound, lighting and band equipment suppliers' names and phone numbers
- Any record company support
- Setup, soundcheck and show times

Then you should call everyone connected with the show; these advance calls establish the tone for the eventual performance. If the promoter dislikes you after this conversation, your gig may go badly. However, try not to react too negatively if you encounter difficulties at this point.

This is also your first chance to to gauge the promoter and discuss his/her responsibilities. A promoter who rushes the conversation is usually trouble. Be prepared to take 20 to 30 minutes to do it right, and make sure the artist pays for these calls.

Next, find out if the local production people can do the job. Realize that your ability to help and teach may become extremely important, since XYZ Productions may never have done a show this big before (and there is no other local choice). The "world's friendliest guy" can get the local crew to perform miracles, but if they dislike you, they can sabotage your efforts just by being slow to cooperate.

A week before the date, try to touch base again with all of the principal parties. This provides time to warn people if storm clouds are forming on the horizon. Keep in mind that people will sometimes reveal more than they might want: A promoter may not tell artist management if ticket

sales are slow, but this is crucial information if the date is being played for a percentage of the door. So pay close attention.

A day or two before the show, check the travel arrangements again. Arrange to have the driver stand at the airport arrival gate (not in baggage claim) with a sign with *your* name on it, *not* the artist's.

On the first day of the tour, go to the management office to pick up plane tickets, per diems for the band members, copies of all contracts, itineraries and "road float" (money for tips, expenses, emergencies, etc.). Having a copy of the contract can be extremely useful. You will be amazed at how many times changes have been agreed to, and then forgotten, by management. When the promoter makes changes, it's a good thing to have your own copy. When your artists object to the changes, at least you have proof that someone agreed to them.

Upon arrival at the airport, check all baggage with the skycaps. Skycaps are convenient, but more importantly, if you are a bag or two over the limit, a skycap will usually let you go; a counterperson can't.

This brings up the question of what baggage to check. You can't carry everything, but hand-carry the one piece that would stop the show if it were lost. With Judy, this is the dress bag.

Next, go to the gate and check in as early as possible. Have the gate agent confirm that all tickets and seat assignments are correct, and that your frequent flier mileage is put on the computer. This is important, because the only person who can use the mileage is *you.*

At the hotel, the RM usually checks everyone in and inspects the star's room. When checking in, give everyone in the band a list with the band's room numbers on it. Next, take the artist to their room. In most instances, you probably could just hand the artist their key and everything would be fine. But 10% of the time something is screwed up, so it's best to go with them. If you really want to impress, send performers shopping while you and the bellhop get the room ready.

After the artist is situated, you're ready to prepare for the show. Once you arrive at the venue, the first ten minutes are crucial. During this time, everyone formulates their opinion of you and decides whether they're going to work with you or against you. I always carry the artist's newest release on cassette and CD so that I have a gift when I meet the promoter. In that meeting, try to establish that you are all going to have a good time and are working toward the same goal: a profitable show everyone would like to do again someday. After all, your artist wants to come back and play this town every few years.

When the promoter is paying a flat rate, I try to arrange to receive the check during the afternoon. Every RM can tell you stories about the promoter leaving without paying you—sometimes on purpose. Remember that concessions are important to any mid-level act. This extra money can often be equivalent to your salary. Concessions will almost always be sold by the theater for a percentage, usually 20%-30%. Recently, a theater asked for 40%. I turned them down because the return for the act was not high enough.

Your first goal with the local crew is to establish a rapport. Never grapple with problems immediately on arrival; you will destroy the tone of the day. Then, ten minutes after you get there, deal with any problems. I occasionally have had to take someone to another room to read them the riot act. It doesn't help for everyone to know you can be a monster, but everyone expects that RMs can hold their own in any situation.

Before soundcheck, see that the dinner arrangements are correct and make sure that the dressing rooms have what you need—mirrors, towels, bathrooms, etc. If your act requires showers, please check them! You don't need the aggravation caused by showers that don't work or moldy shower curtains.

The biggest conflict in being a sound engineer/road manager is *time*. There are no two-hour soundchecks any more. If you can't make it sound great in a song and a half, it's time for a new engineer. My personal goal is always to get drum sounds in under two minutes.

After soundcheck, do a quick lighting check. It's assumed that most sound engineers/road managers do not know a whole lot about lighting. It may or may not be helpful to learn something about the subject, but you should realize that the more you know, the greater chance you have of getting bogged down in what is already a

ROCKY MOUNTAIN PRODUCTIONS
P.O. Box 1298
Cathedral Station
New York, NY 10025
(212) 749 - 7221

TODAY IS Friday   DATE August 30, 1991

TRAVEL: JC, Val, Robyn, Joseph, Zev   DEPART JUDY'S: 10:30am
Frank, Lou & Lisa, Louis.

12:00pm - Depart LGA, United #171
1:12pm - Arrive Dulles

Promoter to provide transportation

HOTEL: Dist. airport/show 20 mins
Sheraton Premiere at Tysons Corner
8661 Leesburg Pike   Dist. to airport   20 mins
Vienna, VA 22180
(703) 448-1234   Dist. to show   10 mins
FAX (703) 790-8091
Contact: Phyllis Bradley   Room Service   24 hours
(703) 506-2501
                                    Restaurant   6:00am - 2:00am

                                    Coffee Shop

                                    Other Facilities   Health Club

                                    Outdoor pools, raquethall, sauna

ROOM RATE: $79 per room
1 suite & 7 singles

VENUE: Wolf Trap - Filene Center
Vienna, VA
                                    Band setup   4:15pm

PROMOTER: Matt Hessberg   Sound Check   5:00pm 4:30pm-5:30pm
(703) 255-1900
                                    Off Stage   5:30pm

TECH. CTC: Showtime 8:45pm - One regular performance
                                              8:00pm - with band. w/Intermission
GBS: There will be a brief   Show Info:
reception backstage
MBL: immediately following the
performance, held for the
major donars (approx 20 people)
Matt Hessberg is in charge of
putting this together.

Judy Collins

very busy day.

Next, see if the guest list is ready. Since guest seats are usually in a prime position, having these seats empty may result in a noticeable hole in the audience. If your show is sold out, giving up these unused seats is the equivalent of handing the promoter extra dollars. They like that!

Have the local crew sweep and wash the stage after soundcheck. Also, write the name of the town you're in on the star's set list, and see that the driver is really going to be there after the show.

And Finally, Ladies and Gentleman, It's Showtime!

The pinnacle has been reached, and it's all downhill from here. If you've forgotten anything, it's too late now.

So now the show's over and the audience has gone home happy. But you're not done yet. Remember the flurry of activity I described at the beginning of this article? Here it comes…the record company, the band, the guests, the promoter, the concessions people and everyone in the world who wants an autograph. Priorities, priori-

ties. Stay in touch with your act and when they're ready to go, have everything set for them. Once everything is put away, you're almost done—just be sure that you thank everyone.

Suppose someone screwed up all day long. It's rarely a good idea to lambast someone in front of other people, if for no other reason than that people will remember you and be lying in wait the next time you arrive. It's better to let sleeping dogs lie and try to psych them into an acceptable performance before the next show.

When you get to the hotel and are safely in your room, you can finally call the band with their pickup times, call the front desk for your wake-up call and set your portable alarm, because hotels sometimes screw up. Now turn on the TV and take a couple of hours to wind down.

Organization is the key to this job. Ideally, you're going to do this perfectly for 40 or 60 days in a row. If you think it's easy, you've obviously never done it; if you think it sounds impossible, just remember that every day of the year a couple hundred of us are out there doing it.

Running a Regional Sound Company

BY
GREGORY A.
DETOGNE

TRYING TO RUN A PROFITABLE REGIONAL sound company in these days of retrenchment and economic malaise may be a strange notion to some. Despite the pitfalls and obstacles, however, there *is* still a breed of person ready to accept the challenge.

In a simple sense, a regional sound company is one that serves a distinct region. That may sound logical enough, but when you consider that a great deal of the sound companies that do most of their work within a specific geographical area also tour nationally and internationally, definitions become blurred. A more comprehensive description is that a regional sound company is one that may indeed tour nationally and internationally but can also be counted on to take care of the production needs of a specific market. For example, in major metropolitan areas such as New York, Chicago and Los Angeles, there are sound companies that can be relied upon to handle the local market's production needs, whether it's for a Fourth of July festival or a top-name concert tour needing additional help. These companies, regardless of whether or not they've been seen regularly with The Judds in Brazil, are what we'll define as regional sound companies.

It's important to consider from a marketing and legal standpoint what it takes to manage a regional sound company successfully. Let's assume you've collected the necessary gear your sound company will need and have the means to haul it around and store it safely. What's next? Other than searching for paying clients, you should look into the matter of contracts.

Contracts

According to Bill Hosch, the logistics manager of Dallas-based Bernhard Brown Inc., a good contract has saved him from many problems. "With a good contract, you can avoid billing questions, labor disputes, payment problems and all kinds of impromptu field negotiations," he says. "Our contract, which was drawn up by a lawyer we keep on retainer, has performance guidelines, an equipment schedule, a payment schedule and exhibit after exhibit of what the client is paying for and what we're sending. It's not a document written in incomprehensible legalese, but it definitely lays all the cards on the table."

Bob Walker of Brisbane, Calif.'s Sound on Stage thinks of a contract in anatomical terms. "A contract is like a skeleton, the bones of a deal," he says. "When you talk about a contract, you're talking about the relationship between yourself and the client, how you perceive your services, what the client wants and how you'll respond to those needs. Once you've established these things, then you send out the paper. It needs to be a good contract, presentable and readable, with all of the information the client needs to make a decision. It also has to have the nuts and bolts spelled out."

Detail is vital to a contract. For example, the number of stage hands to be provided by the promoter should be written out, along with elements such as the times of day for load-in, load-out, soundcheck and final payment. If a deposit is required, the contract should specify the amount, the type of funds and the date and time of payment.

"The worst thing that ever happened to me was when we failed to specify at what time during the day of the show the final payment was to change hands," Hosch adds. "The client wanted to pay after the show, and I maintained that we traditionally collect after soundcheck. That way, if we don't get paid, we can hold the show until the check shows up. In this case, since it wasn't carved in stone, we were forced to go along with the client. Finally, while we were loading the trucks, the payment came, and it was $1,500 short. At that point, we had no viable recourse, since that was all the client was willing to give us. It was simply another $1,500 tuition payment made to the college of hard knocks."

If properly worded, a contract can be invaluable for settling disputes, regardless of whether the friction is caused by events outside of anyone's control (i.e., the truck didn't get there because of an earthquake, flash flood, blizzard, etc.) or involves litigation. In the latter instance, specify the physical location in which litigation, if required, will occur. Any court action that takes place outside of your home state will be costlier, given that you'll spend time and money traveling and will have to hire an out-of-state attorney.

All caveats aside, is there any time you don't need a contract? Sure, a lot of business is still conducted the old-fashioned way with a smile and a handshake, but it's strongly advised that you save those types of deals for long-standing clients with whom you have a good relationship.

With a signature on your contract and a deposit check in hand, it's time to pack the truck and start rolling, right? Well, not yet—the truck, your employees and every other facet of the business need insurance.

Insurance

As a general rule, you can never have enough insurance. Jack Boessneck, direc-

tor of sales and marketing at Cleveland's Eighth Day Sound, strongly agrees. "It costs us somewhere in the neighborhood of $6,000 to $15,000 per year just to maintain $2 million worth of liability and comprehensive insurance, and that may not be enough, given the way juries have handed out punitive damage awards recently."

Boessneck also uses insurance as a sales tool, especially in bidding situations. "If I'm bidding against someone for a job, I always make it a point to ask the client how much insurance my competition has, including workman's compensation," he says. "There have been times when the amounts we carry have made a difference in getting the job. After all, if a sound company is underinsured or uninsured, insurance shouldn't become the client's responsibility. I'm responsible because I'm the one who's in business, and I don't know of any business that would suspend several thousand pounds over a crowd of people and not carry insurance."

Taxes

We've seen that if anything's certain in this business, it's the necessity of contracts and insurance. There is another certainty, and that's taxes. A handy and obvious guideline (useful in preventing the IRS from examining your tax file with a microscope) is to remember that for every dollar you make, the government will want a piece of it. Save accordingly, pay on time, and things will run smoothly. Other areas of taxation are more nebulous and vary from state to state. A quick-witted accountant can help you take advantage of every break possible.

Whether you choose to own or lease your equipment can also have tax repercussions. "In order for leasing to be tax-advantageous, it has to be a true lease," says Gary Mathews of Quickbeam Systems Inc., a regional sound company based in Albuquerque, N.M. "A true lease enables you to write off the entire amount of the lease, which can be good for some. The problem with a true lease is that you'll never actually own the equipment, which means all the money spent on the lease is useless when it comes to building assets. If you're not interested in building assets, a true lease is the way to go. Here at Quickbeam, we generally use lease/purchase programs, which allow us to gain a few tax breaks by amortizing our payments on a schedule, similar to what can be done if you buy a piece of gear outright. At the end of the lease, we usually make a final payment and the equipment is ours, thereby becoming a business asset."

But if you own the equipment, what happens when it becomes obsolete? "Obsolescence isn't really a problem when you own," Mathews explains. "We have components in our shop that are 20 years old, and we still use them. We don't use this stuff for our main gigs, of course, but it still gets around. Eventually we may sell an older piece we never use, but then we have to pay a capital gain tax if we don't reinvest the money we make."

Pricing

Compared to some of the parameters mentioned above, pricing seems to be a more ambiguous, though no less crucial, aspect of a well-run business. How do you set pricing? Bernhard Brown's Bill Hosch feels that voodoo may be a factor. "Pricing is probably something everyone wishes they had some magic formula for," he confides. "Sometimes it seems like voodoo. We'll submit a bid and it will match all of the others almost to the penny. At other times, we're significantly lower or higher. Usually, however, our clients tell us that we're really close to the price structure of the competition. The only reason I can give for this occurring is chance."

If we remove the voodoo factor from the equation, however, logic tells us that it still costs every sound company the same amount to move from point A to point B,

labor is generally the same price, and everyone's gear costs about the same. That being the case, can a universal formula be applied to the pricing dilemma?

"It's not by accident that everyone seems to have the same price," says Al Holman of United Sound Associates USA, based in Yakima, Wash. "From my point of view, pricing should boil down to two components: how much you want to make on the job, and what your expenses are. Clients do have budgets, and you naturally want to stay at the top end of their range, but if a promoter you've been doing business with for 15 or 20 years tells you that they need help on the price of a certain gig, you'd better be prepared to make concessions. In relationships like that, you know you'll make it up down the road."

Bob Walker at Sound on Stage takes a straight-ahead approach to pricing. "Anyone who thinks a client doesn't know what the costs are is a fool," he states flatly. "And anyone who thinks the competition doesn't know what the costs are is also a fool. When I set pricing, I want the client to know that they're getting a fair deal. You can't just keep marking prices up—then the client will think that they're being gouged, and that's certainly no way to build confidence."

Clients

Building client confidence is crucial, as are many other aspects of maintaining good client relations. Providing good service is the best way to keep a client happy. "A lot of smaller companies don't even realize what service is all about," Eighth Day's Jack Boessneck says. "You can get great gear anywhere in the country. What you can't get is good service, and that takes on many forms. Appearance is an important service factor—not only the appearance of the gear itself, but also of the crew. If I'm doing an industrial, I'm not going to send crew members wearing the latest heavy-metal T-shirts. To keep the gear looking good, we continually maintain everything.

Sure, we have components that are a few years old, but we make sure they look like new when they leave the shop. Service also means taking care of the details. When clients use one of our consoles on tour, they can expect to open the box and find that it's all laid out, labeled and so forth. That's what service is about, giving clients a little bit more than they expect to pay for."

Staff

Dealing well with your staff is also important. It almost goes without saying that fair treatment and pay are crucial, along with providing good working tools and equipment, plus benefits like workman's compensation or health insurance. Keeping morale high benefits everyone as well, and a large part of maintaining team spirit depends on what kind of players are on the team.

For Al Holman, good employee qualities start with a good disposition and sense of humor. "We all enjoy our jobs and like to have fun while we're working," he says, "so it's important that new employees have the same outlook. Outside of that, people we employ need to have certain motor skills and physical abilities to take care of the heavy work, and they have to be able to relate to others on a one-on-one basis. Relating to people like that means you have to know how to have a good day even when everyone else isn't, and you have to know how not to make everyone else's bad when yours sucks."

A good way to find employees who are right for your company is to try people out temporarily while working short-term jobs. Based on their performance in these situations, you'll be able to decide whether or not they'd be suitable for a full-time position.

Employing people full-time naturally requires that your company work year-round, which means surviving the winter successfully. How can you make it once the summer season is over? "Don't put yourself in a survival mode," Holman says. "Constantly maintain your workload by working colleges, community Christmas festivals, industrials and anywhere else that generates cash flow. That way you'll stretch the big dollars you made in-season further. You should also stretch the borders of the region you're working. Keep looking for the next biggest town where there's work. Also, don't pigeonhole yourself into thinking that you just have to do music. Think of all the opportunities available in politics, theater, at churches and so forth. Don't be afraid of doing permanent installations either. We've been doing well as of late with sports bars and churches."

Sound on Stage also takes on different work during the off-season. Corporate work they've landed includes jobs with IBM, Apple and Kawasaki. "The real difference between a touring company and a regional company is that a regional company can find work in the winter that doesn't happen in the summer," Bob Walker emphasizes. "Besides the corporate things we do, we've developed a subsidiary company called California Cases that makes road cases in the same shop we use to build our own sound systems. All of this helps us get through the winter."

That, in a nutshell, is what it takes to run a regional sound company. Is there any last bit of wisdom from our experts? "Once you get yourself going, you can't survive for very long by thinking about one account as the real money-maker," Walker says. "If you want to be around for a while, you have to look at things in the long term, and treat everyone the same so that they'll come back. Your business will be built by satisfying one client and then another. The satisfied clients will recommend you to someone else, and then you'll have another client. You can advertise and promote yourself in many other ways, but word of mouth is what works in this business, and nothing else."

Buying Concert Speaker Systems

BY
GEORGE
PETERSEN

R UNNING A SOUND REINFORCEMENT company is no picnic: The hours are long, the ratio of financial return to investment is low, and the risks are great. Yet staying afloat requires making informed decisions in order to stay competitive. Perhaps the most important of these decisions is the selection of the most essential (and expensive) component in any concert sound system: main loudspeaker systems. Here, a number of regional sound reinforcement companies across the country discuss the factors that led them to select their current systems.

CAREY SOUND
Greensboro, North Carolina

This 15-year-old business started out as a concert production company and over the years expanded with sales (retail and contract/install) and rental (staging/lighting/concert audio) divisions. Carey Sound made the jump into arena-size shows in 1985, when the company went from proprietary loudspeakers to the EV Manifold MT-4 system.

Ken Carey: "I've made some strategic alliances with other companies—both local and some farther away. Some time ago, we set up a pseudo-network for owners of EV manifold boxes, with several other users, and now Electro-Voice is finally getting going and making it official. My feeling is that Electro-Voice should take a more active role in making sure that I'm busy—they've got just as much at stake and just as much invested as I do in their equipment.

"When this company started, I had a lot of time and no money. So I started constructing boxes—in fact, for years we built boxes for ourselves and several regional sound companies in the area. When the EV Manifold boxes came out, I was really excited because we had to get more 'oomph' out of smaller boxes. We ordered their first four boxes without even seeing the final versions. Prior to buying the Manifold system, I had never considered buying a piece of equipment that one person couldn't maneuver, because as the owner of a regional sound company, when everybody else disappears, it's up to you. In the 'bad old days,' there were more occasions than I care to remember when I literally had to go out and do a show by myself.

"If you take four times anybody else's system and cram it into one box, you've got the Manifold system. So there was an initial perception that you've shown up with a little system, since there are 32 speakers in one block, and you can't see the 12 drivers in each of the top cabinets.

"We currently have six blocks (12 bottoms/12 tops). We can easily do a 15,000-seat hall with six blocks and have all the SPL we need. We can do 2,000 or 3,000 people outdoors with one block [two bottom and two top cabinets]. We're using the stock [EV] MTX-4 crossovers, and we'll stick with those until we can get the new QSC/MediaLink controllers for our EX-4000 amps. MediaLink is a wonderful protocol, and [computer control] is our future."

JBL Array Series

DALLAS BACKUP
Dallas, Texas

For the past 14 years, Dallas Backup has provided sound, lights, staging and musical equipment to a variety of touring artists, including country superstar George Strait (a regular customer for nearly a decade). According to president Charles Belcher, the company is quite successful in focusing on the production niche, without relying on the usual sound company sidelines such as sales and installation work. Besides a large roster of country acts, the company also handles conventions, special events and pops concerts for the Dallas symphony. Dallas Backup recently purchased a large selection of Clair Brothers 12AM monitors to complement its two main touring systems—a proprietary system using JBL components and an Eastern Acoustic Works system with KF-850s and 300s.

Charles Belcher: "We built our custom system in 1984, and back then Clair Brothers, Showco or any company trying to make a name for themselves would build their own boxes. Since then, of course, the sound reinforcement industry has changed dramatically, and now off-the-shelf speakers are everywhere. We made a decision to offer both our own and a manufactured design, and we chose EAW.

"Buying the EAW system was an orchestrated move when our production business doubled and almost tripled. Fortunately, all the manufacturers have reps here in Dallas, so we rounded up the systems we wanted to listen to in our warehouse—it wasn't too difficult; we listened to them all and picked the one we liked. Now if I was in Boise, Idaho, it would have been a little bit harder. It wasn't too tough, as everything was available to us here. And, of course, if you're going to spend a lot of money, people are going to listen to you [Laughs].

"Proprietary systems don't show up on riders very often, but our system is great for outdoor festivals, and there's always a need for ours. Our regular customers know what our custom system sounds like, because we've had them for so long. The custom system went out with George Strait for the first four years, and when we bought the EAWs, we kept them here for a year and then put them out with George.

"Our two systems are comparable in the size of venues they can handle, and they interchange all of the time. We designed the cabling and amp racks to work with either system, and both have [Yamaha] PM3000 consoles, so there's more to it than just the speakers—you have to consider the whole package. Our boxes take up a lot more truck space than the EAWs, which made more room for lighting, so we could have a bigger lighting show. Truck space is always a consideration."

MORGAN SOUND
Lynnwood, Washington

Located just 15 minutes north of Seattle, Morgan Sound is a multifaceted company, offering retail sales (with two pro audio showrooms), lighting and video sales, audio design/installations, service, small system rentals and, of course, touring and regional sound reinforcement with a 70-box JBL Concert Series system. According to owner Charlie Morgan, the 23-year-old company has also diversified into another market—renovating the sound systems of 18 cruise ships over the past seven years.

Charlie Morgan: "It's been five or six years since I bought the JBL Concert Series system. Before that, I had come off the road for 12 years with Gordon Lightfoot, and one of the ways that I auditioned loudspeakers was when I had a block of three dates with Gordon someplace, I rented loudspeakers or I would subcontract a company to do the gig with me so I could hear their speakers. I owned some Northwest Sound stuff, so I rented from Maryland Sound, Clair, Audio Analysts and tried out other systems.

"I went with a JBL system. Building my own speakers was not an option, because I didn't want to get into that much R&D. Having spent many years looking at equipment riders, I knew that if you didn't have the right equipment names, you wouldn't get the work. And the processor-controlled systems I listened to—such as the Meyer and Renkus-Heinz—didn't sound as natural with a microphone plugged into them as the JBL Concert Series did.

"The final major point was that if I bought S4s or Renkus-Heinz M-4s, then I'd need a pretty big stack of equipment to handle a small gig. The M-4 only operated as a three-box module; the S4s were big, unwieldy and heavy—difficult for one or two guys to manhandle into a hotel. The Concert Series appealed to me because I could break it down into small pieces. I could modularly build it up in increments of two boxes and have the ability to splay, as well as separate and do four rooms with one truck with equipment.

"So I rented. I listened. I considered and wanted to go with something where I'd get strong factory support—and I got far more support from JBL than I ever expected. There's another issue. If I say I own 48 mid/high packs and 22 double-18 subs of JBL Concert Series, then somebody has a pretty good idea of what kind of investment I've made. So even if somebody doesn't know my company—at least coming in—they know what I'm using."

PROMIX
Mt. Vernon, New York
Founded ten years ago, ProMix specializes in audio for theatrical shows, along with installations and special events, such as the 1992 Democratic National Convention. According to project manager Mary Falardeau, ProMix currently keeps its large Meyer complement busy with seven shows on Broadway, several touring companies and a number of industrials.

Mary Falardeau: "When we were called to do *Miss Saigon*, it came as a surprise to much of the industry, because no one knew we were big enough to handle it. At the time, we were thought of as a small company, so *Miss Saigon* served as a proving ground for us. We handled it successfully, and a lot of people who would not normally have come to us with bigger things started calling. It really changed the nature of what we're doing.

"With the big shows, the choice of speakers is completely determined by the show's sound designer. What's out there and working is what gets noticed. The sound designers didn't find Meyer because it was what the rental houses had—they found it because it was out there and was what they wanted. For example, *Miss Saigon* designer Andrew Bruce is adamant about using a Meyer system. Tony Meola, the designer of *Guys and Dolls* and *Five Guys Named Moe*, also wants to use Meyer all the time. On systems we design or install, we have more of a choice: We occasionally use EAW or Apogee, but frequently go with Meyer. It can deal with rough treatment on the road, and it's consistent, reliable and clean-sounding. It's the best thing out there."

Electro-Voice MT-4 loudspeaker system

Turbosound Flashlight
loudspeaker rig

SCORPIO SOUND
West Bridgewater, Massachusetts

Founded in 1979 and located about 20 miles south of Boston, Scorpio Sound handles a variety of local one-offs and corporate events, along with regional and national tour legs. About 18 months ago, the company augmented its 60-box EAW complement (32 KF-550s, 18 split KF-550s and ten SB-550 quad subs) with 32 of the larger KF-850s and eight KF-850 subs. While out with the Tom Tom Club/Soup Dragons/James/Black Sheep tour, head engineer Carl Gagnon reported that Scorpio's system was put to the test at the Boston Garden by WBCN's "The Rock of Boston," a festival event that required not only a 360-degree arena P.A., but also a separate P.A. for a second stage.

Carl Gagnon: "We decided on the EAW system predominantly because we feel it's the best-sounding off-the-shelf box that you can buy at this point. Also, we're [geographically] close to EAW here and get excellent factory support.

"To a certain extent, the EAW [Virtual Array Technology Assocation] users network was a factor because it makes a lot of sense to have a system that's easily expandable [by cross-renting similar gear from other sound reinforcement companies]. One problem with the proprietary speaker systems—like the big touring companies have—is that once you run out of boxes, you can't get them anywhere else. So at that point, if you want to increase your company's business, you have to invest in building more cabinets to keep up with the demand. Of course, we all know that the demand can be quite large one day and quite minimal the next day. With the EAW system, we can keep our relative inventory low and still be able to have the luxury: If we need 100 boxes for one show, we can get 100 boxes for one show.

"On the Soup Dragons tour we did a variety of venues, from small clubs to large arenas. If we had our own proprietary system, we'd have to carry enough boxes to handle the largest arena we'd be doing on the tour. So we would carry a smaller number of cabinets and locally rent boxes to handle the larger shows. I carried enough power amps to double the size of the P.A. system at any one time, so all I had to do was have more boxes brought in and plug them in."

WEST RIVER LIGHT & SOUND
Sanford, Michigan

Located about 30 minutes from Saginaw, Mich., West River Light & Sound is a full-service company specializing in complete production packaging, with staging, lighting, roofing and audio systems, along with sales and contracting. When we contacted Chris Irons, the owner of the 12-year-old company, he was on tour with regular client Sawyer Brown.

Chris Irons: "We've had our Turbosound system for about a year and a half. When we did an installation at the time (a renovation at the Pine Knob Music Theatre in Detroit), Turbosound was a logical choice. There is a noise curfew and sound-level situation with some of the local residents, and we put in the delay system for the theater, which is an outdoor shed. They do about 80 events a year; there's a JBL system for the lawn, but most of the touring acts were carrying production [sound systems] in there with them. There's seating for about 6,000 under the pavilion and another 10,000 on the lawn. We proposed a Turbo system with a Crown IQ system, which was ideal for this application because it allows the stage manager to control the level on the lawn area, so the venue doesn't have problems or complaints from local residents. That installation was the beginning of our involvement

Intersonics Bass Tech 7 Servo-Drive subwoofers

with Turbosound, and now we've got a 40-box system out on the road.

"We had been doing staging and lighting for quite a while, and over the years we've had different brands of speaker systems, including some proprietary systems we put together. But there are a number of things that attracted us to Turbosound: The packaging is good, the flying hardware is good, but most of all it's a good-sounding box. Another thing is that two or three major manufacturers show up all the time on riders, and Turbosound is one of them. After all, we're in the rental business, and we need equipment that is marketable. Ultimately, this stuff has to generate revenue and pay for itself.

"When an artist or client is doing advance work for tours or for one-off dates, it's nice to say that you have a Turbosound, Meyer or EAW system and hear the guy on the other end say, 'It's no problem.' I've also been on the other side of that, doing the advance work. If a local sound company has a proprietary system, trying to figure out what their system sounds like can be a real guessing game. Now, some of those [proprietary] systems work really well, but some of those systems leave you wanting."

Safe Rigging Practices

BY DAVID
(RUDY)
TRUBITT

FOR YEARS A STAPLE OF THE TOURING scene, flown loudspeakers are now becoming commonplace in smaller venues and installations all over the country. Users and manufacturers alike share a concern for the safety of these systems, but, surprisingly, there are no standards for rigging design, nor for accreditation of riggers themselves. Fortunately, those familiar with the dos and don'ts are eager to share their knowledge, in the interest of safety for all involved. The information provided here is intended as food for thought and not explicit design information. When rigging, always seek the advice of qualified experts.

The most basic rule of rigging is this: *Design your rig to support five times the weight of your maximum intended load.* While most sound reinforcement people have heard of this 5:1 factor, not everyone understands why it is so important. If a rigging system is designed with a reduced safety factor—say 2:1 or 3:1—it's still two to three times stronger than it needs to be, isn't it? Harry Donovan, a 22-year veteran of the tour scene, warns, "The speakers won't stay up in the air as long—the rigging will eventually break." Andrew Martin, president of the ATM Group, a manufacturer of loudspeaker flying hardware, agrees. "Everybody's always very interested in the right way to do it," he says. "At the same time, not everyone is ready to build it that way, due to the cost involved. They may not have had accidents using a safety factor of 2:1 or 3:1, but it doesn't mean they won't down the road."

A 5:1 design factor is necessary for a number of reasons. Although only load-rated hardware should be used, it is possible that such a fitting does not meet its published specification. This could be due to wear, a manufacturing defect or other causes. In any case, if the part is being loaded to only one-fifth of its rated capacity, a reduction in its strength is less likely to cause a catastrophic failure.

Another reason for over-design is the dynamic loading put on a rigging system when starting and stopping chain motors. Andrew Martin recently analyzed the problem with a structural engineer and determined that the shock load adds 85% to the weight. "A good rule of thumb is to figure that you're doubling the load when you start things moving," says Martin. "That happens every single time you start a motor or let it drop." Chain motors aren't the only case to consider—earthquakes are a less predictable but clearly potent source of dynamic loading.

If any doubts remain as to the need for a 5:1 safety factor, reflecting on the risks involved should quickly dispel them. "When you think about rigging," Donovan says, "you're thinking about killing people or not killing them. If you put in just one fitting that doesn't work, or put it in the wrong way, you could kill dozens of people. That fact calls for an entirely different level of concern than plugging a microphone in. If you plug a mic in wrong, it's fixable. But most people put the same level of concern into rigging as they do into other things."

Paula Abdul's Maryland Sound Industries system (rigging by Harry Donovan). The total weight of this production's flown gear was 67,000 pounds.

What steps are necessary to ensure that you're working safely? "You have to look at every single element in the system," Donovan says, "and make sure you have that safety factor for each one. You may have decreased the strength of a part somehow. For instance, pulling an eyebolt at an angle will decrease its strength. You have to figure out what angles you're pulling and what the strength loss is due to the way you're using it, and make sure you still have a 5:1 safety factor."

It is a basic fact of rigging that the effective weight of a load can increase greatly depending on the angle of the cables suspending it. Take the simplified example of a 1,000-pound load held by two cables. If the cables are the same length, hang vertically and are balanced between the load's center of gravity, each will be stressed to 500 pounds. This seems intuitive enough, until the angles of the suspending cables deviate from vertical. Rocky Paulson of Stage Rigging explains: "With bridle legs of equal length hanging at an angle of 30 degrees with a 1,000-pound load, you have 1,000 pounds of force in *each* leg. If you decrease the angle

Materials Under Stress

Let's look briefly at the properties of different materials involved in rigging and how they respond to stress and ageing. There are different types of stress, but the two most basic are tension (stretching) and compression (squashing). "Both steel and aluminum react the same way," says Andrew Martin. "They don't like compression. An obvious case is a Coke can. You can step on a Coke can and crush it, but you couldn't pull one apart with a three-ton press."

Different metals and alloys age differently. "Steel simply loses volume [and, correspondingly, strength] as it rusts," says Martin, "but aluminum hardens with age and becomes brittle and cracks. Take a look at a piece of triangular box lighting truss that's been in use a long time. If you look around all the cross-sectional braces, they're cracked right around the weld, because that's where it flexes. Aluminum trusses have a life cycle of about five or ten years, on average. The more brittle your material is, the more susceptible it is to damage from a shock. So you can imagine that aluminum is not too good under shock-loading, especially after it's been used a lot, or after it's been tested.

"Concrete does not like tension at all," Martin says. "But it takes compression like crazy. That's why they build highways out of it. When highways fall down in an earthquake, it's because tension is applied to them." Steel-reinforced concrete behaves better under tension, but Martin urges caution. "Concrete is basically something to be avoided from a rigger's standpoint, unless it's a concrete-wrapped I-beam.

"In a professional venue, you don't see many wood beams," Martin continues, "but you find them in many installs. Wood handles both tension and compression, but the weight rating is greatly reduced. Fastening to wood beams is tough and always should be looked at by a structural engineer—there is no single way to do it. We found that out in a job we bid—we were going to put lag bolts in and when we had the outside engineering done, we found out we had to wrap the beams instead." Of course, wood plays a central role in speaker cabinets, although any flown enclosure should be steel-reinforced. "The cabinet's the weakest link in the chain," Martin says. "Way before any steel will fail, the cabinet will pull apart. It pulls apart in the middle of the cabinet, or two or three inches from the edge. Corners are well-braced, so there's less force on the cabinet seams than on the sides."

15 degrees, it would be roughly 2,000 pounds in each leg. And if you try to make it perfectly horizontal, the load will be an infinite weight."

"You have to calculate this load [angle] and make sure that even with this increase in force you still have the 5:1 safety factor," urges Donovan. (These calculations become quite complex when dealing with different leg lengths and angles. Donovan carries a palm-top computer running a spreadsheet program to facilitate the process.)

"Finally," Donovan continues, "look at the load increase factor from shock-loading [an increase of up to 85%, as men-tioned above] and make sure you still have the 5:1 safety factor. You'll end up with pieces a lot bigger than you thought. In most accidents, several things go wrong simultaneously. The safety factors are so high that doing a single thing wrong usually doesn't cause an accident—usually, you have to do two or three things wrong at once."

With safety in mind, let's turn to a familiar issue—getting your loudspeaker array positioned optimally in the room. "[Touring] sound companies want their speakers in the same place every day," Donovan says. "I'll typically find that it's not safe to get that many speakers up in a certain building, or it's not safe to get the height they want. As the bridles get flatter and flatter, you reach a limit as the tension increases. So between a reasonable bridle angle and the slightly lower beams of a particular building, the speakers are lower than the engineer would like. At that point they'll complain, and the riggers will be under pressure to do things that they think are not safe.

"What happens then depends on personalities," he continues. "How dominant are the sound people and how sure of themselves are the riggers? The trouble is, most riggers can't calculate tensions, forces, loads on beams and what those beams can take. All they can do is estimate—'We did this before and it worked'—but the fact that something's worked before doesn't mean it has a 5:1 safety factor. Because these riggers are guessing and estimating, they are apt to change their minds slightly under a lot of pressure. In some cases, they're doing things that they aren't sure are safe. What's needed is the education so they can do the calculations and tell the sound engineers, 'If we get it two feet higher, it's going to cause 4,700-pound tension on this cable rated at 4,000-pound safe working load, and we can't do that.'" The bottom line? "Don't ask the rigger to do something he doesn't think is safe," Donovan concludes. "It happens frequently, and it's a bad idea, because he's liable to do it if you ask him strongly enough."

Behind this interpersonal dynamic looms the issue of liability. Andrew Martin says, "If I'm a sound company and I pay a rigger to hang my points, I'm responsible for what that person does." If the sound company tells the rigger where and how the points should be set up, they're assuming additional liability by specifying how the job should be done. "If you tell them to get the points however they can," Martin says, "the liability issue is somewhat clouded—it has to be decided in court. But you can bet that in any situation, you are at least 50 percent responsible."

Talk of responsibility quickly leads to thoughts of insurance. "If you give any kind of instruction and it's not your profession," Martin continues, "you're in big trouble, and no one is going to insure you on that. For a contractor to get liability insurance is not a big deal—it's just a general liability policy. But the insurance company does need to be informed that you are hanging things above people's heads so that they can make a notation on the policy. Most of the insurance writers will overlook that and call it a general liability policy, but if it comes to a claim, they'll try to find every loophole they can. In order to protect yourself, you want to make sure [the policy] specifically notes that you are rigging things above populated areas."

The building you are hanging the equipment in also needs to be considered. Most structures are designed to support the extra loads that result from wind, rain and snow, but architects of smaller structures may not have considered the load an average-sized sound system can present for the building's roof. Compared to rigging's 5:1 design factor, building codes typically require far smaller design factors—well under 2:1. "Buildings are not

A loudspeaker cluster constructed with ATM flyware

designed to waste the builder's money," says Martin. "They design them as cheaply as possible for the purpose. If a wall and girder system's purpose is to hold up a ceiling, then it will be designed to use the minimal parts and be the cheapest for the builder, which means they are not going to design for any tensional stress [as created by flown equipment]. In big venues it is considered, but in smaller facilities they don't consider it." Where any doubt exists, it is necessary to consult with a structural engineer to ensure safety.

Even if your sound company hires experienced riggers to set your points, there's still the design of your loudspeaker grid to consider. Those choosing to build their own should follow the same 5:1 design factors. "There are dozens of designs out," Donovan says. "Some of them are extremely flexible and adjustable, and some have no adjustment to them. Some

Rigging Resources

• Harry Donovan and Dr. Randy Davidson periodically present three-day seminars in conjunction with Synergetic Audio Concepts. For information, contact Syn-Aud-Con at 12370 W. Co. Rd., 100 N., Norman, IN 47264, (812) 995-8212.

• ATM Flyware offers free information on proper use of their products and safe rigging in general. For a copy of the Safety Handbook and Rigging Reference Manual, contact ATM at 20960 Brant Ave., Carson, CA 90810, (310) 639-8282.

• The U.S. Institute for Theater Technology oversees independently run seminars on rigging and other aspects of performance facility safety. For information, contact the USITT's commissioner of engineering, Jerry Gorrell, c/o the Phoenix Civic Plaza, 225 East Adams, Phoenix, AZ 85004, (602) 262-7364. According to Gorrell, the Institute is in the process of developing an ANSI standard for rigging design. When completed, the document will be the first such standard written.

• JBL Professional publishes a free white paper detailing many important aspects of rigging safety. For a copy of Tech Note Vol. 1, Number 14, "Basic Principles for Suspending Loudspeaker Systems," contact JBL Professional at 8500 Balboa Blvd., Northridge, CA 91329, (818) 893-8411. This document is also available via the company's FlashFax service; call (818) 895-8190 from a touch-tone phone and request document number 903.

• Chain motor manufacturer Columbus McKinnon offers maintenance training seminars for their products. Contact CM at 140 John James Audubon Parkway, Amherst, New York 14228-1197, (716) 689-5400.

• Community Professional Sound Systems offers "Rigging Information for Flying Systems for Community Loudspeakers." This free booklet also includes some general rigging information and a substantial listing of rigging hardware suppliers. Contact Community at 333 E. 5th St., Chester, PA 19013-4511, (215) 876-3400.

"When you think about rigging, you're thinking about killing people or not killing them."
—Harry Donovan

companies have done a very thorough engineering job on their grids, while some have never been tested and are obviously put together by some apprentice in the metal shop. I wish we could convince all sound companies to get their stuff engineered and tested—it's the ones who aren't making that much money who think they can't afford to do it. These companies are also usually the ones with the least training for their people, so they're the most dangerous."

Testing should always be approached with care. Martin described a situation where testing itself caused a hazardous situation. A sound company designed a loudspeaker grid with only a 2:1 safety factor. To test it, they loaded it to 150%. It held, and out the door it went. If the system had a 5:1 design factor, 150% of the grid's safe working load would have represented 30% of the system's theoretical limit. But with only a 2:1 design factor, their test load was actually 75% of the weight required to cause catastrophic failure. Add to that the shock-load when hoisting the rig, and the maximum load could easily have been reached. Stress like that causes permanent damage to the system. "There's a point in any alloy called the yield point," Martin explains, "where the material gets flexed so far that it doesn't return to its original shape. You've changed the molecular structure of that part and weakened it. It's very bad to test something until it starts to bend and then say, 'This is strong, use it.' But a lot of people will do that."

"Every piece of hardware has to be load-rated by the manufacturer [and be rated] for holding loads over people," Donovan adds. "They should probably also be proof-tested at twice the safe working load so you know there's nothing wrong with it. Some manufacturers proof-test every single piece, some don't test any, some test a few samples from each batch. Standard proof-test is two-fifths of the yield point. You shouldn't test it to anywhere near its yield point, but twice the safe working load [assuming a 5:1 design factor] should be fine."

It's important to note that metal parts will reach their yield point before breaking. The additional force required to reach break-point varies, but is often in the 20% to 30% range. All rigging components should be rated for a maximum load, but whether that value represents the yield or breaking point is a particular often omitted by the manufacturer. Finally, remember that testing won't guarantee that the part won't fail someday. Unless a part is tested to its destruction, the test will only prove the part is capable of supporting the weight you've tested it to, and since that point should not be over two-fifths of its maximum load, you can't be sure how the part will perform under extraordinary conditions while in use.

Finally, safety requires maintenance, which means keeping a watchful eye on all your equipment. For example, experienced riggers will throw away any metal fitting or part which falls from a distance onto a concrete floor, as hidden damage can result from the fall. "If *any* equipment shows *any* kind of abuse or wear, don't take chances—*throw it away*," says Stan Miller of Stage Manufacturing. "A $5 fitting or a $20 SpanSet or $50 Aeroquip part is cheap. Throw it away." Miller takes the extra precaution of destroying potentially damaged parts before disposal to prevent their reuse. Hoist motors also need looking after from time to time. Wally Blount of hoist manufacturer CM says, "One thing we stress is proper maintenance of the hoists. These are mechanical devices, and they require periodic maintenance and inspection. If people don't do that, it could ultimately lead to an accident."

Detail of the Maryland Sound Industries/Paula Abdul system

So what's a conscientious would-be rigger to do? Those looking to further their education in safe rigging practices could start with some of the options listed in the sidebar "Rigging Resources" (previous page). Rig safely.

53

Noise Regulations and Sheds

BY
GREGORY A.
DETOGNE

CAN THE TWO PEACEFULLY COEXIST? AGAINST *the current backdrop of bewildering state and local ordinances, one often wonders...*

In the great dictionary of human conflict, the ongoing debate over how noise regulations should be applied to outdoor amphitheaters can be defined as a nebulous war at best. As battle lines are drawn between communities and various venues, each side is faced with confusion when it comes down to the rules of engagement. What is noise, after all, but a subjective experience? If anyone thinks they have an answer to that quandary, try tackling the issue of how much noise is too much, and then come up with a way to measure that noise—providing, of course, that you can establish where the measurements should be made and over what length of time.

The question of whose ordinances actually apply is cause for additional discord in many disputes. In some cases, alleged violations occur in one jurisdiction, yet the complainants live in another, where ordinances are different. To further complicate matters, some sheds are owned by state agencies, which brings up the question of whether state rules apply or those of the hosting municipality. Sometimes when litigation has been brought against a shed on the state level, it is done through an agency like a pollution control board, which has little experience in dealing with these kinds of cases. For the permanent record, then, it is apparent that the current situation represents a Pandora's box of complexities that have yet to be sorted out. The intent of this article is not to advocate an ultimate set of solutions, but to make an attempt at defining the real issues at hand and to offer the expert viewpoints of professionals who have been dealing with these problems in some of the major outdoor venues around the country.

That said, the best place to begin this discussion is with a general overview of the regulations most sheds are faced with at both a state and community level. To help distinguish the types of ordinances, we spoke with Dr. Marshall Long of Marshall Long Acoustics, a firm that has worked with California's Pacific Amphitheatre and other prominent sheds facing noise problems.

At the low end of the spectrum is what's commonly referred to as a "reasonable man" type of ordinance. Generally, a reasonable man ordinance will have a core section worded something like this: "It shall be unlawful for any person to willfully make, continue, or cause to be made any loud, unnecessary or unusual noise that unreasonably disturbs the peace and quiet of any neighborhood or causes discomfort to any reasonable person of normal sensitivities." This type of clause is normally tacked onto other ordinances that mention specific dB levels and is favored by police organizations because they can be enforced without having to carry any measuring devices around. The problems with this type of ordinance are obvious. First of all, who is this reasonable person? And even if you find one who is disturbed, it's hard to prove a violation

PLEASE NOTE:
THE SHORELINE
HAS A D.B. LIMIT
PLEASE DO NOT
EXCEED 98 DECIBELS
AT THE BACK WALL
OF THE LAWN
FINES (MINIMUM
$3000) WILL BE
IMPOSED AND
DEDUCTED AT
SETTLEMENT.

Punchline R

occurred, since no measurements are available. Primarily aimed at the noise offender level inhabited by garage bands, drunken parties and mufflerless cement trucks, this ordinance is of little use in regulating sheds, because it can easily be picked apart in court.

Moving up through the noise ordinance hierarchy, we come to a class that can be described as the "thou shalt not make more than (fill in amount here) dB" category. Like the reasonable man clause, these ordinances have many different structures. Most are similar to the City of Los Angeles ordinance that prohibits making five dB over the ambient level of noise at any location. The ambient, in turn, is defined as 50 dB, or whatever the existing noise level is at the area in question. Therefore, if noise cops travel to a site in the daytime and it's quiet, the ambient is assumed to be 50 dB.

As a producer of "noise," then, you can make 55 dB's worth before a violation occurs. If there's a high ambient at the site already—say 55 dB—you can make 60 dB, and so forth. The problem with this type of ordinance is that it does not define what a noise level is. Is it an average taken over a specific time period? If so, over what time period is it measured? Then again, it could be based upon a single measurement, but there's no definition as to what that measurement is.

Shoreline Amphitheater, Mountain View, CA during Lollapalooza 1; this ominous note was posted backstage during that show.

Wolf Trap Farm Park

In the late seventies, the problems posed by the previous ordinances prompted the state of California to commission an acoustical consultant to provide a model ordinance for the state. The consultant came up with what is informally called a "stair-step" ordinance. In essence, a stair-step ordinance says, for example, that you can generate 50 dB for 30 minutes per hour, 55 dB for 15 minutes per hour, 60 dB for 7 1/2 minutes per hour and so on. With this type of ordinance, an acknowledgement is made that noise isn't always steady, and higher SPLs are allowed for shorter periods of time. Where things get difficult is during enforcement, because very few people have the type of equipment needed to do the necessary monitoring. Providing the tools are at hand, a measurement would have to be made over a 30-minute period in at least the lowest category to prove a violation existed. When these types of ordinances reach the courtroom, there is often misunderstanding regarding how they are applied and how ambient noise levels are measured.

Which brings us to the latest generation of ordinances, which are based upon L_{eq}s. "The nice thing about ordinances based upon L_{eq}s is that they can be expressed both as a stair-step and a single-number metric," says Marshall Long. "L_{eq}-based ordinances can also be written that prohibit specified dB levels above a certain L_{eq}. If you defend a case like this, however, you must make sure that the noise was measured from the source that is alleged to be in violation and not everything else. The ambient must be taken into account, or at least subtracted from the source that is being measured. A way to refine this type of ordinance would be to allow a specified L_{eq} above the ambient, which would also be measured in L_{eq}."

To help sheds meet various ordinance requirements, Long and other consultants have developed noise monitoring systems. At the Pacific Amphitheatre, Marshall Long Acoustics installed a permanent monitoring system that enables the operator to know what the actual noise levels in the community are. The system consists of microphones located on two poles, one by the nearest residence and the second at the rear of the amphitheater on top of the berm. These microphones are linked by dedicated lines to a computer located in the amphitheater office. The computer collects the stream of noise level data, which can be analyzed in a number of ways to determine the various noise metrics that might apply. Because the data is stored as an ASCII file of consecutive levels, L_{eq}s can be calculated as well as any stair-step ordinance for any given time period.

Located in Tinley Park, a suburban area southwest of Chicago, the World Music Theater was first faced with a noise-related lawsuit early in this decade. Filed by the neighboring communities of Matteson and Country Club Hills, the suit was brought at a state level before the Illinois Pollution Control Board. In response, the board suggested that the World monitor sound pressure levels at two sites, one in each of the communities named in the suit. Eager to comply and work out an amicable solution with their neighbors, the World contracted Evanston, Illinois-based Electro Acoustic Systems Inc. to make the necessary measurements during the summer seasons of 1991 and 1992. "Making standard measurements in the field isn't all that complicated," says EASI's Doug Jones. "Our problems with this project began when we took a look at the Illinois Environmental Protection Agency's regulations and the methodology that was required for measurements made in these types of cases. Recently, the rules were changed so that they required us to post one-hour L_{eq}s within specified octave bands. Generally speaking, however, L_{eq}s are taken in a broad-band fashion, and within integration periods much shorter than one hour. As a result, this was a fairly unusual assignment, and it wasn't immediately obvious how we would accomplish the task. We ended up this past summer making precision DAT recordings at each of the sites and then bringing them back to the lab, where they were analyzed."

Jones, like other acoustical consultants who have found themselves in similar situations, feels that agencies like the Illinois Pollution Control Board suffer from lack of experience when hearing suits such as those filed against the World Music Theatre. "In most cases, agencies such as the IPCB deal with manufacturing noise, which is fairly constant. As a result, they are used to monitoring noises like those you get from a forging hammer going *thunk…thunk…thunk* steadily all day long. With noise like that, you can be fairly sure that if you go out and take a sample of it and then integrate it over an hour or so, you'll get something meaningful. With music, it's not nearly as clean, so it's very hard to measure and make it relate to an annoyance factor."

After determining what the measurement protocol should be and obtaining

the IPCB's blessing on proceeding with the project, EASI took to the field and began making their DAT recordings on evenings when concerts were held at the World. One-hour L_{eq}s were to be used as measurement standards, but EASI technicians were only rarely able to collect more than a few minutes of audible noise coming from the World, and some of that was fragmented. Without enough source data to produce an hour-long L_{eq}, EASI was given a mathematical formula that would enable them to create one from the data they had. Then, if this corrected value of the one-hour L_{eq} was 10 dB or more above the legal limits, they were to correct them for ambient noise. In those cases where the final calculated one-hour L_{eq} was less than 3 dB above the existing ambient, it was determined that there was no contribution from the World, and the value was not reported.

"What we did took forever, and it was tedious and expensive," Jones adds. "Ultimately, the IPCB said enough was enough. We weren't producing the results they needed, and in a sense, they were right. Even with continuous monitoring in the field, we weren't showing anything, because the problem is just too close to the ambient noise to get anything legitimate out of it. Overall, there were only about two times during the shows when we were in the field that we were actually able to report any levels at all that met the criteria for being worth reporting. And in those cases, the alleged violation barely squeaked above the ambient, so was it really a violation?"

Despite what some in the surrounding communities may think, the World Music Theater seeks to maintain good relations with its neighbors by keeping a lid on disturbing SPLs. This thinking manifests itself across the country at most other sheds too, usually in the form of level restrictions that are placed upon visiting mixing engineers. Located in Vienna, Virginia, the Wolf Trap Farm Park for the

"In most cases, agencies are used to monitoring noises like those you get from a forging hammer going *thunk… thunk…thunk* steadily all day long. With music, it's not nearly as clean, so it's very hard to measure and make it relate to an annoyance factor."—EASI's Doug Jones

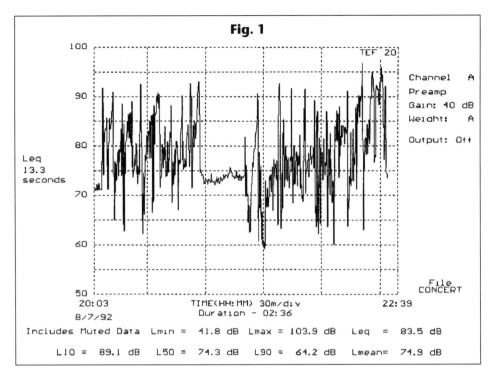

Fig. 1

Leq 13.3 seconds

TEF 20

Channel A
Preamp
Gain: 40 dB
Weight: A

Output: Off

File CONCERT

TIME(HH:MM) 30m/div
Duration - 02:36

20:03   8/7/92   22:39

Includes Muted Data   Lmin = 41.8 dB   Lmax = 103.9 dB   Leq = 83.5 dB

L10 = 89.1 dB   L50 = 74.3 dB   L90 = 64.2 dB   Lmean= 74.9 dB

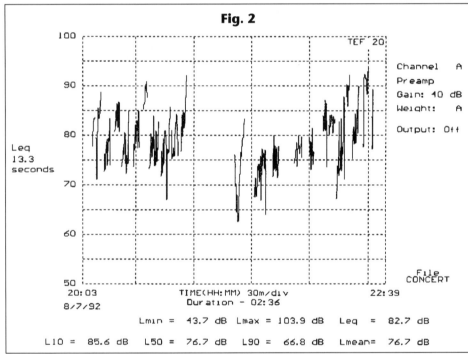

Fig. 2

Leq 13.3 seconds

TEF 20

Channel A
Preamp
Gain: 40 dB
Weight: A

Output: Off

File CONCERT

TIME(HH:MM) 30m/div
Duration - 02:36

20:03   8/7/92   22:39

Lmin = 43.7 dB   Lmax = 103.9 dB   Leq = 82.7 dB

L10 = 85.6 dB   L50 = 76.7 dB   L90 = 66.8 dB   Lmean= 76.7 dB

artist's contract, we ask that SPL not exceed 95 dBA at the house mixing console, as well as at a second location onstage. SPLs are monitored and displayed on a video screen at each location. Data appears as an integrated level in real time in bar-graph form. There's also a numeric display that shows the integrated level over the last 30 seconds. We consider that if the level exceeds 95 dBA for three consecutive 30-second intervals, that a violation of the contract clause has occurred."

Wolf Trap has experimented over the years with ways to deal with offenders. At one time a $1,000 fine was levied for each violation. Today, however, Gray admits that a kinder, gentler enforcement technique has been established. "We've eliminated the fine, but have made it clear that we will not be responsible for any damage suits brought by anyone, that the artist is responsible for any refund requests and that the artist's return to this venue may be contingent upon dBA levels and sound quality during their performance."

With limits being imposed upon house and monitor engineers, new ways to monitor their

Performing Arts is no exception. Owned by the National Park Service, Wolf Trap is a national park in the same sense that Yellowstone is, only it has the distinction of housing an outdoor amphitheater. "At Wolf Trap, there are guidelines for visiting artists with regards to sound pressure levels," relates John Gray, Wolf Trap's production manager and one of the few National Park Service employees to come to the agency with a theatrical background. "In a technical rider that is appended to an

work are being devised. "I've mixed at Wolf Trap and elsewhere, and I know what it's like if someone tells me I can't exceed an L_{eq} of 95 for the duration of the show," says Farrel Becker, an acoustical consultant and TEF programmer based in Laytonsville, Maryland. Of course, the subjective nature of hearing is at the root of this entire conflict, so playing it entirely by ear is probably insufficient. "To be fair," Becker continues, "[a mixer must] be given a way to know what [their] levels are. Just as it would be unfair for the state police to tell me I couldn't drive faster than 55 mph on the expressway and then provide me with a car without a speedometer, the same holds true for the engineer who is faced with limits on L_{eq} and finds he has no way of monitoring himself."

To create a proficient level-monitoring device, Becker first wrote Noise Level Analysis software designed to run on Techron's TEF 10 analyzer. Extremely useful for recording sound levels, the original software could also be used for recording concert sound levels, but a few inherent glitches kept it from being ideal. All that changed recently, however, when he upgraded it specifically for use as a measurement device for concert levels, and it was incorporated into Techron's Sound Lab software for TEF 20 and TEF 20HI analyzers.

"When it came to measuring concert levels, one of the biggest problems with the NLA software I originally wrote was that you had to set it to run for the length of the concert. If you set it to run for a scheduled two-hour performance and the show ran for two and a half, you'd lose half an hour of data. Now, the NLA program will run in an auto-repeating mode. I usually set it to run for twelve minutes at a time. In that mode, it puts a data point on the screen once every second, so once per second you are shown the sound level. It does that for twelve minutes, saves the data, and starts over again, continuing until you stop it. At the end of a concert, you have stored a series of data files to disk that are each 12 minutes long. Another new NLA feature allows you to combine all of these files into a single overview showing all of the sound levels as a function of time, the equivalent level, minimum level, and maximum, mean and excessive levels, too."

A pair of cursors can also be used to go to any particular point on the screen to see what the level was and at what time

the level occurred. If the operator needs to see more detail, he or she can go back and pull up the file that was providing data once every second and zoom in on it anywhere on the screen.

Besides its obvious advantages for those in charge of enforcing shed regulations, the NLA program provides the mixing engineer with equal benefits. As the engineer watches the program draw a graph at one data point per second, exact levels can be observed from moment to moment. But more importantly, the engineer is able to view the maximum and minimum levels that have occurred so far, along with the L_{eq} up to that point, at the bottom of the screen. "Being able to view the L_{eq} in this fashion is the critical feature," Becker says, "because if you're told that you may not exceed an L_{eq} of 95 for the duration of a concert, and suddenly you see that the L_{eq} is at 95, and you still want to get louder for a finale or whatever, you'll have the opportunity to let the L_{eq} drop for a few numbers to provide the headroom necessary. If the updating moment-to-moment graph is your speedometer, then the updating L_{eq} feature is your odometer, because it shows you how far you've gone. It provides you with an excellent way to monitor yourself and survive under the rules and regulations that will increasingly govern live performances."

To compensate for the fact that the audience is often as loud or louder than the performance, Becker's NLA program is equipped with a muting feature that can be used to exclude unwanted crowd noise from the L_{eq} data. "If you press 'M' on the keypad, the mute feature is activated," Becker says. "When this function is working, NLA continues to run, but it draws the graph in a different color, and the data collected isn't included in the L_{eq} or any other measurement. This feature provides an element of fairness to the mixer, who shouldn't have to be held to an L_{eq} that includes crowd noise. However, if you

An entire concert is shown in Fig. 1, measured from the house mix position. Each horizontal division represents 30 minutes. An intermission and the gradual level buildup toward the end of the show can clearly be seen. The numerical data in Fig. 1 includes noise generated by the band as well as the audience. In Fig. 2, the audience noise is muted in the graphical and numeric display. Note that, although the band was responsible for loudest instantaneous peak (Lmax of 103.9 dB is unchanged), the crowd noise significantly raised the level of the loudest 10% of the show (L10 increases from 85.6 to 89.1 dB).

Reading the plots: Lmin: The lowest instantaneous noise level during the measurement period. Lmax: The highest instantaneous noise level during the measurement period. Leq: Averaged sound level derived from the Leq method. L10: During 10% of the measured period, the instantaneous level exceeded this value. If L10=85.6 dB, 10% of the total show was above 85.6 dB. L50: As above, 50% of the total show. L90: As above, 90%. Lmean: The statistical mean of the three previous values.

should want to include this data later to see its effects, it can be done by setting a menu item."

As measurement and monitoring capabilities become more refined, others are looking at how existing noise ordinances governing sheds can be improved. Most notable is an Audio Engineering Society study group officially known as Working Group WG-11, or the AES Working Group on Music Sound Levels, chaired by Jesse Klapholz. Among the volunteers on the committee is Peter McDonald, an acoustical engineer and member of the California firm Smith, Fuse and McDonald. McDonald feels that the audio industry has a vested interest in seeing that sheds don't go the way of the dinosaur. "There are several ways to look at this issue," he confides from his Bay Area office. "One of them is to try to describe what's wrong with existing ordinances, while recognizing that there is a unique aspect to music. It has been the collective experience of the committee that many local sound ordinances are asking that sound levels be turned down to the point where a performance can't carry on. Therefore, one of the things we'll try to accomplish is describing some of the typical levels found in a typical shed, so that there is a standard reference available that lists levels at the house console and other appropriate points. When ordinances are considered against this reference, they can be compared with what has become a standard expectation for outdoor sound."

McDonald feels that perhaps the key issue the committee will examine is how levels should be measured, both in the facility and out in the neighborhood. "We need to come up with a way that sound levels created by music can be described in an intelligible fashion to both the community noise control officer and the console operator," he believes. "There needs to be a common language that both can agree upon and that isn't excessively elaborate. With this accomplished, we can then move past the inappropriate ordinances that are on the books, and all will hopefully realize that these facilities are a good source of entertainment for the larger community around them."

The Ear is a Terrible Thing to Waste

BY
DAVID
SCHWARTZ
AND
PENNY
RIKER
JACOB

MANY AUDIO PROFESSIONALS USE THE WORD "insidious" to describe the hazard of high sound pressure levels. This is because there is a massive gray area between temporary threshold shift and permanent hearing damage. High noise levels can damage the fine inner ear structure, the nerve endings that respond to sound. Steve Otto, research audiologist for the House Ear Institute of Los Angeles, says, "One of the first signs of temporary hearing loss due to noise exposure is ringing in the ears. In many cases, the ears will recover and the ringing will go away after a period of time. But with repeated exposure, recovery is less and less, until there is none at all."

Guidelines for noise exposure levels in the workplace have been in existence since the Occupational Safety and Health Administration (OSHA) developed recommended sound level criteria based on research done in the 1940s by Dr. Aram Glorig of the House Ear Institute. Music professionals, however, have rarely embraced these guidelines because of their lack of specific attention to the complexities of music monitoring.

Of course, ignoring the problem doesn't make it go away. For many people, overexposure to noise manifests itself as tinnitus, a high-pitched ringing, whistling, whining or hissing sound. An estimated 36 million Americans, ages 14 to 85, experience these unwanted sounds in their heads to a disturbing extent. "It can keep some people awake and it interferes with listening," audiologist Otto explains. "It

can be extremely bad in some people. I've seen a lot of people who were driven to distraction and felt that they needed some kind of psychotherapy because they were bothered so much by it. There are other diseases of the ear that cause tinnitus, and to the extent that these conditions are surgically treatable—a punctured ear drum, for instance—the tinnitus can be cured. But the type of tinnitus associated with noise-induced loss is typically permanent.

"Almost everyone will have some tinnitus after a rock concert, unless they have taken some precautions like getting away from the loudspeakers or wearing ear protection," Otto continues. "Tinnitus is its own warning sign. When you leave a concert and your ears ring and you can't quite hear the people next to you speaking, or the background sounds are unclear, this is a sign of some damage. The major problem is that this damage is cumulative. You may only do a small amount of damage at one show, but each successive exposure can cause a little more damage until you have lost a good portion of your hearing.

"Rest periods during high levels of exposure can make a big difference," says Otto. "If you can keep a set to 30 or 45 minutes and take a 15-minute break to allow your ears to recover a little, that's great. You can't always do that, so you need to think about using some hearing protection. Almost anything is better than nothing."

Although not all crew members are able to work with hearing protectors, many can. These devices come in three

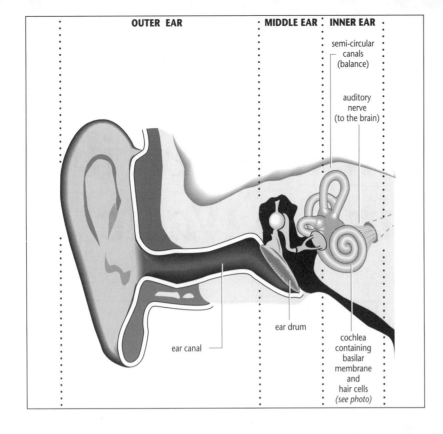

OUTER EAR | MIDDLE EAR | INNER EAR

semi-circular canals (balance)

auditory nerve (to the brain)

ear drum

ear canal

cochlea containing basilar membrane and hair cells *(see photo)*

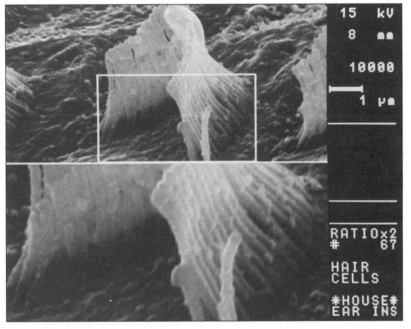

15 kV
8 mm
10000
1 μm

RATIO×2
67

HAIR CELLS

HOUSE EAR INS

Noise-induced hearing damage typically occurs in the hair cells of the cochlea (location shown in the drawing at top). These hair cells vibrate in response to sound waves and transmit the signals to the auditory nerve endings. After excessive noise exposure, these hair cells degenerate; this damage often results in a dip in the upper midrange (often between 2.5 and 5 kHz), as shown in the audiogram on the facing page.

styles: earplugs, which are inserted directly into the ear canal; earmuffs, worn over the head with a cup over each ear; and canal caps, which are held against the outer ear by a headband. Most sound professionals choose earplugs, which are available in foam, rubber, wax, plastic and fine mineral-fiber forms.

"The foam type is fine for non-critical listening," Otto explains, "and provides quite a bit of attenuation, about 27 dB. The acoustic filters that are specifically molded to your ear offer about 15 dB of noise reduction across all frequencies."

(These custom plugs have a much smoother, though still noticeable, high-frequency roll-off than foam plugs—ed.) "These are available through any hearing-aid dispenser and cost under $100. But even the acoustic filters allow some sound through if you are playing or listening at extremely high levels for long periods, so it's important to remember to take a rest or get yourself out of the direct sound path of the loudspeakers."

Dr. John House, president of the House Ear Institute, notes that the institution is currently doing research on "former patients who have willed us their temporal bones to study, so that we can look at the fine, delicate structures of the inner ear to determine the extent of noise-induced damage and exactly how it affects the inner ear. We are beginning to see a phenomenon that is not necessarily associated with an extreme hearing loss, but with an extreme sensitivity to noise. There are certain patients whose problems stem from one rock concert or one loud gunshot. This one-time exposure to an extremely loud sound can damage the inner ear and cause these people to become so extremely sensitive to normal, loud environmental sounds—a door slam, cars going by on the freeway—that they have to wear earplugs just to survive in the normal environment.

"We are very active in the prevention of noise-induced loss," House explains. "This is frustrating in that it is totally preventable, and yet we're seeing more and more of it. This type of loss is not correctable. It's not something where we can go in and put in a transplant or new nerve endings. Once the little delicate hair cells in the inner ear are damaged or lost, they are lost forever. But it's very easy to prevent—either by eliminating the extremely loud sound at the source or by wearing ear protection. Now of course, with music, the ideal situation is to play it at a volume that's safe.

"People who make their living [in professional audio] need to be especially aware of the dangers," House adds. "We have engineers as patients who are very sensitive to this problem. And fortunately many of the younger ones seem to be more aware. The big problem lies with the older engineers who have been in the business ten to 20 years and find that they're 40 years old and beginning to have hearing problems. Naturally, this affects their professional life.

"The other thing that happens to engineers," House warns, "is that they'll lose their high frequencies first, so when they mix, they add high frequencies because it sounds better to them, although it does not necessarily sound better to everyone else."

"By the way," House adds, "the guidelines we helped establish are a quantitative measure and a universal standard for everything, whether a machine or music or an airplane engine. Higher-frequency sounds cause more damage, so if someone were listening to noise at between 2,000 and 4,000 Hz, that person would suffer much more damage than someone listening at 1,000 to 2,000 Hz, for example. This is why when we talk about noise level, we are talking about dB on the A scale. The dBA weighting filters out the lower-frequency sounds below about 250 Hz, which we know are not particularly dangerous. So we want to weight it more toward the higher frequencies.

"The general OSHA rules are that someone could be exposed to noise levels of 90 dBA for eight continuous hours, and do that safely five days a week all their lives. Then as the noise level goes up by 5 dB, you must decrease the exposure time by half in order to avoid damage—so at 95 dBA, you could be exposed for four hours, and at 100 dBA you could be exposed for two hours. A rock concert at 120 to 125 dBA only suggests a few minutes of really safe levels. Assuming someone is an engineer in a nightclub or for a stage performance, they are going to need ear protection if the show goes on for two hours at 110 to 120 dBA."

According to House, "Our research has shown that a five- to 15-minute break every hour does make a difference, allowing you to continue the exposure a little longer than you would otherwise."

So what advice does an audiologist give a sound engineer for setting safe, yet effective levels at a concert? "Set a limit of 110 dBA as the maximum—the peak level—at concerts," says House. "The average would be between 100 and 110 dBA for a normal concert. That would be a reasonable compromise. I believe that 90 dBA would be too low because people don't go to concerts eight hours a day, five days a week. Anything over 110 dBA is not necessary from a listening standpoint, and would be potentially harmful."

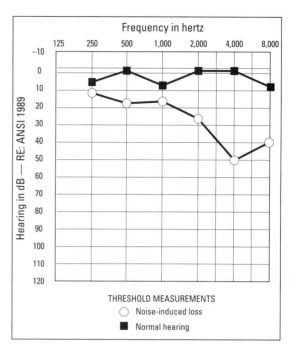

Sound Mixers On Levels

HOW LOUD IS TOO LOUD? WE ASKED several busy engineers, "How do you set levels? What are your criteria?" We also asked each soundman if his company issues any written volume guidelines to its new engineers. The answer from all was "no." Maybe it's time: The only guidelines are those ancient unwritten tenets, "If it's too loud, you're too old" (regarding indoor concerts and sound control) and "If the neighbors can hear it, it's too loud" (regarding outdoor concerts and noise abatement). Before the law gets involved inside the halls of rock, we want to know: When is loud too loud?

Gungi Paterson, independent engineer

"I tend to set levels by the amount of system—lows, mids and highs and coverage, rather than dB level. You can make it too loud. But I like to mix powerfully; I don't want the audience to know how loud it is until they leave! The bass drum needs to be caving your chest in; you use power to mask harshness and give a big sound without giving people headaches. But I think [excessive sound pressure level] is going to come back to bite us. We'll have to come up against it with more coverage rather than pure power." Paterson, who has his hearing checked "occasionally," says, "I do have a little hole at 4 kHz on one side, but it was caused by doing monitors, not what I'm doing now."

Albert Leccese, Audio Analysts, Colorado Springs, CO

"You can't just set a maximum SPL figure, because that number is irrelevant of circumstance, musical style or band. The SPL gets up there for bands that are not considered loud. Billy Joel's not 'loud,' but his SPL gets to 116 dB at the mix position. This isn't continuous all night, but some tunes and refrains get up there. Some metal acts go to 120 dB SPL at the mix position. Metal acts aren't the only ones; the so-called midline rockers like Van Halen want it just as loud.

"So the idea to police ourselves is a good one. It's up to the P.A. company and system engineer to say to the band's manager, 'Don't you think it's a little too loud?' But if the manager says 'Turn it up,' well…we are a service company. At what point is [level-setting] a value judgment, and at what point is it a safety judgment? Who are we to tell the band it's too loud? We don't know them. Our responsibility, as far as service, is to give them the maximum SPL and flattest response at the lowest distortion. Once that's achieved, it turns into a value judgment.

"If sound engineers value hearing, please don't mix with earplugs. If you have to wear earplugs, what about the 20,000 people there? If you have to wear earplugs, turn it down. Basically, 116 dB at the mix

position is a comfortable loud level. Up above 120 it starts getting ridiculous. 105 to 110 dB gives you reasonable dynamic range and doesn't hurt anybody in the audience. A rock band playing two or three hours at that level is no worse than people who work in industry who are subjected to heavy machinery noise for eight hours."

Trip Khalaf, Clair Bros., Lititz, Pennsylvania

"There are lots of dynamics in Madonna's show, which I recently finished. There are some very quiet pieces. At her show there are a lot of 15-year-old girls in the audience. They don't want to be deafened. And they're all there with their mothers, and they don't want their brains blown out! You need to gauge your audience. The secret there is to turn down the level of the P.A.—the girls will stop screaming. Don't turn up the P.A. to go over the screaming; they'll just scream louder! I also did a year and a half mixing Elton John's show. If you start blowing heads off when the audience has stockbrokers in it, and the demographics are ages 15 to 50, half the audience will demand their money back. For the good of the artist, you must gauge the tolerance of the audience.

"Our job is to bring the artist's music across as best we can and also make people think they enjoyed it so they buy tickets again. When I'm setting up, I arrive at a certain physical sensation, and that's as loud as it's going to get. Then I do dynamics down from there. There's a certain amount of satisfaction in feeling that kick drum in your chest and having your pancreas move around—transcending audio from the aural to the physical. But there is a point of diminishing return, as in, 'It was very pleasant, but the patient died.'"

Dave Kob, Clair Bros.

"I recently returned from South America, where I did two shows with Sting. I get to work with bands that are more interested in high fidelity than in pinning people's heads to the back wall of the hall. Sting's more jazz-oriented, but even when he does Police songs, I don't want them to hurt me at the board. I mix about 125 feet from the P.A. in indoor coliseums. I spend lots of time turning down amps on the sides where people are real close to the speakers. I always know how loud it is and can tell how loud the show should go: peak [SPLs] at the console at 110 dB, averaging around 100, 105, maybe peaks 10 dB higher. Ballads are in the 90s.

"But usually figures are pretty meaningless, because what matters is duration, frequency and level all together. A kick drum at 130 dB doesn't hurt your ears, but a 5kHz oscillator tone can hurt pretty bad. The shows I work have dynamics, where the artist performs a loud song, then a softer one like a ballad at half the volume. Your ears need the rest.

"I've heard [band] management telling engineers to turn up the P.A. until it hurts people. If you're a mixer and the manager tells you to do that and you say, 'Get lost,' then you're fired and you go home. Luckily, I'm not required to push levels to pain level. I've been doing this five days a week for 19 years. I don't want to hurt myself. I want to keep on working."

David Scheirman, Concert Sound Consultants, Julian, CA

David Scheirman has been a live sound mixer for the past 20 years and has toured with Linda Ronstadt, Glenn Frey, Sheena Easton and Jimmy Buffett. Scheirman has strong concerns about high sound levels. "I keep a handful of cheap, throwaway foam earplugs to offer to those persons who might need them—gray-haired men, moms with babies, etc. I usually tell ushers who are working the audience to make sure that their building manager makes such earplugs available.

"But realistically, the way I personally deal with the issue is to not ever work on the really loud hard rock or heavy metal projects. I am just not interested in being exposed to super-high levels, and don't want to be involved in subjecting audiences to it. I make my living with my hearing, and I want to keep it for a long, long time. I've worked professionally for more than 15 years, and by carefully choosing my work projects and the type of audio environments that I'm exposed to, I've safeguarded it so far."

Note: For more information about hearing tests, protection and treatment, contact the following organizations:

Charlie Lahaie, House Ear Institute, 2100 W. 3rd Street, Los Angeles, CA 90057; (213) 483-4431.

Kathy Peck, Hearing Awareness for Rockers (HEAR), P.O. Box 460847, San Francisco, CA 94146; 24-hour hotline (415) 773-9590.

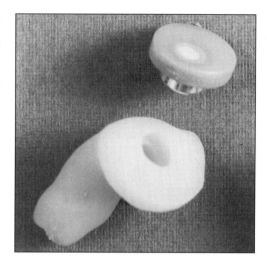

Custom molded earplugs by Etymotic Research provide flatter response than disposable foam plugs, with a uniform 15 or 25dB cut up to about 8 kHz, after which they roll off more steeply. The removable disk provides the attenuation when snapped into the custom mold.

Digital Technology and Live Sound

BY DAVID (RUDY) TRUBITT

WHILE THE USE OF DIGITAL AUDIO SYSTEMS is well-established in recording and production studios, digital applications in sound reinforcement are another matter. Those developing digital gear for live settings are focusing on several areas: DSP as a replacement for current analog gear, semi-automated mixing, acoustical measurement, and computer control and transmission of digital audio between equipment. Following is a look at current developments that could set the future direction of sound reinforcement.

Digital Signal Processing

DSP has been a part of live sound since the first digital reverb escaped the confines of the studio. Since then, digital audio technology has dominated the effects complement of nearly all live systems. Now, as digital specs improve, the technology is making inroads into drive electronics, once solely the domain of analog gear.

"We see DSP as a requirement for loudspeaker [processing] because it works so well," says JBL's Bill Gelow. "It helps clean things up in arrays. [With very steep crossover slopes made possible through DSP,] you're out of the woofer and into the horn so rapidly that they don't really know that the other [driver] exists. In the vertical plane, if they're mounted on a vertical axis, you don't end up with the usual lobing and tilting. Analog crossovers can't sum [to flat] power response and not have tilt. With digital, you can get both flat power and very predictable polar response. Our 52000 [digital controller] allows you to fine-tune things that you couldn't otherwise do in the analog domain."

"We can perform many of the functions [like EQ and crossovers] better using DSP," agrees Rane's Bob Moses. "There's also a lot of other benefits. Every system is different in terms of how much EQ, crossovers or limiters you need. [Today] we have analog modular systems. The reason they're in separate boxes is due to the constraints of analog technology, not because that's the only way it should be. In the future, since DSP products are software-based, we can still provide the same modularity within a single box. Then, you wouldn't necessarily need an EQ box, a crossover box, a limiter box, etc.

"You could have one box with all these resources in it, and the required modularity becomes a software function that lets you patch together what you need. There's a lot of economy in that [design approach] because you don't have all the metal, interconnects and power supplies."

Gelow agrees. "Instead of having a collection of analog boxes," he says, "I think you'll have a digital box for the drive system that'll do the time correction, equalization frequency-dividing and limiter functions."

Mixing Automation

Digital technology is also making inroads into live mix automation. MIDI offered one of the first practical live applications in this area, making it a simple matter to instantly call up a complete group of effects settings with a single program-change command. Today, there is a movement toward more sophistication, but not without some skepticism.

"People have traditionally resisted [live automation]," says Charlie Richmond of Richmond Sound Design, "because the nature of live sound is so variable. You can't predict from one moment to the next what you'll need to change. You can memorize all the mix parameters, but many people are uncomfortable if they can't instantly grab a particular control to adjust."

And what will you grab when the instant arrives? "People prefer moving faders as visual feedback," Richmond says. "But I think moving faders haven't caught on in sound reinforcement because setting live levels is very different than in a studio. Automated mixes are usually referenced to time code, and live sound, if anything, is done on a snapshot or cue basis. And it's more than just the faders you want to control—it's the EQ, the sends, the matrices. You can have control over all of this, but how easy is it to alter a setting in a show that has been preset?

"It's a question of applying digital control technology where it's appropriate," Richmond offers. "A lot of people fail to understand this initially. They think, 'My God, they want to take all my controls away from me!' That's not what it's all about. A good, but hardly typical, example is an industrial I recently worked on where the audience sat in two groups of 700 people each on two huge turntables, which rotated to four different positions. There was a huge matrix of speakers above the audience, aimed in all different directions. The delays had to be changed for each audience position, and the stereo image had to track as the audience moved. It meant changing relative levels, delays and mixes of all the loudspeakers.

"We created cues that made these changes dynamically while the audience moved. No operator in their right mind would want to manually control that. But at the same time, we chose to keep the live mic levels under manual control."

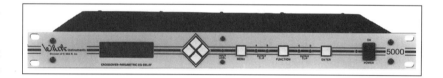

Improved Measurement Systems

DSP also should influence the development of better test equipment for measuring system performance and room acoustics.

"I think there's going to be a point where you put up your loudspeaker system in any venue and tell your computer to make it right," Gelow muses. "It'll apply test signal monitored by an array of microphones spaced in the room, and it will adapt the loudspeaker array to the venue. It will do what it needs to in the time domain to have correct frequency response and coverage for the venue."

TOA's John Murray concurs. "I think the next generation will provide devices capable of creating the inverse transfer function of your entire system," he says, "from the mic to electronics and right on through the speakers.

"Then do you just do it for the signal chain with the speaker in an anechoic chamber, or do you back out into the venue and try to fix some room problems?

Digital gear is finding its way into drive racks, combining the once-separate tasks of limiting, equalization, crossover and alignment delays. Shown from top to bottom are the TOA Saori, Yamaha D2040 and White Instruments DSP 5000.

> **"I think there's going to be a point where you put up your loudspeaker system in any venue and tell your computer to make it right."**
> **—JBL's Bill Gelow**

And what would you fix? Everybody's so busy trying to remove room acoustics from the signal, but if you've ever heard a speaker in an anechoic chamber, you're glad we have room acoustics! When we do this adaptive filtering, we have to decide what part of the signal chain we are going to correct for."

Digital Snakes

Another area of interest is the use of digital snakes, both fiber-optic and copper. Michael Creamer of BEC Technologies sees several applications: "One is a digital snake as a replacement for incoming mic signals. The other is drive-line technology for amp racks and cross-stage patching. Let's say you have ten or 20 amplifier racks, and you need the same crossover signals to arrive at four amps in each rack. The problem is one of noise floor related to the distribution and regeneration of that signal. With a digital snake, you can regenerate the same quality over and over, and each amp can receive an analog signal from a converter less than a foot away.

"I think that we can improve the dynamic range and performance of an overall touring system more dramatically on the return line side, rather than on the mic input side," he adds.

If the approach proves successful, we can expect to see digital ins and outs on mixers, amplifiers and other gear. "All the little links in the chain we have now are gradually going to change," TOA's Murray predicts. "The different signal processors we have now are going to boil down to one box, although you might use multiple copies of it. Everything will be digital from the output, or even the input, of the console, until it hits a power amp."

Toward The Future

So how do we progress from here? One direction seems likely: As more and more gear goes digital, the need for control across manufacturers' lines will grow. JBL's Gelow probably speaks for many when he says, "There's going to have to be an interface standard. The problem is, of course, who defines it?"

"If we're going to get any benefits from this technology," adds Creamer, "various manufacturers are going to have to take an active role in the definition of interface and system integration standards and protocols. Some people are inventing platforms to keep tight hold of the marketplace. We're seeing that in the video world, and I'd hate to think audio will go that way."

Rane's Bob Moses is a key player in the AES Working Group addressing the problem of standards and protocols. "Systems that need more than one box will be sharing data with each other," he says. "That's inherently a networking problem that is much more complex than MIDI or PA-422. Instead of just telling something to change its level, you're sending segments of programs and real-time digital audio between boxes."

"We're moving towards digital control of loudspeakers and electronics," concludes Murray, "because it enables you to have better control. Instead of tweaking a potentiometer that has a variance of 20 percent, you can adjust down to a gnat's ass with DSP. We've been using analog level controls for years and years, and we don't know what the levels are until we get an SPL measurement from a calibrated mic. Digital equipment gives you much more exacting control over your signal."

Computer Control: What Can It Do for Me?

BY DAVID (RUDY) TRUBITT

WHAT DOES COMPUTER CONTROL HAVE TO do with sound reinforcement? Well, why does a mixer have knobs? Because sound system operators must be able to manipulate audio equipment to do their job. For decades, knobs and faders have been the tools we've used to control our audio gear.

Essentially, computer control of audio equipment serves the same purpose. The difference is that a "knob" in a computer-controlled sound system is not limited to changing just one parameter, such as the level of a single channel on one mixing console. Using computer control, sound system operators can make extensive changes or total reconfigurations of an entire sound system, even if its individual components are spread throughout a large venue.

At its heart, computer control is an electronic link between pieces of audio equipment connected to an optional master controller, such as a personal computer. This electronic link can be copper wire or even fiber-optic cable. It carries specific messages which the interconnected equipment understands, such as "Turn up the left channel 3 dB," or "Are you clipping?" The ability to check the current operating condition of a piece of audio gear (and get a quick, accurate answer) opens a wide range of options.

Amplifiers are an obvious target for computer control. Most simply, connecting a computer to an amplifier allows the remote monitoring of the amp's status (if the amp is overheating, clipping, etc.). Furthermore, computer control can let you make changes that would otherwise require a hike to the amp rack, like adjusting input level or inverting channel polarity. The amp control system that people are most familiar with is Crown's proprietary IQ system. One company that's been using IQ for several years is Eighth Day Sound of Cleveland, Ohio.

"The thing with computer control," says Eighth Day's Jack Boessneck, "is that if people use it as a tool instead of a video game, it works real well. We use it on Sinatra a lot. It's a 360-degree show, and we'll use the IQ to set the level of each fly ring from top to bottom. We did the same thing with Jethro Tull. It also came in real handy when we did the Special Olympics. There were things going on all over the place, and they would switch stages on us. I had a podium right in front of the speakers, and I could turn those speakers off when that podium was live. It also works real well in industrials where you have multi-matrixed outputs. You can treat the matrices as zones, and turn them on and off and control levels. What else could you do? Have eight people out there turning amp racks down on cue? How many times have you sat there on the intercom trying to get hold of the stage engineer to find out what's going on up there? Now I can do it with a click of the old mouse."

Computer control systems are capable of connecting more than simply amplifiers, bringing additional benefits to sound engineers. One big advantage is simplifying the operation of a complex sound system. Tom Roseberry of IED (who also happens

to be chairman of the AES standards comittee on the subject) offers an example: "[Computer control] took a whole system that was very complex and required a lot of people to operate, and brought it to the level where it could be handled easily," he says. "For instance, you might be able to operate a huge convention complex with three or four guys, where it used to take 14 or 15. It becomes an easier thing to get your hands on the system and keep it working smoothly."

Computer control also offers benefits as a troubleshooting tool. "A computer-controlled customer of ours had a problem with an amp," says Gary Hardesty of JBL

Professional. "All they had to do was call us and say, 'We're showing this symptom on this amplifier.' We identified the problem and had them send the unit back for repair. It makes troubleshooting much easier."

Roseberry agrees. "[Without it] you had to manually go around and test," he notes. "Now, with our system, you can sit at the computer and test everything from the very front end all the way to each individual speaker. If you've got a fault at a major event with 50,000 people sitting out there and something goes wrong, you get an instantaneous report of where the problem is so you can respond to it."

For the industrious, there are enough existing pieces to put together really large touring systems. The most ambitious to date is Neil Diamond's current touring system, assembled by Stanley R. Miller, Diamond's longtime FOH mixer and chief audio engineer. Putting it together was not always easy. "I have the Crown IQ system controlling all 96 amplifiers," Miller explains. "That's worked exceptionally well so far. But I've had problems getting certain programs to run together on the same computer—I've now got three Macintosh computers to run it all!" MIDI software developer Opcode's Cue Sheet program, which changes mute configurations on his two Ramsa consoles, and Crown's IQ software had problems coexisting peacefully, although both were happy to run on their own Macs.

MIDI plays a significant role in Miller's system design. "I'm receiving program changes from the musicians onstage to set up the console for the next song," he says. "I'm also using TC Electronic MIDI-controlled equalizers. I'm triggering a Forat drum sampler with the MIDI outputs of a BSS noise gate. All this stuff is interconnected."

There are as many other applications as there are system designs. Computer control

isn't a panacea, and it's certainly not required or even desirable for many situations. But you should expect to see more of it in the future, and any effort spent thinking about our needs today will be more than repaid by improved product designs tomorrow.

The TC Electronic 1128 graphic equalizer and 6032 motorized fader head provide a single master controller (with programmable memory) for an entire rack of equalizers.

Computer Control Applications

BY
BOB
MOSES

IS COMPUTER CONTROL AND ITS ACCOMPANYING hype merely snake oil created by overzealous marketing cowboys with a tireless need to make you buy things? Or is it a sign that our industry (along with the rest of the real world) is facing a major transformation into the information age? No matter which camp you subscribe to, it is hard to deny that we are witnessing the evolution of sound systems based on distributed intelligence and automation, with more comfortable and predictable operator controls. If you haven't seen the writing on the wall, please read on. I'll elaborate with three short examples.

Control and Monitoring

A primary feature of computer-controlled audio systems is the ability to remotely "twist the knobs" on all the equipment and remotely monitor the status of equipment. The key to this is small computers (microprocessors) that live in every device in the system. Often called "distributed intelligence," these computers control each device's parameters based on your commands.

Computers are generally more accurate than humans, so when you tell them to set a fader to 10 dB you get 10 dB, not 9 1/2. And they are really fast, so when you tell them to move 64 faders to various settings, you get exactly those settings in a fraction of a second. Computers can pass messages to each other over a communications network, so you can tell one to make all the adjustments and it will spread the word to all the other computers in the system. Computer control provides accurate, repeatable, rapid control over all equipment, no matter where it is located.

Computer control also can give you a staggering amount of diagnostic information about a system. In today's world, systems based on Crown's IQ, Crest's NexSys and Lone Wolf's MediaLink networks allow the sound engineer to monitor a power amplifier's signal levels, temperature, loading and other status elements in real time. When an amp fails you instantly know which one, how, why, when and where. Indeed, the ability to monitor an amp's status means you can take preventive measures (e.g., turn the amp down) before failures even occur. When they do occur, computer-controlled signal routing lets you patch in a backup amp without leaving the mix island.

Idiot-Proof P.A. Sytems

Many sound systems are destined to a life of abuse by people who don't know how to operate them properly. Take, for example, sound systems in places of worship. These systems are generally operated by laypeople, often the proverbial minister's son. Inevitably, these systems wind up fighting their human operators. The system rarely wins, and requires constant maintenance by a professional. This is not a healthy relationship: Sound system abuse causes damage requiring constant remedial attention.

Preventing people from misusing equipment and making the system easier to operate are paramount goals. Computer control can simplify the human interface by hiding details of how every piece of equipment must be adjusted for every application. All the layperson needs to do is push a button, and the entire system reconfigures itself according to setups pre-programmed by a professional. By ignoring bizarre input, computer control keeps the operator from unwittingly (or maliciously) messing with the equipment. Operation of the system is foolproof. Professionals will spend less time troubleshooting abused equipment, and more time developing programmable functionality.

System Automation

It's 7:00 p.m. and you have just arrived at a posh dinner club with your date. Soft music lingers in the background while you eat and make pleasant conversation. At 8:30 p.m. the house lights dim, the background music fades away, the mirror ball spins, the bubble machine burps, the subwoofers come up and the music starts swinging. The transition from "dinner" mode to "dancing" mode could be executed automatically.

This hypothetical system ties all the equipment together with a small local area network (LAN). Each piece of equipment watches the LAN's master clock, and when 8:30 p.m. rolls around, everything performs its preprogrammed task. Alternately, the LAN could have a single master controller and a number of dependent devices. When the master decides it's 8:30 p.m., it commands all its dependents to change their status. In either case, no person lays a finger on a button. The multimedia entertainment system is as automatic as the outdoor lights that turn on after the sun sets.

Toward The Future

Most of the technology required to implement the above systems is available today. The process of transforming from all-analog systems to all-digital systems has been

happening, somewhat subtly, for a number of years. Indeed, digital technology was first applied to audio signal processing back in the '60s. That's over 30 years ago! It's been over ten years since MIDI ushered in the age of interdevice communications and moved the industry from expensive proprietary systems to one slick integrated environment. PA-422 followed a few years ago and gave fixed sound systems a control network.

Behind the scenes today, the MIDI Manufacturer's Association (MMA) and the Audio Engineering Society (AES) have been standardizing Local Area Networking technologies to control, monitor and distribute multichannel digital audio *on the same cable*. Signal processing manufacturers are introducing digital audio processors that talk on LANs, blow your mind with new processing capabilities and promise all kinds of exotic new human interfaces. This stuff is real, and it's coming at us like a speeding train.

Though it's fun to fantasize about the systems of the future, it is time to roll up our sleeves and get down to the business of actually creating and using these systems. Of course, we must not be seduced by meaningless hype. Our challenge today is to visualize the future and work toward making it a reality.

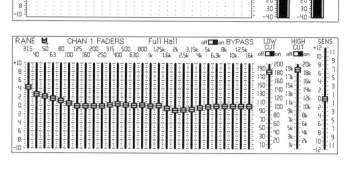

Computer-controlled equipment can display a more flexible arrangement of operator controls on the computer's monitor. The Rane Network equalizer can be displayed with traditional sliders (top) or as an editable curve representing the actual frequency response of the unit's current settings.

The control panel for Crown's IQ amplifiers (below) includes individual amp controls such as level and polarity, as well as global commands such as "all amps on."

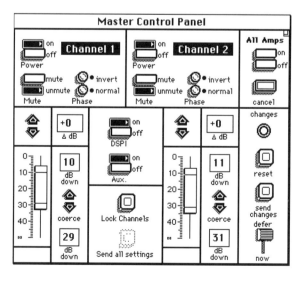

Profiles

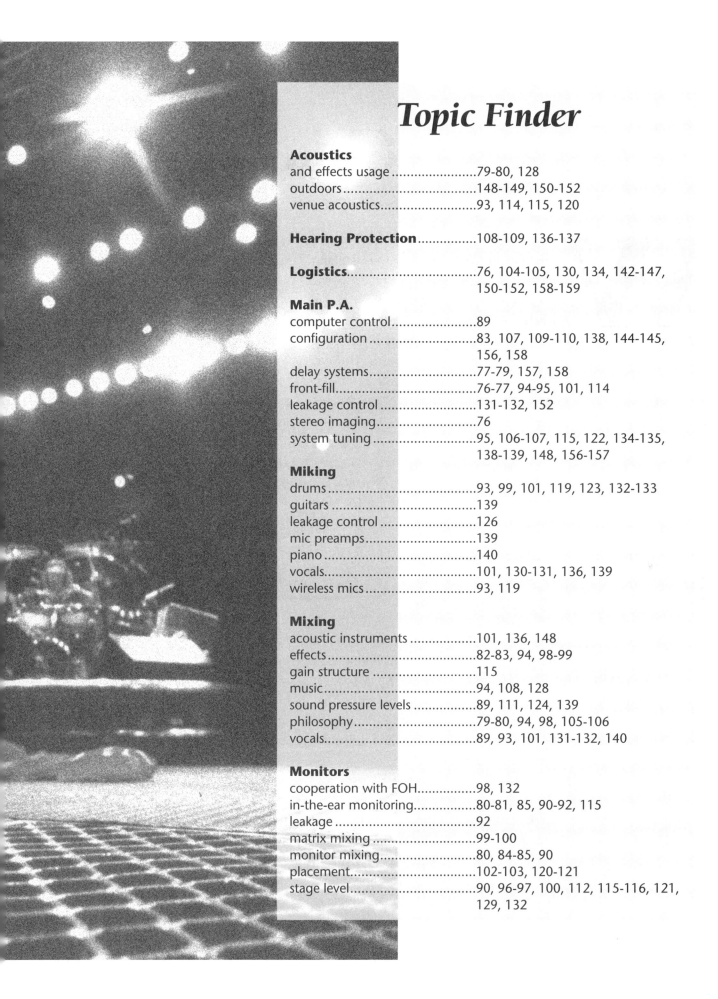

Topic Finder

Genesis

WHEN GENESIS BEGAN PLANNING THEIR first tour in five years, they were looking for something different. "They didn't want it to look like a normal stadium show, where from 200 feet away they look like stick figures playing in a box," says Showco's VP of field operations, Howard Page. Instead, the band wanted an open look that would also improve sightlines and free up more seating. "One of the things we did to achieve that," Page says, "was to make the sound system free-standing and move it 140 feet between inside corners."

Moving the arrays that far apart required some experimentation. "Last August we set up the whole system at the Dallas Stadium," explains the band's house mixer, Rob "Cubby" Colby. "I was there to listen to the P.A. and find a good position for mixing. I ended up at 165 feet back, which I'm really happy with. That distance accommodates a lot of seats in front of the mix position, which helps the sightline problem."

After the concept was tested, pre-production began overseas. "We had four weeks in England getting the songs tight, listening and recording," Page says. "That was mostly for the band's benefit." Back in the States, they moved to an empty blimp hangar in Houston for full production rehearsals. "We spent two and a half weeks there fine-tuning things, but we never took the full P.A. in—there was no point."

"I only listened to very small amounts of P.A. ten feet away," Cubby explains. "It wasn't a great place, but at least we knew it wouldn't get any worse." The full P.A. was finally added to rehearsals at Dallas Stadium during the four days leading up to opening night.

The tour's itinerary includes numerous overnighters. Although some parts of the set exist in duplicate or triplicate for leap-frogging between venues, there is only one set of sound gear. Quick setup and teardown is necessary to meet each day's schedule. Free-standing arrays and the interlocking cabinet design of Showco's Prism loudspeakers help make it happen. "We roll the boxes underneath and pin them exactly the same way we would on a flat arena floor," Page says [see photos on p. 78]. "We're achieving better times on setups and load-ins than we often get with half the amount of gear in an arena configuration." The main system consists of a left and right array, 13 wide by 6 deep, using the Prism "stadium" system, which presumably contains longer-throw mids and highs (Showco considers information about their system proprietary, and does not discuss its inner workings). The main enclosures are complemented by 64 subwoofers. Everything is Crown-powered.

A front fill and small delay system are also used. "Obviously," Page says, "at 140 feet apart you've got the potential for a big hole in the middle. We delay the front fill so that it blends with the main P.A., rather

BY DAVID (RUDY) TRUBITT

> *Venue:* **Oakland Coliseum**
> *Rental Company:* **Showco**
> *FOH Mixer:* **Rob "Cubby" Colby**
> *Monitor Mixer:* **Phil Christensen**
> *System Engineers:* **Cowboy Conyers/Howard Page**

Phil Collins unplugged with Beyer wireless vocal mic and Future Sonics Ear Monitors

"When I first started singing with the band, I was quite happy to be stuck behind two wedges and a mic stand, since I was used to the security blanket of the drum kit between me and the audience. I never took the microphone off the stand, because I didn't really know what to do. I didn't want to wiggle me bum like everybody else."
— Phil Collins

than it being an isolated source. You can walk down the corridor and the image doesn't shift."

"I wanted to make sure that the infield P.A. made the most expensive seats sound really tight with a lot of impact," Cubby says. "The stereo separation is, of course, phenomenal because of the width of the P.A. I started using much broader pans, but I wasn't able to keep that because I was losing level at the center [compared to] the outsides. So I've been bringing keyboards and guitar and vocal harmonies tighter in and giving the drums the full

pan effect. And of course there are all the stereo effects, so you start to create a sort of three-dimensional sound. It's new having the P.A. so far apart, but I adjusted to it right away."

One delay tower was erected behind the FOH position at the Oakland show. "They clean up the high-end projection," Page says. "The [main] system itself is quite capable of covering back there in the configuration we've got; on shorter fields we don't even put it up. My philosophy with delay systems is that unless you get them dead right, they create more problems

77

"We can put it up as fast as we can get it," says crew chief Cowboy Conyers. This sequence of photos shows one hour of work.

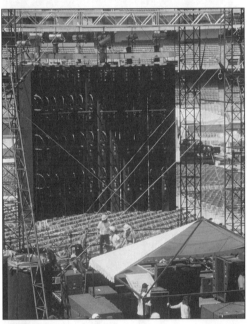

than they solve. It's often better to have someone get used to a sound that's a little distant than to have a delay in their face that's wrong. I try to be discreet."

FOH centers around two Midas XL-3s. "It is a wonderful console," Page says. "They're incredibly reliable. The company did its homework on connecting two boards. The control voltages and signals that could fight between the two power supplies for ground reference are opto-isolated. You can connect anything to anything and never get a ground loop or a problem."

Page also uses a Mackie CR1604 mixer to create a mix for TV crews. "They like to get a shot of the show for their news that night," Page says. "Rather than give them a dry board mix, we put some audience mics up and create a mix that matches their [video] image. That gets fed to isolated outputs here at the FOH and up in the pit." The mixer's alternate stereo bus is used to submix the FOH playback devices (CD, DAT and audio for pre-show videos). "It gives me a lot of flexibility without tying up channels on the XL-3," Page adds.

And what of microphones? "We're using the newest series of Beyer UHF wireless," Cubby says, "and we're really happy with those. The two drum kits are mainly Beyer-outfitted—201s, 420s, M88 in the bass drum and their big studio condensers on the overheads. On guitar are [Shure] SM57s, and there are two [EV] RE20s on the bass amplifiers, which we take direct as well."

"Because we're working outdoors at pretty strong SPL levels," Page says, "gates play an important part in keeping the stage sound under control. Limiters, and in some cases de-essers in series, are used on the vocals. The effects are dictated by the album's sound—Eventide Ultra-Harmonizers, AMS reverbs and the SPX900s."

The venue also dictates effects usage to some extent. "We've been doing a lot of domes," Cubby says. "In the domes, you've got to use the bare minimum [of effects]

and get into the enunciation of the show and the music mix. We use more compression on the P.A. than we would outdoors, where you need everything you have. Indoors you get a little relief because the reverb in the room gives you that extra volume. You have to meet the domes with just enough saturation from the P.A. that you hear only the P.A., but hopefully not the room.

"I go for excitement and impact to get people energized," Cubby continues. "I

The house mix position—Midas XL-3s (top) and processing from Eventide, Yamaha, Klark-Teknik, Aphex, BSS and dbx, a Mackie CR1604 mixer and Showco's Prism drive rack.

TOUR PROFILES: ARENAS

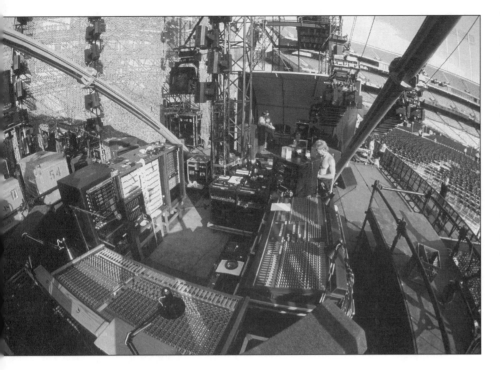

Stage monitor mix position

"I go for excitement and impact to get people energized. I build from that point—I never let go of the fact that the music mix is very important."
—Rob "Cubby" Colby

build from that point—I never let go of the fact that the music mix is very important. Then I wait for the opportunity to get some impact: drum rolls, snare stuff. Most important for me is that people can always understand what Phil's singing and saying between songs. I try to get as much reverb on him as I can without getting in the way. I do a lot of long reverb slams where he holds notes and sometimes harmonizes with himself. It's a matter of getting excitement into the mix and having a good time for myself, as well as the audience. I do love my job!"

In the early '80s, Genesis developed a matrix monitor mixing system that allows each musician to mix himself. A mix is created for each instrument (guitar, keyboard or a full drum kit) at the monitor console and fed to a small fader box at each stage monitoring position. Monitor engineer Phil Christensen explains: "The whole band has to agree on what [the balance within] each mix is going to be, but each musician can adjust his level of that particular mix. It was invented by one of my predecessors because Phil Collins demands a lot of attention during the show, and the other fellows felt left out. This solution got around having two mix engineers. It works really well for this

band—they're all responsible musicians, and they know that if they push something too far it will be a problem."

Christensen uses two main consoles—a Harrison SM-5 and a Yamaha PM3000. The PM3000 console is used to submix the three drum kits and guitars, and also to generate individual instrumental mixes for the Genesis monitor mixing system. "The subgroup outs on the Yamaha are for Phil's mix," Christensen says, "so he gets mixed on the faders, and the rest of the band gets mixed on the pre-fader aux sends."

Two Yamaha DMP7 automated mixers are interposed between the PM3000's outputs and the matrix monitor system. "These are the inputs that change the most," Christensen says. "Rather than doing the cues [manually], I have a MIDI controller that sets the whole thing up for each song." The individual mixes from the Genesis matrix system return to the Harrison, where they are assigned to the appropriate stage wedges. The Harrison is also used to create a stereo mix for Phil Collins, who is using Future Sonics' wireless Ear Monitors for the first time on this tour.

"On previous tours, I found myself always struggling for level and the right sound," Christensen says. Collins adds, "Every night we'd have this autopsy afterwards, trying to work out how we could get more volume at the piano or whatever. Most people dread the load-in and think the gig's the easy part. I'm sure Christensen was starting to dread the gig, because it became a series of finger signals—a sort of Morse code. One was vocal, two was effect; you'll see that all the way through the *But Seriously* live video. Now some nights go by without me saying a thing.

"I can't believe I'm not having more trouble with my voice on a tour like this," Collins continues. "Open-air shows are usually lethal for singers. I prefer singing in an environment where there's natural

The house mix position, stage and main P.A. The production's three large video screens are draped in black, poised above the stage.

reverb. In an outdoor situation, it's very dry, and the sound just falls off the stage. With [the Ear Monitors], I get the same environment every night."

Finding the optimum gain structure for the Future Sonics system can be tricky, according to Christensen. "I'm not certain I've accomplished that yet. We've only been out a month now—it's a whole new world. I'm learning how to mix it, and he's learning how to listen to it. But we both decided that it's a hell of a lot better than it was."

The Ear Monitors have also added to the show visually. "When I first started singing with the band," Collins explains, "I was quite happy to be stuck behind two wedges and a mic stand, since I was used

to the security blanket of the drum kit between me and the audience. I never took the microphone off the stand, because I didn't really know what to do. I didn't want to wiggle me bum like everybody else. On my last tour, we used a radio mic for a couple of songs, and that started to feel easier. But I was still tied to monitors. Now I'm all over the place. I've got the radio mic and the headset, and I can go anywhere I want."

This tour meets its demanding schedule on the backs of the crew, a fact Cubby doesn't overlook. "The crew has been exceptional. The Showco guys have done a fantastic job. My hat's off to them for doing it every day, because we're using the same P.A. every night."

The house mix position, stage and main P.A. The production's three large video screens are draped in black, poised above the stage.

TOUR PROFILES: ARENAS

U2 Zoo TV

U2'S MASSIVE ZOO TV TOUR ROLLED INTO Oakland near the end of their U.S. arena leg, carrying a veritable showcase of new equipment and techniques. Gear highlights included an ATI Paragon console, Clair P-4 front-fill loudspeakers and Future Sonics Ear Monitors, not to mention an enormous video production rig. From a technique point of view, some of the show's most dramatic and intimate moments took place *in front* of the P.A. on the "B stage," a small stage and runway dozens of rows into the audience. At the helm of the mammoth production's sound is Joe O'Herlihy, who's been with the band since 1978.

BY DAVID (RUDY) TRUBITT

> Venue: **Oakland Coliseum**
> Sound Company: **Clair Brothers**
> FOH Crew: **Joe O'Herlihy, Robbie Adams, Jo Ravitch**
> Monitor Crew: **Steve McCale, Dave Skaff**

"Production-wise, we've always had the P.A. system, a few lights and, as Bono used to say, 'three chords and a throat,'" O'Herlihy comments. "Now we've got the ultimate in production values. When taking all those aspects into consideration, the sound is still a huge part, but there are a whole network of priorities. It's U2's response, as the *Achtung Baby* album was, to the '90s.

"It's a performance mix," continues O'Herlihy. "There's three of us working—it's heads, hands and feet, legs, elbows and arms." Joining O'Herlihy in the tangle of limbs at FOH is Clair system engineer Jo Ravitch and second engineer Robbie Adams. "Jo and I have worked together for the last ten years—it's a long-standing partnership," O'Herlihy explains. "Robbie worked as an assistant engineer on the album and he documented everything, so he's responsible for recalling all the effects, and he serves as a good buffer for me, watching what's going on because there's so much activity." Adams agrees: "Sometimes you lose the bigger picture. It works quite well to have somebody who can stand back and [listen]. I also get a chance to walk [the room] and make sure everything's happening up there as well."

The centerpiece of the house position is the Paragon console. "I think it's a step in the right direction," says O'Herlihy. "All the onboard dynamics give you everything right there in front of you. In my case, I have to have visual contact with Bono at all times. Sometimes he sticks the microphone right in [to the deck speakers] to see if I'm awake! It's difficult to chase him if you're looking at stuff that's over your shoulder in a rack. The Paragon seems to be designed from an engineer's point of view—it's very practical. I also find the EQ to be very musical, very transparent. Some consoles you dial up +16 before you hear a hair of difference. [The Paragon] is right on the money. It reminds me a bit of the Clair board (the tour's second house console) in the transparency of the EQ section. And, of course, you've got those 16 auxes, and *Achtung Baby* is treatments a-go-go!"

The crew does a remarkable job of re-creating the album's tones, although many

Bono

of the effects needed tweaking to work in an arena setting. "You have to roll off a lot of brightness from the distortion effects we used on the album," Adams explains. "You've got to use lower, harder sounds to create the same effect. The high, sizzly distortion stuff just doesn't do it—it just sounds like something's broken." An SPX1000 with a chorused-distortion patch was used for the distorted processing on Bono's vocals.

On the loudspeaker side, the tour is using an S-4 rig (see photo) in a 360-degree hang, as all the seats around the back of the stage were sold out. On the

deck, a very tightly wrapped group of Clair full-range P-4s sat above four Intersonics subwoofers on either side of the stage. "The Piston boxes [P-4s]," O'Herlihy says, "cover all the front-fill area. It has an incredible effect from an image point of view—it brings the image from overhead right down to you. The [Intersonics] subwoofers are quite devastating, to say the least! They're used for effect. They're used with the kick drum, and Adam [Clayton, the bass player] uses Taurus bass pedals. Overall, it's the Rolls-Royce model we got from Clair, so we've been getting good sounds."

Clair Brother's P.A. for the indoor U.S. leg of the Zoo TV tour; note the runway jutting out from the left side of the stage

"It's a performance mix. There's three of us working—it's heads, hands and feet, legs, elbows and arms."
—Joe O'Herlihy

The afternoon's soundcheck gave the band a chance to fine-tune some video camera moves and spend time jamming, the source of much of their music. "We record all the shows and all the soundchecks—everything as soon as the guys step onstage," confides O'Herlihy. "When I finish a tour it takes me months to go through the tapes and put together the jams and concepts. 'Pride,' for instance, was [first] recorded at a soundcheck at the NBC Arena in Honolulu."

Surprisingly, the FOH's complexities pale in comparison to the two monitor mix positions. Steve McCale and Dave Skaff provide dozens of monitor mixes to the band's four players. McCale mixes for Bono and Edge (vocal and guitar) while Skaff covers Adam Clayton and Larry Mullen Jr. (bass and drums). The pair use seven consoles and a *lot* of inputs. "The number of channels is actually theoretical—we can't count that high," laughs Skaff. "We were in Ireland trying to figure

this out—we were making phone calls and sending faxes back to the shop, and they were saying, 'What? Are you nuts?' "

"There are a lot of inputs that are used only once during the show," McCale explains. "The band tries to make themselves perfect, and [they want their monitors] to be perfect. So just having something in the mix isn't good enough—it needs to be proper, which is fine, but it takes a lot of channels. Bono really likes a full house mix. That's why I'm here, actually—because I don't normally do monitors, I'm a house mixer. But Bono is looking for a house mix with lots of effects, so I spend most of my time mixing for him."

The stage's open, 360-degree look ended up requiring both monitor positions to be beneath the stage. And how is it being out of eye contact with the players? "In a word, horrible," McCale says. "It's like watching the show through a peephole. But the band knows I can't see, and if I miss something I'm not expected to work miracles. And we've got good coverage: I've got three cameras watching the show all the time."

The design of the monitor system is continually being refined, even at this late point in the tour. Part of the system's ongoing changes are related to the tour's increasing use of Future Sonics' Ear Monitors. "They came in very late in the game," says McCale. "For the first few shows, they were strictly used for B-stage stuff. But Bono started liking them, and they went from a very small sideline specialty thing to being a very large part of the show. Bono now wears his for anywhere from half to three-quarters of the set, and Edge is starting to wear his more and more. With the earphones on, all the effects and real subtle stuff that you do to a vocal is very clear and apparent—it doesn't get lost in the wash. So actually, I do a lot more for him in his earphones than I can without.

"[The Ear Monitors] take some finesse," McCale continues. "It took me several weeks to feel like I really knew the units. I get kick and bass into the earphones, but only their top end, because the sidefills and P.A. carry so much of the low end. But the most critical thing is getting the gain structure throughout the entire system, from the way you drive it to the Aphex Dominator, which comes with the system, to how hard you drive the transmitter input and the actual gain on the beltpack. It's possible to overload one stage of it, but once you get it dialed in it does real good."

However, wedges and sidefills have not been completely displaced. "These guys always want the flexibility of being able to pick and choose from different feels all the time," Skaff says. "You can get something that they like in the wedges or something they like in the ear monitors. It's a question of deciding which paintbrush to use today."

"It's a difficult tour that we're doing," McCale concludes. "If it wasn't for the band's drive to do the best that they can, it wouldn't push all of us to do our best. The

main thing is it's not just me or Dave or Jo out there. We've got nine people on sound for this show, and everyone puts in long hours and does a really good job. It's all a big teamwork thing, and I want to make sure that the credit gets passed down the line where it's deserved."

Although the show's technological bombast had the potential to swamp the music's rich emotional content, that didn't happen. Instead, the sound and visual elements of the production contributed to the ultimate purpose. "The intention is to communicate," O'Herlihy notes. "I just look around and see the expression on people's faces, and to me, that fulfillment is worth its weight in gold. That's why I do what I do."

The Zoo crew (left to right): Steve McCale (monitors), Jo Ravitch (system engineer), Joe O'Herlihy (house mix), Jimmy Hores (house tech), Robbie Adams (house effects mix) and Dave Skaff (monitors); O'Herlihy and Adams during the show

Garth Brooks

"**I** LOVE TO KNOCK PEOPLE OFF THEIR SEATS," says red-hot crossover country singer Garth Brooks. "I like to see people come to the show, go nuts, and then talk about it until we come around again."

Brooks has been successful at knocking people off their seats, as well as keeping other country artists off the top of the charts. His second album, *No Fences*, logged 42 weeks at Number One on the *Billboard* country charts before being knocked back to Number Two by the release of his next CD, *Ropin' the Wind*. More impressively, his new record exploded onto the pop charts at Number One on the first week of release, certainly an unheard-of achievement for a "country" artist. It is the first crossover country record to reach the top of the pops since *Kenny Rogers' Greatest Hits*.

BY
DAVID
SCHWARTZ

Representing a new generation of country artist, raised on tradition but influenced and inspired by the power, excitement and technology of modern rock concerts, Brooks has created a fusion between country and popular music that reaches out to a broad cross-section of music fans in search of music with meaning. "Our concert is country music," says Brooks, "but with a late-'70s rock show mood, and it's the '90s as far as the mobility onstage—without any wires or mic stands.

"It's a melting pot, as my whole life has been," he adds. "George Strait was the guy who made me know country music was where I wanted to go. But seeing a Queen concert when I was in high school showed me how important the general power of the show was in connecting with the audience. Groups like Kansas and Styx showed us how exciting and well-staged a show can be, and we're always drawing influences from all kinds of artists, where we see and hear things that turn us on—Billy Joel, Cinderella, even Megadeth. We try to put together an all-star event, a whole concert of things, so that by the end of it, people are worn out."

Audiences are not the only worn-out people at a Garth Brooks concert. With the band using wireless instruments and wireless headset microphones, constantly and unpredictably running around onstage, the sound and light technicians don't have a moment to relax. The most unfortunate is monitor mixer Brent Dannen, who has the insane task of trying to mix stage sound for a pack of musicians who are continually rearranging themselves onstage. "See this T-shirt?" says production manager John McBride, pointing proudly to his "Workin' for a Madman" shirt. "There's a reason for that!"

McBride, who started MD Systems in 1984 in Wichita, Kan., with a borrowed $6,000 worth of amps, speakers and a 12-channel mixer, notes that despite the challenges of this kind of show, the effort is well worth it. "With Garth, we care more. Garth ruined us for working for anyone else because he treats us so well. But he

> Sound Company:
> **MD Systems**
> House Mixer: **Dan Heins**
> Monitor Mixer:
> **Brent Dannen**

expects his people to work hard. We're carrying fewer people on the road than other tours doing the same kind of job. We work harder, but we get taken care of."

"Mixing Garth requires you to stay on your toes and be ready for anything to happen," says house mixer Dan Heins. "Like last night (the first of two sold-out shows at Dallas' Reunion Arena being taped for an NBC network special), I wasn't aware that Garth and Ty England, his other acoustic guitar player, were going to smash their guitars against each other at the end of 'Friends in Low Places' until five minutes before showtime. I'd heard

something about it, but I thought I'd better ask, because if they were, I'd better mute them. Other shows seem to be more rehearsed and choreographed, but with Garth's show it's always a free-for-all. We don't have a set list that we use for the whole tour—every night's different, and he could throw something in at any moment. You've got to stay on your toes."

After graduating from the University of Kansas in the mid-'80s, Heins joined MD Systems because "John (McBride) was the regional sound god around Kansas and had the best system." The two worked a variety of Midwestern shows for artists as

MD Systems' house mix position and two ATI Paragon consoles

diverse as Yngwie Malmsteen and Cameo, until in September 1989, while handling sound for a Ricky Van Shelton show, they encountered Brooks as an opening act. "Garth had just come out with his first album and didn't have a house mixer," says Heins. "It was just luck that I made an inquiry into who was going to mix him and got the job. Garth pretty much stole the show."

By January 1990, McBride, Heins and MD Systems had relocated to Nashville, betting on the continued growth of Brooks' career, though McBride admits that at first Brooks wasn't able to carry production. "But within about six months," McBride says, "I needed to expand to keep up with him. His career was skyrocketing."

Brooks' success has moved MD Systems into the big leagues of equipment operation in a relatively short time. This has brought a certain amount of freedom, along with the great challenge of matching technology to the intense demands of this unique artist. "When Garth has an idea," says Heins, "you never want to say to him, 'That's never been done before,' because that's just what he's trying to do out there. He's trying to expand every aspect of the

show to the point where it's right on the edge. And he wants people behind him who'll say, 'I don't know, but we'll find out, and we'll try it.'" MD Systems recently added the technical expertise of Wally Bigbee (head tech on the "Monsters of Rock" tour) and has received considerable technical support from Crown International, Systems Wireless and Brock Jabara, P.E.

For the Dallas arena shows, as well as the balance of the "Ropin' the Wind" tour, MD upgraded to 48 full-range flown cabinets, each composed of two 18-inch speakers, two horn-loaded 10-inch drivers and one 2-inch tweeter. The cabinets were built by JTB Associates of Wichita, a group normally employed to remodel interiors of jet aircraft.

With rigging safety in mind, MD asked for high-test precision work. "We took the cabinets to Pittsburgh Testing Labs," says McBride. "They weigh 250 pounds apiece, and we fly them four deep, maximum. With 150 pounds for the motor and 100 pounds for the bar, that's 1,250 pounds split between two support points, or 625 pounds per point. We had them tested at 5,000 pounds per point for 12 hours. When it comes to flying systems, you can't be too careful—especially if you're over seating. If that stuff ever falls, I hope I'm the first one in line. I hope I get crushed, because I can't imagine causing harm to anyone over this business."

Driving the cabinets are Crown 2400 and 3600 Macrotech amplifiers, with house sound mixed by two Yamaha PM3000s. Recently, the company began using a Crown IQ 2000 for control and monitoring of the amplifiers during the shows, to give total access from the house mix position and a faster balance, especially when working in the round. Says McBride: "One of the advantages of the IQ is that in a hall like Reunion Arena, Dan can sit at the house console and I'll walk the room with a radio, and he can turn down certain amplifiers and speakers in areas that may be closer to the audience so we get a better overall coverage. Then we can save those settings on disk, and the next time we come to Reunion, as long as we're flying the same configuration, we'll know where we are."

Bringing the vocal above the adoring crowd noise at a Garth Brooks concert is one of the sound crew's more serious considerations. "Competing with the crowd for volume gets into a snowball effect," Heins says. "I try to keep it down to a non-fatiguing level. We run an average of about 100 dB at the house console. Last night the crowd was louder than the P.A. a lot of the time. The crowd on the floor was hurting my ears, but the P.A. wasn't."

Brooks' vocal mic—as well as that of the rest of his mobile band—is the AKG 410, the best-sounding mic the crew found for this demanding application. To keep a reign on Brooks' dynamic voice, "We constantly use a good deal of compression, anywhere from 3 to 6 dB of gain reduction," says Heins, "because the proximity of his mic to his mouth never changes. And he can go from something that's really soft to bam!—something that really pushes it into compression. We also use a Klark-

House mixer Dan Heins

Teknik DN405 parametric EQ to take out some mid-low, to control popping and to bring out intelligibility."

Garth Brooks certainly doesn't take the technical side of his show lightly. "The band has always said that the most important man at any concert is the man at the house mixing board," Brooks says, "because you can be playing your ass off, and if the engineer isn't picking it up, the audience will never hear it. The MVP of any concert is the engineer."

Brooks' show also caught lighting operators off-guard in the early days. "When we first started running around onstage," says Brooks, "it would take a while for spotlight operators to catch up with us, because they were used to just setting the spots on a certain point and going to get some popcorn or something. But now they watch every move we make. And if they're doing that, then they're focused in on us. So that's when the message of the song comes through, and it's a way to keep people's attention. When they're watching you, they're listening to you.

"I like to move around to keep people's attention, to keep them into what I'm saying and doing, so that there's no lull in the show," he continues. "The mobility brings attention, and attention allows you to deliver the messages you came to deliver.

"Mixing Garth requires you to stay on your toes and be ready for anything to happen. Other shows seem to be more rehearsed and choreographed, but with Garth's show it's always a free-for-all."—Dan Heins

Gloria Estefan

G LORIA ESTEFAN'S "INTO THE LIGHT" TOUR opened in Florida, hopped to Japan and Europe and then began working the States. From the audience's perspective, the most notable piece of tour equipment is probably the huge stage, which includes a large, second-story catwalk, part of which separates and flies forward over the crowd. However, the biggest impact on the sound system has probably come from its smallest component, the in-the-ear Ear Monitors (manufactured by Future Sonics, Newton, PA). These devices are custom-molded to the individual performer's ear, providing a headphone-style mix which is relatively free from many limitations of conventional wedge monitor mixes. In this case, the devices are run via wires to the band's drummer and percussionist, and are wireless for Estefan and the four background singers.

Although initially skeptical, Estefan quickly became a fan of the Ear Monitors. "They're great," she says. "They've saved my voice, that's for sure. My voice is right there. One of the main problems you have as a singer is fighting everything onstage. Especially in this show, where I have to be in so many different places—we'd be looking at a nightmare of monitors, from side-fills hanging up on top, across the whole front and side [of the stage], and that would have just increased the noise level 5,000 percent."

"Stage level has become much less of a problem with the Ear Monitors," says FOH mixer Mark Dowdle. "The drummer and percussionist play on them with no wedges. That allows us to have open condenser microphones all over the drums and percussion without a lot of bleed. Also, the backing vocalists use them, so there's no real sidefill volume. The rest of the wedges [Meyer UM Ultra Monitors] are for the keyboard and horn players, and they don't amount to much, volume-wise."

MSI monitor engineer Craig Melvin concurs: "It's brought the overall stage level down. The previous tour had pretty big sidefills—four Turbosound TMS3s per side, or double [MSI] high-pack/low-packs per side. Her voice was loud, and that drove up the level overall. It's changed things a lot onstage; it's really comfortable. Not only that, it's given us the ability to get great audio out front."

The tour is extensively wireless (using mostly Audio-Technica wireless equipment), including Estefan's vocal mic, four backing vocalists, three horn players (each with several packs), bass and guitar. On top of that are two channels for two wireless Ear Monitor mixes, bringing the total to 14 working frequencies on a given night (not including six spares). Assistant monitor engineer Mark Bradley mans the wireless rigs.

The 13-piece band requires a lot of inputs. "What I really needed," says Melvin, "was a 60x24 console, but I couldn't find anything that would do it, so I made two Ramsa WRS-840s [40x18 consoles]

Venue: **Oakland Coliseum**
Sound Company:
Maryland Sound Industries
FOH Mixer: **Mark Dowdle**
Monitor Mixer: **Craig Melvin**

BY DAVID
(RUDY)
TRUBITT

"One of the main problems you have as a singer is fighting [the level of] everything onstage."
—Gloria Estefan

work. Basically, one console is a wedge console, and the other is an Ear Monitor console—I needed different processing for each. The Ear Monitors require a lot more compression, for instance. I normally wouldn't compress drums for monitors, but it's needed to get it present in the Ear Monitors and to avoid overloading the transmitter.

"It took me a while to sort out the routing to make this work," Melvin continues. "For instance, I've got Gloria separate for anyone with Ear Monitors—it's de-essed and compressed with a BSS 402. I ride her gain naturally for ballads, and that works well for the drummer and percussionist, who don't want to hear her too loud [in the Ear Monitors] all the time. On the

Monitor engineer Craig
Melvin

wedges, I've got some outboard EQ but no compression. There's tons of these sorts of splits and mixes, back and forth between the two consoles." Input to both monitor consoles comes from 96 channels of Brooke-Siren active mic splitters.

The Ear Monitors have removable ports, which come in different sizes. "The smaller port appears to load the transducer better," Melvin notes, "which gives a little more output and slightly brighter sound. But rather than going with both small ports, which would be a little too bright, I've got one of each [a smaller and larger port in either ear]."

A hard limiter provides protection on all the Ear Monitor mixes. Melvin uses old- and new-model Aphex Dominators, although he prefers the sound of the original unit, which is no longer made. "I spent some time playing with the new one before I was comfortable with it, where the old one was kind of idiot-proof. I talked with Aphex at some length, because I really wanted the old one. They said, 'give this a try,' and it's working fine for me now. I was concerned about protecting Gloria's hearing, and the Dominator's the best device I could find for the job."

Using a combination of in-the-ear and conventional monitors created some interesting challenges. For instance, the physical

distance between the wedge and the Ear Monitors resulted in a short delay, creating an undesired small-room sound. By reducing the overall vocal level in the monitors, wedge leakage into the lead vocal mic was reduced, solving the problem.

On the other hand, vocal mic pickup of the stage sound (and the ports in the Ear Monitors themselves) provides a natural mix of the band for Gloria. However, this is lost when she moves onto the stage's upper level. To compensate, Melvin creates a stereo submix of the entire band, which he rides up and down as she travels the large stage's two floors. It's proved an interesting challenge, according to Melvin. "It's all very different—combining the Ear Monitor with regular wedges has been a learning experience for me."

Mark Dowdle was on the group's last tour, but this time around his FOH equipment roster is quite different. "The high points out front are the two Gamble EX 56 consoles and everything that goes along with them, insert- and effects-wise," Dowdle says. "It's the first time that the consoles have been linked so that you can use the muting, auxes and subgroups in tandem."

Again, spare inputs are at a premium. "They are doing some [sub]mixing up there with the keyboards, which helps me out," Dowdle continues, who notes that his 112 inputs are full. "I get a left and right feed from the keyboard player. The horn players also play keys through the same rack and another mixer, and then give me a feed from that. Because we have so many inputs onstage, we've got two snakes running down to me with inputs. And those inputs don't necessarily go to one particular console. I had an XLR mic scrambler built [housed inside the rack], so I can patch any input to either console.

Once that's done, it remains that way through the entire tour. The only mic cables involved [outside the scrambler] are talkback and intercom. It all goes together in a matter of minutes.

"Most of the drums are miked with Ramsa S5s: snare, top and bottom; piccolo snare; all the rack toms; the congas and bongos. You can't see it—it clips on the rim—and it's shock-mounted. It's a wonderful microphone," according to Dowdle. "In the kick, I've got a B&K [Bruel & Kjaer] and a Shure SM91 PZM. You get the attack from the 91 and the roundness from the B&K." AKG 414s are used for drum overheads and Sennheiser 421s on timbales.

Horns are miked with more R5 capsules adapted to Audio-Technica belt packs, and run through Summit Tube leveling amps. "[The Summits] do a fine job," Dowdle continues. "They smooth out the section very well and make it easy to get a nice blend. There's a sweet spot with these units, around -7. Anywhere [on] either side of it, you start lopping off the high end a little. At the shop, we analyzed these and found that we could actually see what we were hearing."

The Audio-Technica vocal mics have updated capsules, and everyone agreed they were smoother and warmer than the previous version, which had a peak in the 4kHz region. Vocals run through Drawmer 1960 tube compressor/limiters. "These make it easy for me to get a nice, smooth vocal sound," says Dowdle, "because you can't hear them working at all. She [Estefan] can max them right down, and you can't hear the compressor at all."

Dowdle describes his room-handling philosophy: "A room like this is approached with caution. You try to anticipate what you'll run into, as far as resonant frequencies are concerned. To start with, [it's important to] aim speakers properly and trim them at the right height to give you optimum results before you even get into tuning [the system]."

The main loudspeaker system is MSI's high-pack/low-pack system, loaded with TAD 4001s on the high end, followed by JBL 12-, 15- and 18-inch subs. High and mid components are grouped in one enclosure and low frequencies are handled in a separate box, hence the "high-pack/low-pack" designation. Crest power amps are used for everything except the highs, which are covered with Ramsa amps. Dowdle is pleased with the new TAD drivers. "They're really nice," he says,

House mixer Mark Dowdle

"and our own horn design augments them to a point where it works out very nicely."

The high/mid and low FOH cabinets are arrayed in vertical columns. The sidewrap is arranged in a checkerboard configuration to break things up for the closer side seats. The system is run stereo, with the sidewrap being fed signal from the opposite side of the rig, providing stereo (albeit a reversed image) for those on the fringe. Dual-ported, 18-inch subs were stacked on the floor, along with a few more high and low cabinets to fill the floor seats closest to the stage. Stage level was noticeably lower than one would expect, especially considering the size of the band. And the Ear Monitors did their thing. "I think they're the future of performing," concludes Estefan, "because they're great for your voice, and that's the bottom line."

Elton John

CLIVE FRANKS HAS MIXED ALL BUT TWO OF Elton John's tours over the past 20 years, as well as The Who, Peter Gabriel and others. Franks' approach is a decidedly musical one. "Don't get too bogged down technically," he advises. "I've stood on the sidelines of stages where the sound has been incredible and the band was cooking. But you get out front and something isn't right—the energy doesn't get across to the audience, and that's a shame. I'm not saying that it's bad sound. You can have good sound but not get a feel for the music. That's the whole thing—to be able to get that energy across.

"I don't believe in a lot of effects," he continues. "The more you add in a live situation, [the more] you can just get yourself into trouble. So many engineers spend so much time worrying technically that they lose out on the real meaning of what's happening onstage. Your system has to be fine-tuned, but once that's done, you've got to let go and just listen to the music. If the band suddenly goes in a different direction, you don't want to just carry on mixing and not listen to the music. If the voice isn't loud enough, I won't push it up. I'll pull everything else down to create another dynamic. With Elton, it's great because there's a lot of room to create dynamics and moods in his songs. I seem to anticipate what they're going to do sometimes—especially with Elton. I guess after 20 years you do get in tune."

BY DAVID
(RUDY)
TRUBITT

> Venue: **Oakland Coliseum**
> Rental Company:
> **Clair Brothers Audio**
> FOH Mixer: **Clive Franks**
> Monitor Mixer: **Keith Carroll**
> System Engineer: **Mike Wolf**
> Crew: **Cliff Downey (house), Tom Foehlinger (stage)**

Mike Wolf is Clair Brothers' system engineer for the tour. He's worked with Elton and Franks for ten years and mixed the '84 tour while Franks was off the road. "We're carrying 72 Clair S-4 cabinets with us right now," Wolf explains, "and we had 128 in Europe. We take out what we need and leave as much in the truck as we can." Sixteen of the S-4s are P-type cabinets, the company's long-throw configuration. No subwoofers are used in the rig.

"Front fill is always a problem, no matter what you do," he continues. "Hang it from the stacks above you and it sprays the stage too much, unless you've got real narrow horns, which create their own problems. If you put something high enough on the side to cover the center, you still have spill on the stage, plus you're blocking sightlines from the side. And production doesn't want you to put anything in front because it blocks their set. But the people up front are the people the band sees. If you make the show sound better for them and they have a good time, the band does the same."

This tour's solution is to use Clair's P-4 piston cabinets lying flat on their sides between stage wedges (the P-4s are about 4 feet tall and one foot wide, tapering to just a few inches at their rear panel. "They're the same height [on their sides] as our 12AM monitors," Wolf notes, "which are very small. They're spread out across the front, and they do a good job

filling in. They're turned way down to not hurt the people who stand up right in front of them—safety first. They blend in, and the set designers aren't that worried about them. It'd be nice to be able to get two more up there, but production won't let us!" (On the other hand, the tour's production manager scored some audio points by skipping the originally proposed metal grates that would have covered the monitors.)

Once the system is up, final tuning is left to Franks, who relies in large part on the sound of his voice booming throughout the empty hall. "[The Oakland Coliseum] is a tough room when it's empty; it should be better when the people come in," he says. "There's a lot of rumble all through the spectrum. I'll keep sounding the room out until it sounds smooth, then walk around. I try to get everything from

the house graphic. I'll do all my work there, and I find that I need very little EQ on the board. But my graphic looks like, 'No room can be that bad, surely!'"

New on this tour is a Yamaha PM4000 console. "Basically," Wolf says, "it has everything the 3000 did, plus additional things that make it more flexible. It's been reliable, and it's been working out real well. The biggest advantage is the stereo input channels—it comes with four and we added another eight. We started with a PM3000 and a side board for effects returns, and we're now down to one console with some open channels."

"We thought we'd have the 4000 at the beginning of the tour in Europe," adds Franks, "but it wasn't quite ready. When it did come out, [Clair] kept the 3000 just to make sure I was happy, because we were changing it in the middle of the tour. But

Elton's position on what the crew refers to as "the riser of doom." The entire assembly lifts and rotates during the show.

"Your system has to be fine-tuned, but once that's done, you've got to let go and just listen to the music."—Clive Franks

it was great—it felt comfortable straight away. It's a little bit bigger, to accommodate the extra channels. The EQ is so much better. It's still very sharp, but I can fine-tune it now and just get right in and pull out frequencies.

"I like working on the VCAs," Franks continues. "They're right in front of me in the right spot. It's comfortable, and that's the way I mix. Luckily, within this band, everything fits nicely onto its own submix." (The eight VCA groups are assigned to lead vocal, piano, guitar, one for each of the two other keyboard players, backing vocals, bass and drums.)

As might be expected, the focal point of the show is the artist and his piano. In contrast to past tours, which used acoustic grands, a Roland electronic piano is John's ax this time around. "It took us 18 years to get a great piano sound, and then he ditched it!" quips Franks.

Elton's seat at the keys also marks the focal point of cooperation between house and monitor systems. Keith Carroll handles monitor duties. This is his second tour with Elton but "this is our first time working together," says Carroll, referring to himself and Franks. "It's a very complementary [relationship]. What I do can drastically affect the vocal sound. On the other hand, except for the keyboardist and bass guitarist, I'm not using any big low end—I'm getting all that from the P.A. So I depend on how Clive tunes the P.A." Carroll runs 13 band mixes (in addition to meeting Elton's needs) from a Harrison desk, using TC Electronic equalizers with the TC/Clair moving-fader EQ controller.

Elton's stage position is atop a circular platform, which can move upstage and downstage, plus lift eight feet into the air and rotate 360°. Carroll provides Elton with four monitor mixes—stereo vocal and instrumental, spread between two pairs of monitors held in place by a welded aluminum frame. Clair 12AMs are used on top for vocals, with older Clair single

15-inch/2-inch wedges for the instruments. While the rigid frame and fixed mic position keep the spatial relationship between mic and monitors consistent (removing that variable), Elton's exceedingly high monitoring levels and heavy vocal effects processing keep Carroll and Franks on their toes.

"I cannot sit down and tap more than a few keys—it's pretty loud. I know what it should sound like and what frequencies should close my ears down," Carroll says. "During 'Saturday Night's Alright for Fighting,'" adds Franks, "the guitarist and the bassist run up onto Elton's riser. Every night back in the dressing room they say, 'Jesus! We wanted to get off as soon as we got on!' And Elton's just pumping away. It's amazing that we've got such a tight sound—that mic (a Milab LC25 condenser) helps immensely. It is not necessarily the mic that I wanted to use, but it's the best for rejection."

"He used to use an SM58," says Carroll, "but he grew to dislike the sound of it. We tried an SM57, some Sennheisers, some Beyer stuff. The Beta 58 has the peak frequencies that he likes to hear, and that really suited him for a while. But he wanted something different for this tour." (Beta 58s are still used by the three female backing vocalists.)

Even with the tight rejection pattern of the Milab, there are still times when Franks will ask Carroll to pull back certain troublesome frequencies in Elton's monitors. Sometimes it works, but sometimes... "You can't fool him," says Carroll. "You think you can get away with a little bit, but then you get your wrist slapped! But that's good. I prefer working with people you can't fool because we can talk on a more equal basis. He knows what he wants. He's demanding, but he's also understanding. If there's something that can't be done right this minute, as long as we can make it right in a given space of time, it's okay. It's

nice to have that relationship, rather than there being a problem and you find out from the tour manager, or you wake up on the bus one morning and there's this guy out there—'Here's your replacement.' The thing for me that makes this one so special," concludes Carroll, "is the respect that I get back from the artist. We have real feedback with each other, which I don't always get with some artists. Everybody's got a different aura about them, but this is the one I enjoy most."

Clair Brothers' P.A. (note the long, narrow P4 cabinets lying between 12AM monitors at the lip of the stage); engineer Keith Carroll.

Van Halen

AN HALEN'S TWO SHORELINE AMPHITHEATER dates were near the end of the first leg of the band's successful summer shed tour. Providing sound for the band was Audio Analysts, which coincidentally was in the middle of a move from Plattsburgh, N.Y. to Colorado Springs, Colo. While previous outings with the band had been more extravagant, on this tour a "less is more" philosophy prevailed. FOH mixer Jon Ostrin explains: "I had a conversation with Eddie [Van Halen] at the beginning where he said, 'It doesn't have to be a wall of thunder. Let's get this thing clean and distinct. Let's understand every word Sammy [Hagar] is saying and all the notes to all the riffs.' [On the last tour] I'm told they were running from 24 to 30 inputs on the drum kit. [This time] we're doing the whole band on 30 inputs: The simpler, the better."

It's always easier to please a client who knows what they want. "From day one in rehearsals, I got the idea they wanted it to sound like a band playing," says monitor engineer Jim Yakabuski. "Eddie's sound has changed a little over the years, but it's pretty similar. I don't think Alex's drum sound has ever changed—he knows the frequency he likes, 500 Hz, and likes that boosted on the snare—a lot of 'wood' and that's all he wants to hear. There's no reverb on anything [in the monitors]. It's really just a balance. It's almost like an FOH system down low."

Ostrin agrees. "We get very similar sounds—the sound out front is very similar to the sound they're looking for onstage." Cooperation between house and monitor systems makes that goal easier to reach. "We work together," says Yakabuski. "Just a couple of days ago we spent half an hour on the vocals. I wound up taking just about everything below 200 Hz off all the vocals to let Jon do the warming and filling up in the house. It keeps things really dry and tight onstage, and it really worked out well."

The FOH position centers around Audio Analysts' custom-designed CADD console. Ostrin notes, "It has features that can keep you busy for months, as far as routing and A/B switching for effects, but since we're doing the band with only 30 inputs, it's set up pretty straightforward. It's not a band where you can get away with big snare reverb shots, 'cause there are no ballads. I keep all my reverb times below 2 seconds, around 1.4 or 1.7 seconds, and let the cymbal overheads keep everything grooving. It's not a real effects-heavy band. I've got a couple of slap echoes on Sammy's vocal, which vary from song to song, but I'm not doing much changing, especially for the first leg." A Lexicon 224 and Eventide 3000 Harmonizer are the house effects highlights. Instrument effects, when used, come directly off the stage, with L/R and dry feeds provided to FOH from both bass and guitar rigs.

BY DAVID (RUDY) TRUBITT

Venue: **Shoreline Amphitheater, Mountain View, CA**
Rental Company: **Audio Analysts**
FOH Mixer: **Jon Ostrin**
Monitor Mixer: **Jim Yakabuski**
System Engineer: **Mario Leccese**

"This album has probably the most effects they've had," says Yakabuski. "Andy Johns came in and beefed the drums up. But Alex came into rehearsals and said, 'It's a great sound for the album, but I still want my drums to sound the way they have for 15 years.'" Drum mics are mounted inside the drums themselves, including Sennheiser 509s in the toms and 421s in the kick. This makes getting a consistent drum sound easier for everyone, and, of course, helps reduce leakage.

"I started out with noise gates on everything," says Yakabuski, "but they're not on anymore. I don't even use the mute groups on the board. Everything is open during the show—it's a low enough level that you can pull it off."

A CADD console is used for monitors as well. "I don't think I have anything on the board cut or boosted more than 3 dB.

But if you do need to boost or cut a frequency, it's right there. It's a nice EQ. I have a graphic and a five-way parametric on each mix, but the way it's turned out, everything's almost flat. Some of the mixes have a little cut at 2.5 or boost at 10 kHz. You could almost do it off the board and the outboard parametrics, but for me the graphics are like a security blanket! The board also has an aux matrix remix section, which lets you take any one of the four aux mixes and reroute it to any stage mix. I use this when Eddie and Mike [Anthony,

Eddie Van Halen and Sammy Hagar (inset)

Monitor engineer Jim Yakabuski (left) and house mixer Jon Ostrin; Sammy & Eddie at Cabo Wabo

"We're doing the whole band on 30 inputs: The simpler, the better."
—Jon Ostrin

the bassist] come to the center to sing with Sammy. I just set up a little mix of Eddie's guitar and drums, and bring that in Sammy's mix. You don't have to turn on four or five channels, just one matrix. The only thing about it that isn't great is that it weighs a lot. Four stagehands can lift a

Series 4, but this takes at least six or eight guys. It's probably twice as heavy."

With this band's style of music, one might expect stage level to be pretty high. Fortunately, this is not the case. Yakabuski explains: "Mike is probably the loudest thing up there. He goes for that bassy tone, without a lot of cut in it, so to hear himself he has to be quite loud. But Eddie's real reasonable—he just uses three bottom cabinets at the end of his stack. He doesn't like to hear those straight on. And I put a little of him in his sidefill." Sidefills are Audio Analysts' A-3s, with one hung for lead vocal and two on the floor carrying a full mix on each side of the stage.

Analysts' crew chief Mario Leccese notes the absence of subwoofers in the the tour's 56-cabinet, Crown-powered rig. For the arena leg of the tour they will increase the box count to 72, eight of which will be subs. Leccese felt subs weren't required for the band's sound in the sheds, taking into consideration the full-range response provided by the HDS-4's dual 18-inchers. To prevent buildup in the lower seating area of the venue, Leccese tilted the bottom row of HDS-4 cabinets up toward the grass seats, rather than using the typical downward orientation.

"At this point in the tour, we've done about 15 shows," says Ostrin. "We've done totally outdoor ones and a lot of difficult venues, but it's at a point now where we're pretty locked in. The first week was pressure, with the guys out front every day or doing an hour and a half just on monitors. But we're relaxed now, we've gotten over the big hump and finished the first leg pretty successfully. Now they don't have to worry about what we're doing—they can just concentrate on playing their music, which is exactly how it should be."

Tom Petty and the Heartbreakers

"**I**T'S THE MOST STRAIGHT-AHEAD THING I'VE done since Glen Campbell," says house mixer Mark Deadman, on his second outing with Tom Petty and the Heartbreakers' "Touring the Great Wide Open." Deadman's previous work includes ten years with Huey Lewis, The Cars and others, as well as spending the last year and a half as a studio engineer at Nickelodeon's Orlando production facility. Electrotec (Canoga Park, Calif.) is providing equipment for the tour, including its new LAB Q-2 loudspeaker system. "It's definitely better-sounding than the old system," Deadman notes. "Every cabinet is fixed, which makes for a much more even sound when you walk the hall. But the fact that we were able to tilt individual cabinets in the old P.A. was handy, because you could still point something down."

Instead, the new rig addresses this need with wedge-shaped, under-hung cabinets. "They cover the whole front section," Electrotec FOH tech Peter Downey comments. "If you're using groundfills on a stage this size, you can lose seats. These fill in that section." The system crossover is a BSS unit; Klark-Teknik EQ is used on the main LAB Q-2 boxes and a White EQ tweaks the under-hung cabs. A BSS limiter is used to tighten up the sub-bass.

Deadman describes his no-frills approach to Petty's FOH vocal: "I'm running him through the Summit [tube] limiter, which I really like a lot. I put a little 60ms delay on his vocal left and right through the Eventide, just to fatten it up a little bit and help get it above our monitor levels, which are extremely high. On a couple of songs, I put a 120ms or 175ms delay, similar to what they had on the earlier albums. I put a little delay on the backing vocals and a short reverb on the snare, which is the only reverb I use." A little more subtlety is used to get the band's full, ringing acoustic guitar sound. "I put a little Eventide Harmonizer on the acoustic guitars," he says, "one cent down on the left and one cent up on the right side. I'll use one or the other—it's better to take it up if the hall is kind of boomy, but if the hall's real bright, I'll take it down. Sometimes I use both.

"It's nice to actually mike a kick drum again," Deadman adds. "Of course, it gets frustrating some nights when it would be a lot easier to be triggering a sample!" Drum mics include a Beyer 88 on the kick, Beyer 201 on hi-hat and Shure SM57s on snare (top and bottom). Ramsa WM Series miniature mics are used on the toms, with AKG 414s for overheads. An EV PL10 and a DI are on the bass. "Everything else is 57s," Deadman notes, "all the guitars and vocals. We tried a Beta 57 on Tom last year, and I kind of liked it better, but our monitor engineer didn't like it as much. I'd like to try an EV 1776—I used one with Bette Midler a couple of weeks ago; it's a real tight-pattern mic with a lot of rejection.

"I've been with Tom for a long time—since '78," notes monitor engineer Dave

BY DAVID (RUDY) TRUBITT

Venue: **Oakland Coliseum**	
Rental Company: **Electrotec**	
House Mixer: **Mark Deadman**	
Monitor Mixer: **Dave Bryson**	
System Engineer: **Chris East**	

"To get his intonation when he sings, you have to get it really loud, but you have to get the tonal quality, too."
—Dave Bryson

Bryson, who provides Petty plenty of level with over 50 drivers pointed at the singer. "There are sidefills on either side, the overheads [LAB Q-2 under-hungs at center stage, pointed back] and four monitors on the floor. So he has five mixes. I do stereo on the floor for the echo [only on ballads], left and right sidefill, and the overhead. That's all vocal mixes. To get his intonation when he sings, you have to get it really loud, but you have to get the tonal quality, too. Basically, I shoot for how loud I can get it, with the best quality I can get. That's why you need those drivers.

"The rest of them just have these floor monitors," Bryson continues. "[Keyboardist] Ben Tench has two mixes—band and vocal mix; drummer Stan Lynch has the

same." Lynch doesn't require extra sub-bass monitors; Bryson says the TAD 1601 600-watt drivers powered by Crown amplifiers provide plenty of lows, while JBL 2241s are used for the wedge's high end. A Soundcraft console rounds out the monitor system, running a total of 39 inputs, 14 mixes and a couple of effects sends. Effects are used sparingly. "The Lexicon LXP-15 is a really neat unit," Bryson says. "They've come a long way in the last few years as far as dynamic range is concerned."

One of the band's strengths is the spontaneity of their live show. "There's no set list," Deadman explains. "We have the first four songs, a big open space, and the last four songs. I really enjoy it. They're all real steady players, especially Howie Epstein, the bass player. He's the easiest guy to get a tone from I've ever had. Bass is

always the toughest in these big halls."

"The basic thing to this band is simplicity," Deadman concludes. "It's a simple, straight-ahead rock 'n' roll mix. That makes it a challenge—to go back to the roots. Except I have a Gamble console!"

Petty's stage (note Electrotec's wedge-shaped front-fill cabinets silhouetted above center stage); house mixer Mark Deadman

The Rolling Stones

**BY
GREGORY A.
DETOGNE**

HISTORICALLY, MEDIOCRITY HAS NEVER BEEN something associated with the Rolling Stones, and their "Steel Wheels" tour was no exception. Sizable in form, function and profit, their foray across the continent was a spectacle of monstrous proportions featuring Mick and the boys frolicking in an elegantly industrial, stylized landscape. The band looked and sounded great, offering a broad cross-section of their best material from the past quarter-century.

Visually, fans got their money's worth in the form of a truly innovative stage, continuously awash in a sea of color from a state-of-the art lighting system. Giant video screens at stage right and left supplemented the already larger-than-life display. Halfway through the show you could count on an appearance by two inflatable 55-foot-tall Honky-Tonk Women, and to cap things off, before you left, an ample dose of fireworks exploded in the sky during an encore performance of "Jumping Jack Flash."

All the visuals in the world wouldn't make much difference, however, if the sound reinforcement system failed to live up to expectations. To fill the bill, the Stones relied upon Dallas-based Showco's Prism Concert System to take on the rigors of the 36-city tour.

Requiring an 18-person crew to operate and eight tractor-trailers to transport, the system can be viewed as three separate entities. To distinguish these three groups,

> *Venue:*
> **North American stadiums**
> *Rental Company:* **Showco**
> *FOH Mixer:* **Benji Lefevre**
> *Monitor Mixer:*
> **Chris Wade-Evans**
> *System Engineers:* **Jeff McGinnis, David "Cowboy" Conyers and Gary Epstein**

Showco assigned three different "team" leaders to each: Jeff McGinnis oversaw the operations of the Red Team System, David Conyers the Blue Team System, and Gary Epstein the Universal Team System. The first two groups of equipment are identical leapfrogging main speaker systems (i.e., one system is used for one show while the other is torn down and sent to the next concert site). Each package consists of entire speaker arrays, including subwoofer systems and front-fills, a large portion of the monitor system, and amps and effects for opening act Living Colour. By contrast, the Universal System, which travels to every show, includes the house and monitor mixing consoles, along with the main effects rack, featuring two AMS reverb units, two AMS digital delays, two Yamaha REV7s and four "antique" UREI 1176 limiters, among other things.

While design credit for the Prism Concert System goes to Showco's Clay Powers, Jim Brawley and Lee Hardesty, the title of chief audio engineer falls squarely on the shoulders of Benji Lefevre, who has logged 21 years in the business and worked with the likes of Jack Bruce, Led Zeppelin, Peter Gabriel, James Taylor and George Michael. Lefevre, a Showco employee for more than a decade, chose two Harrison HM-5 consoles to serve his mixing efforts, while monitor engineer Chris Wade-Evans sat behind a Harrison SM-5 (also outfitted with a 20-channel expander).

Once given the job, Lefevre concerned himself with getting all the practical things out of the way. "I wanted to plan the whole thing out so it would be as easy as possible for the crew to install the large amounts of equipment we were dealing with," he said, while preparing for one of the tour's New York City dates. "Together with some key people, I came up with methods of installation that were simply delightful for the guys working on the tour."

To facilitate load-in and load-out, a passageway that ran the entire length of the stage from left to right was built underneath. Elevator bays extended from this passageway to the stage floor, which allowed the P.A. to be installed without the roadies ever having to touch the stage surface itself. As a result, the lighting could be installed overhead while the P.A. was set up from underneath, and getting ready for each show was accomplished in what Lefevre refers to as "record time."

With logistics out of the way, Lefevre began thinking about how he would approach his work. Initially, he spoke with the group while they were finishing the *Steel Wheels* album, and he expressed an interest in becoming involved in rehearsals as early as possible. Shortly thereafter, he found himself working with the band at Wykeham Rise, a former girls' boarding school in Washington, Connecticut. Sequestered in a separate area with his Harrison console, effects rack and small amounts of other gear, away from the main rehearsal room, he plotted exactly what he wanted to do and when. After the first couple of weeks, he was satisfied with his choice of microphones and their placement, and started to conceive of how he wanted to project the Stones to the public.

"On the tour, I wanted to make the large stadiums we were playing as intimate as possible," he recalls. "I clearly wanted to steer away from the massive big-stadium sound that gives people a feeling of

Mick Jagger, Keith Richards (inset)

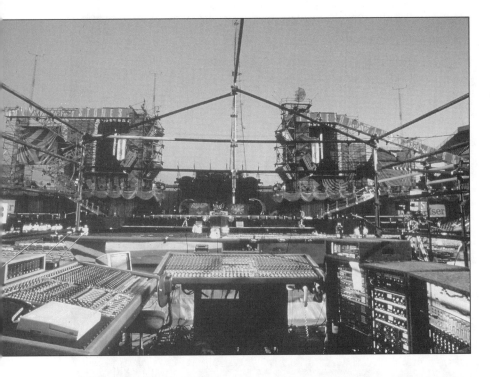

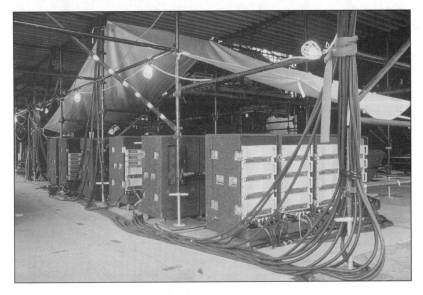

Harrison HM-5 consoles and outboard gear at the Dallas shows, Crown amp racks (below).

manufacturer's Macro-Tech 1200 and PSA-2 amplifiers. The Crown amplifiers drove a version of Showco's Prism Concert System, which was configured carefully just for this tour.

"Everything about the rigging scheme of the Stones' system was integrated into the overall show," says Showco's Robin Magruder. "We've worked with the band since the "Some Girls" tour in '78, and became involved in the preliminary production discussions for this tour. To properly fit the Prism Concert System into the scheme of things, we held a series of meetings in London, Dallas, New York and Connecticut to work out every detail of the logistics, from taking the system from the trucks to operating conditions. Throughout the process, it was imperative that we maintain a correct relationship with the rest of the set, because in this case, the Prism arrays were actually a scenic element, and we didn't have the luxury of hiding everything behind scrims."

Aesthetics aside, Showco's underlying performance philosophy was to achieve predictability and accuracy. To help attain these goals and predict how the system would perform in a live environment, they used computer modeling. According to Clay Powers, one of the three Showco designers working on the project, they began their studies by defining the sound field in a model stadium. Next, the geometry of the seating area was considered and a radiation pattern specified. They then matched hardware to that pattern, with other factors such as levels of distortion, reliability and service taken into account.

"We developed the modeling programs ourselves," Powers says. "But they aren't some sort of magic piece of software capable of doing something you couldn't calculate with pen and paper. They simply allow us to crank through many calculations at a very fast pace. Based upon our calculations, the system was optimally designed, constructed and verified with the aid of Techron's TEF technology."

being remote and distant. My reasoning was that basically, the Rolling Stones are an R&B band, just like many bands you see in local bars. I wanted to project them just that way, even though we were working with a very sophisticated sound reinforcement system. I didn't want them sounding very polished or hi-fi; I wanted to have a raw edge, while at the same time being able to project over the entire audience in a uniform fashion."

Lefevre's power to project over huge audiences is aided in no small part by 500,000 watts of Crown power, served up over 250 of the Elkhart, Indiana-based

It is Showco's policy to maintain a tight lip when it comes to questions about the Prism arrays' contents, and they would admit only to "using the very best professional sound reinforcement products available today." For each show on the tour (with the exception of the Alpine Valley [East Troy, Wisconsin] performance, which, due to spatial considerations, used a scaled-down version of the system), two main Prism arrays are constructed on each side of the stage. They cover the entire audio spectrum, ranging from bass through frequencies in excess of 15 kHz. The grey-black cylindrical arrays are composed of 84 individual enclosures. A rigging scheme allows the cabinets to be interlocked in a flush fashion that also leaves them physically aligned for optimum performance [see Genesis profile for related photos]. Each side contains 32 subwoofers, and five more enclosures are mounted in front-fill positions to provide coverage for fans seated directly in front of the stage.

To further realize Lefevre's vision of an intimate atmosphere in a large stadium, the setup includes custom-made delay towers. In stadiums where the structures can't be flown, they are placed 200 feet out from the main P.A., and reach even the most remote seats.

As might be expected, power distribution for the tour is extremely complex. Provided by a company called Show Power, two 300-kilowatt diesel-fueled generators mounted on trailers—essentially a small power station—drive the entire sound system (house and monitor). Snakes and cables are also given careful consideration, using the best components available for the more than 2,000 interlocks.

Newsweek succinctly described a concert on the Stones tour by writing "the volume level was properly deafening, fireworks properly blinding, the band sounded fine." For Benji Lefevre and Showco, the last part of the review was probably the best compliment.

"I wanted to make the large stadiums as intimate as possible. My reasoning was that basically, the Rolling Stones are an R&B band, just like many bands you see in local bars. I wanted to project them just that way even though we were working with a very sophisticated sound reinforcement system."
—Benji Lefevre

Kiss

IRST THEY TAKE OFF THEIR MASKS, DUMP the excessive theatrics and focus on improved musicianship. Then they clean up their sound and go on the road with a brand new touring concert system, specially designed to present extended-range coverage evenly throughout the audience area. What's going on here?

The show is still "Kiss," but it now sports a new production package that has been impressing promoters and rock fans alike. During the spring and summer of 1990, the tour played to major venues nationwide, such as Nassau Veterans' Coliseum in New York, Tampa's Sun Dome and Atlanta's Lakewood Amphitheatre. The flashpots, the lasers, the acrobatic guitar solos and the impressive stage set are still here, but a new, high-end sound system was assembled by heavy-metal sound specialist Tasco for the tour. [Note that assets and many personnel from Tasco's U.S. operation were acquired by A-1 Audio of Hollywood, CA two years after this tour—Ed.]

Live sound specialist Greg Price, who began his mixing career more than a dozen years ago working with pop and MOR acts like Pablo Cruise and Glen Campbell, is in charge. Metal Lite? Not exactly. Price's powerful but precise musical approach to live mixing has definitely complemented both this show and Tasco's new arena sound system, which features Midas consoles, Crest power amplifiers and speaker enclosures from Eastern Acoustic Works.

Rental Company: **Tasco**
FOH Mixer: **Greg Price**

"I came from a pop background," notes Price, who has previously toured with acts like Night Ranger and Poison. "I try to manage a metal mix the same way I would a pop show. It's much more challenging when you add some finesse, instead of just turning everything up. Maybe that's why a lot of metal music sounds so boring to a lot of people…it's just a volume thing for some sound mixers.

"Basically, what we do is remove the harmonic distortion points that are inherent with a hard-edged guitar band," he continues, "and then focus on blending the whole mix, from vocal harmonies to percussion accents, so that you hear *music*, not just noise. The kids notice the difference. They know the tunes; they want to hear the words. They know how pleasing it can sound. So why not work to give it to them? That means a high-fidelity sound system, cleaned-up instrumental inputs and a focus on musical mixing."

Price found that hearing protection is an important aspect of doing his job. "When setting up during the day," he says, "a lot of guys will open the system up wide, play their favorite compact discs at crush or whatever. Or maybe put pink noise through the system for an hour just to annoy the lighting crew. That's not really where it's at. You can totally ruin yourself for the show if you abuse your hearing early on in the day. I already know what the system can do. I know what the band can do. So I don't need to prove anything. And soundcheck is not the time to beat

BY
MIKE
STANDE

against the walls of an empty arena with high SPLs. I wait until showtime, keep the sound of the show at a manageable level, and it works well for everyone."

The system Price has at his disposal was packaged by Tasco after a lengthy examination of available amplifiers and loudspeaker systems. Working with EAW designer Kenton Forsythe, Tasco engineers assembled a modular, packaged sound system that also could include long-throw components. The result of this collaboration is the new KF1000, identical in size and shape to the popular KF850 but designed with far-throw applications in mind. Featuring new components, including a twin 12-inch, long-throw, low-midrange horn chamber, the KF1000 gives Tasco's KF850 arena systems more punch. "The comments we are getting back from out on the road are very good on the KF1000," noted Tasco's then-vice president of operations, Steve "Griff" Griffiths.

Price's mixing strategy on the Kiss tour makes interesting use of the long-throw speaker packages. "We put the KF1000s on the top row of the flying arrays," he says. "They are fed with separate left and right crossovers directly from the stereo vocal subgroup and the stereo effects group. This gives me an 'overlay' of sweetened vocals on top of the full music mix. The vocal harmonies reach the farthest seats, even in the largest arenas. I can achieve good penetration of the crowd noise and reach way back, even in bad, boomy halls. It gives me a variable speaker system to work with on top of the regular full-range mix."

Tasco supplied the Kiss tour with 48 EAW KF850 full-range enclosures, 24 SB850 subwoofers and eight of the new long-throw KF1000s. A dozen of the subs are stacked two high in front of each audience corner of the stage; portions of the scenic stage set, looking like a high-tech junkyard, are stacked atop these. Twenty-three KF850s are flown on each side with

Gene Simmons

Stage, with Tasco's EAW
loudspeaker rig

three chain motors, using compact aluminum hanging beams. "We've specified a beefier hanging hardware package, so that we can now fly our cabinets six deep when we need to," Griffiths explains. "This is a quick and easy system to get off the ground and in the air, and we get excellent full-frequency throw for large audiences."

The system drive package features EAW's MX800 CCEP™ (Closely Coupled Electronic Processor) with customized cards for Tasco. Thirty-two Crest Model 8001 power amplifiers, packaged four per compact rack, power the system. Three separate 30-ampere circuits are provided for each amp rack. A newly fabricated snake cabling system and beefy 10-gauge speaker wiring harnesses tie the system package together.

On this Kiss tour, Price relies on a few signal processing "tricks" to achieve a powerful yet well-blended mix. A dbx 120X Subharmonic Synthesizer is fed an auxiliary mix, made up of instruments intended to have low-bass impact, to the subwoofer arrays. Vocal and stereo effects subgroups pass through Klark-Teknik DN410 parametric equalizers before going to the separate long-throw components.

The usual channel-insertable compressors and noise gates are available for vocal and drum inputs (dbx 903 and 904, and Drawmer DS201s). The arsenal of special effects devices includes two Eventide H910 Harmonizers, a Roland SDE-3000A digital delay, Lexicon 224XL, 200 and PCM70, Yamaha REV7, and the TC Electronic TC 2290 digital delay and effects control processor. The main left and right system drive package includes three EAW stereo MX800s, Klark-Teknik DN27A graphic equalizers and dbx 165A Over-Easy compressor-limiters.

Price runs the show from a 40-channel split-frame Midas mixing console. A separate Midas desk is available for the opening act. "You have to have the right stuff to achieve a certain consistent level of results," Price says. "But I don't like to get stuck on the hardware itself. They're just tools of the trade. Where it really happens is out there in the room—the way the sound system interacts with the acoustics of a given venue. Getting a good mix is the first step; managing how the mix is presented to the audience through the sound reinforcement system is just as important."

With years of experience working with a variety of acts like Huey Lewis & The News, Jefferson Starship and others, Price found that high-SPL shows are particularly challenging. "Metal music is really no different from anything else, when it gets right down to it," he offers. "You have melody, rhythm and a harmony structure. You have to find a place for each voice and instrument that *works*, so it can be heard and it blends without sticking out too far. In terms of managing high volume, I try to hold things back. I like to use the different sound textures like accents, maybe a guitar riff or a drum crescendo, punching them up a bit to make a point and then backing off. If you let everything just creep up and up, pretty soon you don't have a mix anymore. And that means noise instead of music."

With a mixing philosophy based on taste and dramatic effect, and a new arena sound system to work with that is intended to offer better audience-area coverage, Price was prepared to do what he does best. "When I first came into this situation," Price recalls, "everyone was telling me that all I had to do was turn it up and be on auto-pilot, because it was just guitars, guitars and more distorted guitars.

Engineer Greg Price

But I thought to myself, 'Maybe no one has ever taken a fresh, new look at this band's sound and what all there might be to work with!' Rather than just have the whole show be the same, I'm focusing on the melody and harmony aspects of the different tunes. As a group starts to sound better for its audiences, they are inspired to play to their highest potential. When the players know they are getting across—even despite difficult acoustical situations—then they start to make every show a peak performance."

Kiss have been active on the concert stage for well over a decade, and as the band has matured, so has its audience's expectations. This tour demonstrated a commitment to a higher-level sound, lighting and staging production, and the addition of Tasco's new sound system and Greg Price's mixing strategies made the concert audio one of the event's highlights. As far as arena concerts go, this one delivered what the fans came for: a dynamic, highly visual, high-energy show.

**"When I first came into this situation, everyone was telling me that I [could just] be on auto-pilot, because it was just guitars, guitars and more distorted guitars. But I thought to myself, 'Maybe no one has ever taken a fresh, new look at this band's sound and what all there might be to work with!'"
—Greg Price**

Bruce Springsteen

WHILE CLOUDY SKIES LOOMED OVER THE small Chicago suburb of Tinley Park, Bruce Springsteen's crew prepared for the first of two sold-out shows at The World Music Theater, a massive, state-of-the-art shed that saw its first concert season in the summer of 1990. It has the largest outdoor seating capacity under one roof (12,000), with a total capacity of 33,000. The World's enormous steel roof makes the venue an acoustical challenge.

By 7 a.m. on the morning of the first show, stage hands and crew were busy replacing the venue's 96x68-foot stage with the tour's own bi-level platform. Springsteen's stage is equally impressive in size, but is contoured at the two upstage corners, allowing for approximately 12 extra rows of seating wrapped around each side. Before the stage was half-constructed, the Audio Analysts sound crew had flown the 64 HD S-4 speaker enclosures they were to use for the next two days. Crew chief Mario Leccese oversaw the rigging of the system while monitor engineer Fred (Gumby) Jackson and FOH engineer John Kerns were busy at their respective stations.

Springsteen's monitor mix position is in a ground-level pit, squeezed between the audience and the stage. There is just enough room for Fred Jackson's Audio Analysts-designed CADD SM-1M monitor console and a Gamble 36x16 custom desk. "I sit less than two feet away from one performer and less than four feet away

Venue: **The World Music Theater, Tinley Park, Ill.**
Sound Company: **Audio Analysts**
House Mixer: **John Kerns**
Monitor Mixer: **Fred (Gumby) Jackson**
Crew Chief: **Mario Leccese**

from another," Jackson says. "The crowd is three feet behind me, and two monitors are directly in front of me. I also have my cue wedge behind me and a sidefill above my head. It's like trying to have a conversation in a crowded room. Somehow, you have to keep track of everything that's happening. I mix every night at about +5 over nominal, just to get over the top of the other information that's bouncing around the room. After three and a half hours of all that, you can become pretty disoriented."

The need to keep clear sightlines precludes the use of monitors or sidefills on-stage. "Instead, we developed a box that incorporates a compression 10- and 2-inch, which we blasted from the center, almost like an HD S-4," Jackson says. "When Bruce steps out of the center pocket, there is another set of monitors buried in the runway that comes around the front of the stage. There's also a set of long-throw sidefills in the air on the side of the stage. It's not a wash like what you'd do with normal sidefills and a bunch of wedges across the front. There are certain positions you wait for him to walk to, and then you hit him with it. You can't just sit back and watch—you have to punch up each mix. He can be unpredictable."

The house mix position at The World is a 32x16-foot area centered 115 feet from the stage, just in front of the first-level pedestrian walkway. House engineer John Kerns uses an AA/CADD SM-1H

BY NORT JOHNSON

house board, along with a Soundcraft 500. "The CADD console has a lot of inputs and great sound," Kerns says. "Once I started using it, I never wanted anything else. There's a lot of headroom and flexibility. It's got 40 inputs, both with A and B mic inputs and a line input on each channel, eight stereo returns, eight auxiliary inputs, eight matrices, eight stereo group outs, three stereo mix outs, three mono mix outs, eight mono sends and four stereo sends."

Kerns also showed off three impressive effects racks. "I'm using a few TC Electronic 2290 delays," he notes. "One is just for effects, and the other is a vocal thickener. I also have an AMS reverb and AMS delay harmonizer, which are only for Bruce's vocals, and three Lexicon PCM70s for drum and instrument reverbs. All the background vocals get Eventide H3000. I'm switching [presets via MIDI] on everything with a Digital Music Corp. MX-8 MIDI patch bay and a little Roland controller. It's extremely easy—just punch in your program number. Some drum sounds come from two Wendel Jr.'s [sample-playback devices] here [at the FOH] and a

"The crowd is three feet behind me, and two monitors are directly in front of me. I also have my cue wedge behind me and a sidefill above my head. It's like trying to have a conversation in a crowded room."
—Fred (Gumby) Jackson, monitor mixer

Audio Analysts' rig flying at the World; John Kerns (left) and Fred (Gumby) Jackson at the Shoreline Amphitheater

folks in the middle. Those are the people who either paid the big money or slept in line all night. It's important for them to hear the house sound, not just the monitors. The speakers have two 12s and a horn inside and are tuned to 40 Hz. I don't try to get that much bottom out of them because there's a lot of bottom end thrown around, and you have the stage volume right there." The entire system is powered by 12 racks of Crown amps. Each rack holds a mixture of Macro-Tech 2400s and Macro-Tech 1200s and is located at ground level, stage left and right.

Jackson notes that a new mic capsule on Springsteen's wireless helps with the monitors as well as with the house. "We got a custom Audix OM 7 capsule and had them put it on a Sony transmitter. It's got a hypercardioid pattern, and rejection is incredible. It sounds like a wired microphone. It makes it a little bit easier for John and me, with the amount of stage volume that's going on."

Springsteen's first night at The World went well. Thunderstorms were predicted all day, but luckily the skies didn't open up on the crowd. The lightning strikes seen on either side of the stage during "Thunder Road" were not produced by special effects, but by nature. The next day, Kerns talked about his first night under the World's immense roof: "The bottom end will not go away. It just sort of rumbles. It's about six seconds out here at the mix position, somewhere between 80 and 100 cycles. And it's tough with these skyboxes here. It's tough to get even coverage on the top end. If we could put a lot more sound on the ground, I would have taken the whole rig up higher to cover that specifically. It's very important to Bruce and everybody involved with this production that everyone in the audience gets the best sound possible, and I agree with that. After all, the audience are the people who pay the big bucks."

couple of Akai S1000 samplers backstage. They're occasionally used for kick and snare, but not that often."

Besides the 64 flown HD S-4s and six HD S-4s per side onstage, there are what appear to be two monitors hanging from each cluster, angled down at the audience. Kerns says that the motivation behind the position of AA's new nearfill cabinets is to provide clear sightlines. "With this design, the bottom cabinets hang down at a slight angle and cover the first ten or 15 rows," he says. "We also have one onstage for the

Reba McEntire

"I'VE BEEN MIXING REBA FOR EIGHT YEARS—from rodeos and county fairs to the big time," house engineer Ricky Moeller says. As with many country acts, McEntire tours constantly—about ten months each year. This time out they've played sellout shows at everything from theaters and state fairs to 15,000-seat arenas, with the occasional plane ride to corporate dates.

Moeller describes his daily routine: "First, we do a systems check and make sure all of our components are happening. Then I run it up with 60 Hz and set the delays between the sub-bass and the array." He sets the delay time by listening for the largest level peak while watching 60 Hz on a real-time analyzer. "Some people go by set formulas," he continues, "but I like to listen to the room. If you walk it off with the formula, it works out about the same. Then I run pink noise up and look at what the room's doing before EQ." Moeller runs the Showco EQs uniformly boosted across the band, which leaves extra range for up to 20dB cuts when required.

The slightly inverted domed ceiling of the Coliseum presented a challenge to Moeller. "The main problem in this room," he says, "is throwing HF up to the very top. With the low trim, I couldn't go much higher. The beauty about the Prism system is that if you get your points and get trimmed, you can fill up the room. I also like the way it loads into—and how much you can get in—the truck."

Venue: **Oakland Coliseum**
Rental Company: **Showco**
FOH Mixer: **Ricky Moeller**
Monitor Mixer: **Robert Kosloskie**
System Engineer: **Doug Hall**

A Yamaha PM3000 is shared by Reba and her support acts at the FOH. "I like to run that console low," Moeller says, "because the summing amps on the main outputs get a little grainy—that's why everybody seems to mix the output and the cue buses in the same range, so your summing amp's not sitting up there freaking out." Stage volume of the nine-piece band is also held to moderate levels. "We don't have any onstage amplifiers, and Reba's using Future Sonics Ear Monitors. We may move the vocalists and wind players to them soon."

However, Moeller's not looking to replace all the stage monitors. "If you put everybody on them, you just have drums sticking out. You want a nice little rhythm balance up there. People who need high-volume monitors should go on Ear Monitors, and their troubles will be over."

Robert "Kosmo" Kosloskie has been mixing Reba's monitors for more than five years. Until recently, he practically surrounded her with monitors. "I had them everywhere—on the floor, in the sky, front and back—it was really loud." Switching to the Ear Monitors dropped the stage level and reduced the box count. The transition took a little adjustment: "She and I are both getting used to it a little more," says Kosmo. "We know what to expect and what we can and can't get out of it." Initially, Reba wanted only her vocal in her ears, but gradually asked for more and

BY DAVID (RUDY) TRUBITT

"Learn to work with every piece of gear and any console, because if setup runs late, that time comes out of your soundcheck."
—opening act mixer Tim Prince

more instruments. "I have a full band mix going in there," Kosmo says. "I try to make it sound as much like the record as I can." An Aphex Dominator limits the Ear Monitor levels. "I'm using 15 sends [on the Harrison monitor console]," he adds. "She's got a left, right and a reverb send. I've got 11 band mixes and a sub for the drum monitor. I've got a PCM70 on her

reverb, an SPX90 as a delay for the background vocals, and a Brooke-Siren DPR 402 dual limiter. I've got a couple of 904s on the drums and 903s on the backing vocals. It's pretty straightforward."

Mix duties during the show are shared by system engineer Doug Hall. "There's a lot of movement happening on the faders," Hall says. "I have half a dozen faders that I run for just solos, acoustic guitar, steel guitar and one of the electric guitars. There's a lot more blending of levels in this type of show than in a lot of rock shows." Levels are in keeping with the music's varied audience. "The acoustic stuff is 90 db, and we go over 100 db for some of the hot numbers," Hall adds.

Already, Moeller is looking ahead. "Next year we'll go with the Harrison," he says. "We'll either keep the 3000 or add another for the opening acts. I'm going to add more effects. I just have the bare essentials—a Lexicon 224, an Eventide 910. Next year I'll be going to a Yamaha DMP-7 with the two SPXs built in. I'm going to MIDI everything and go to a Lexicon 480, three PCMs and an Eventide H3000. We'll label the songs on the PCM70 and just step through them with a MIDI footpedal [using program change messages]. We'll also add a delay and equalizer for tying into shed lawn systems." However, Moeller keeps an eye on his own wish list. "I try to give her as much fidelity as I can and stay within the budget. We don't want to price ourselves out of venues, because that's our bread and butter. We try to cooperate with the big picture but still not compromise any details."

The bill at the Oakland show started with Aaron Tippin, followed by Vince Gill. Tippin's FOH mixer, Tim Prince, added a word of advice for would-be opening act mixers. "Learn to work with every piece of gear and any console," he cautions, "because if setup runs late, that time comes out of your soundcheck. You can work on instrument sounds during the set, but make sure your lead vocal is happening during soundcheck, because that's the

most important thing."

"This is a combat audio gig," says Gill's FOH man, Hugh Johnson. "It's a different P.A. just about every night. We're fortunate to work with a P.A. like this one. Next year we'll probably have [our own] production for 50 to 75 percent of our shows." Gill's monitor engineer, Sam Parker, adds, "Trying to get the level of consistency that the band and Vince want on different stuff every day is quite challenging."

McEntire's stage monitor position, with Harrison console, Crown amp racks and Showco wedge monitors.

117

AC/DC

BY DAVID
(RUDY)
TRUBITT

"I'M HERE AS A SOUND ENGINEER THROUGH dB Sound, but chosen by the band—it's one of those complicated situations," says house mixer Robbie McGrath. When dB bid on the job, they also put forward names of several potential mixers, including McGrath. "I was really shocked at the phone call to even put my resume in, because I'd been doing Simply Red, Tears for Fears, Sinéad O'Connor and Art of Noise—it's a different ball game. But I spoke with the guitar player, and he said he was quite fed up with going to hear bands that were too loud, with not enough distinction. I think it's worked. At least, they haven't gotten rid of me! The main problem with mixing a band like this is to keep it loud but separated, and try to make the halls sound a little smaller than they are. I'm using the TAC SR9000 [a 42x16 board with an optional 24-input extension], which I've used before, and I find the desk is amazing. It gives me everything I need."

Electro-Voice MT-4s are McGrath's loudspeakers of choice; he's used them on previous tours as well. MT stands for Manifold Technology, meaning the output from multiple drivers is combined (through a manifold) within the cabinet. This results in an high-output enclosure that is very compact in relation to the actual number of drivers it contains. "The EV is a very unforgiving system, in the sense that it's real easy to mess up. It's not like a Meyer [Sound Labs] rig, where you always get a Meyer feel from it, or a Clair Brothers [Audio S-4 system], where it's always a Clair Brothers feel. You can get anything out of it, so you really want to know what you're looking for. All in all, I think it's a very good rig. I think a lot of people are frightened of it—it's got a few problems, but nothing you can't get over." A Meyer CP10 stereo five-band parametric equalizer provides overall system EQ, with a broad 4dB boost at the low end and a 2dB dip around 2-3 kHz. "The high mids can be quite bitey—you have to be careful that your volume isn't [in that frequency band], because that will destroy everything below it."

"EV is doing some modifications on these boxes for us," says dB Sound crew chief Scott Pike. "The DH-2 high-mid driver and manifold has been redesigned, because it's kind of peaky in the 2.5k range. These will all be changed next week. EV has been really supportive as far as taking criticism and actually *doing* something about it."

Pike describes the rig's layout: "The first two rows are three-ways hanging with horns on, then the next row is bass. They're all in columns until you get around to the side-hang where they checkerboard to split it up, because you don't need it quite so beamy. When you get it in columns like this, it's really high-powered."

> *Venue:* **Oakland Coliseum, Shoreline Amphitheater (Mountain View, CA)**
> *Sound Company:* **dB Sound**
> *House Mixer:* **Robbie McGrath**
> *Monitor Mixer:* **Paul Owen**
> *Crew Chief:* **Scott Pike**

Like most, McGrath enjoys experimenting with new outboard gear, although he shows considerable restraint when mixing. His current fave? "The Eventide H3000 Harmonizer is an amazing machine. I recommend it highly. Before that, it was the Lexicon 480—some of the programs in that are amazing. I like the BSS compressors; I want to try the new one. They've also got a nice delay with a temperature probe for adjusting delay settings."

Stage miking is fairly straightforward, but McGrath offers a few twists. "I mic the top snare with two Shure SM-57s [in a crossed-pair configuration], so the pickup area on the drum is much wider than with a single mic. I get a lot more tone out of the snare before cranking the gain. Also, I use an Aphex Exciter on one of them, which gives me a processed sound on one mic." A third SM-57 on the bottom head finishes the job. "I'm using a [Beyer] M88 on the bass drum—it's got a real sweet low end. A lot of people who do this kind of music go for a lot of that 5kHz attack in the bass drum sound, which, to be honest, I don't like, because I think it takes the bass drum too far out of the mix."

Also notable is the Sony wireless microphone system used by singer Brian Johnson. "I have a love/hate relationship with that thing. Some nights it's great, and some nights…I'd prefer to use Samson or Shure, but Brian likes it, and he's the one out there in front of 16,000 people."

McGrath believes in adapting to the situation. "Every hall sounds different; as

Singer/ringer Brian Johnson and Angus Young (inset)

dB Sound's Electro-Voice
MT-4 rig

long as you apply a bit of care, you can get the hall to sound good within itself. Use whatever the hall is giving you—you don't bring your own sound in there. If you do, it'll drive you mad, 'cause you'll never get every room to sound the same, as we all know. I think using the excuse that the room was bad is a bit lame. We've landed a man on the moon, lads; surely we can hear the guitar at the end of the hall!" His approach to the Oakland Coliseum was to start off slow and build. "If I were to power up too hard in here, it wouldn't work. I'll set the mix up first before bringing it out." He pauses and laughs. "If not, I'll have plan B!"

Monitor duties are covered by Paul Owen, who was last out with Metallica. "I started in rehearsals with AC/DC in September 1990," he explains. "I did two weeks with them, which gave me a fair bit of insight into the band. In the studio, we had conventional wedges on the floor, and they sounded great. But as soon as I put them under the metal grilles on this stage, they didn't happen at all. The grilles have a 3/4-inch gap, but it's like looking through a venetian blind: No matter where you put the horns, the sound will only come out one way, and it makes everything bright and sparkly. I had to revamp the whole monitor system during production rehearsals, so I changed to the Electro-Voice DeltaMax, which responded better under there. I think the processor (a combined crossover/limiter designed specifically to complement the system's enclosures) makes them more efficient, and the overall sound of the cabinet works well, although I don't think the low-end response is that wonderful. Single DeltaMaxes sound totally different than two that are within, say, six inches of each other, because you get the coupling at the low end." The monitors are powered by Crown MT2400s for the low end and PSA-2s for the highs.

"I'm using a Ramsa board," Owen continues, "but I'm going to change that to a [Midas] XL3, because I find that on the Ramsa, the EQ isn't that superior. You end up taking so much away on the board that you find you are using the outboard EQ to compensate. So I've inserted parametrics

on Brian's vocal and the backing vocals, which has helped to a certain degree, but the biggest problem with this band is the actual volume. At the backing vocal position alone, it's 120 dB A-weighted—just the volume of the guitars. So if they're not [singing] any louder than the guitars at the mic, and they ask for the vocals to be turned up, you just end up increasing the stage volume around them. Brian has been pretty consistent [-3 to +3 VU at input], but toward the end of the tour, he can drop down to just above the stage level [-10]. It's an impossible situation, because he isn't singing louder than the stage."

Of course, AC/DC is a *guitar* band. Malcolm and Angus Young each use eight guitar cabinets—four on each side of the stage. There are no guitars in the monitors. "They rely mainly on the backline," says Owen, "and they've been doing it so long that they're not really willing to compromise backline-wise. It's always the monitors

that have to compete against their level. I find I have to emphasize the high end, probably from 3k to 10k, which hurts my ears, but these guys will say it sounds really dull onstage. But the frequencies that sound very harsh are the ones that cut through over the loud guitars." Overall, Owen runs 12 channels of monitors. In addition to the DeltaMaxes, EV MT-2s (half-sized versions of the above-mentioned MT-4s) are also being used for sidefills.

Keeping the whole operation running is crew chief Scott Pike, who also mixes opening act L.A. Guns. I asked if the two responsibilities create any conflicts. "Quite a bit, actually," he says. "I spend a lot of my day making sure things are right for Robbie, and then I have to do the opening act on top of that. You have to kind of separate yourself from that side of it to get into a mixing mode. A lot of the time, I won't get 15 minutes before I walk up to the desk, so it can be difficult."

"We've landed a man on the moon, lads; surely we can hear the guitar at the end of the hall!" — Robbie McGrath

George Strait

"I'VE BASICALLY GOT THREE JOBS," PAUL Rogers says. "Production manager, sound engineer and systems tech/crew chief. That happens in country music. It's not like rock 'n' roll acts, where they can have one person do each job. But the good part is when the show is over every night and I talk to George. Any complaints about anything—lights, sound—is all my responsibility. It takes a lot of pressure off the crew, and it gives George one guy to deal with for everything. It works great."

Rogers began his relationship with George Strait through the Dallas Backup sound company, which Strait worked with in the Texas/Five States region. In 1984, Rogers left his chief engineer position with Dallas Backup and went full-time to the Strait organization. In '86, Dallas Backup began touring nationally with Strait.

BY DAVID (RUDY) TRUBITT

Rogers describes a normal day: "We come in at 10 in the morning, and by 3, with an hour break, we're ready for soundcheck. That's hanging all the stuff, pink-noising and checking everything. We've got EAW, which I love to death." The tour carries 30 EAW KF850s (22 flown, eight on deck) and eight EAW subs and processors. "We're very limited in what we can carry," Rogers explains. "We've got one semi and a bobtail for all the sound, lighting and band gear. There are some rooms we get into, like the Arco Arena in Sacramento, where it's almost not enough. But the system's good enough that you can get

it all the way up to red-line, and it'll get you through the night.

"I use an analyzer to set the house EQ up," Rogers continues. "I won't even pink-noise if we're on the third or fourth night in a row—I'll just 'ear-ball' it. But on the first night [in a room], I'll analyze it immediately to make sure everything's working. Then I'll find three or four points that are a problem and fix them. I don't necessarily go for a flat [spectrum]. With the EAWs, the first thing I notice is a 200-250Hz bump. I really have to dig on those frequencies. There's also a little 400 and 500, and for my own ear, 2 and 2.5 kHz. I don't care *what* system it is—if I want to be loud and punchy, I've got to get rid of those frequencies. Then I can pump it up, and it's not going to hurt your ears."

Crest 8001s are the amps of choice. "We've been using Crest a long time," Rogers says. "When the PSA-2 came out, we sat down with a Crest and a Crown and listened to them naked, and we really liked the sound of the Crest better. That was back when they had the 4001 and 5001. The only thing I don't like is that they come up with something new every year—next thing you know, you have a bunch of stuff that doesn't match up exactly.

"George's vocal mic is a Beyer," Rogers explains. "It's great as far as monitor rejection. The one thing I don't like is that as soon as he walks away from the mic, it picks up all kinds of high-end stuff from

Rental Company:
Dallas Backup

FOH Mixer/System Engineer: Paul Rogers

Monitor Mixer: Dale Trout

the stage. I don't even hook his guitar up to the P.A. system—it's more of a prop than anything. If he walks away from the mic and really gets into playing, his guitar goes flying through the vocal mic—I just turn it off. I'm using your standard array of mics on drums—an EV RE-20 and a ddrums kick trigger, Shure SM57 on the snare, SM81 on the hi-hat, Sennheiser 421 on the toms and SM81 on the overheads. I use 57s on a couple of guitar amps, but everything else is direct: the steel, the fiddle, the piano and acoustic guitars."

When the show starts, Rogers has a golden opportunity to nail the details. "George doesn't hit the stage until the third song," he explains. "The band does two songs. They have lead breaks in both songs that go right down my [Yamaha PM3000] console. It goes steel, fiddle, guitar, guitar

Sound engineer Paul Rogers

"I start with the kick drum. Once that sounds good, I know everything else is going to fall into place."
—Paul Rogers

and piano. Then they do it again! After those two songs, I'm where I should be.

"I mix the way I want to mix. I don't have anybody over my shoulder, and I haven't in the eight years I've been with him. I've learned to see who the crowd consists of. On the East Coast we saw nothing but people 55 and older. They're very pleasant and quiet, and those rooms let you achieve a good, quiet mix—you won't get a big, punchy mix with these little P.A. systems, anyway. I don't want anybody up here bitching about [levels].

"When we do our normal situation in an arena, the crowd is 25 and under and screaming at the top of their lungs. It needs a punchy mix. I start with the kick drum. Once that sounds good, I know everything else is going to fall into place. Some people would probably say I'm a little heavy-handed on drums, but it works in situations where we've got our regular crowd. We do a big stereo mix."

Dale Trout, another Strait/Dallas Backup veteran, handles the nine stage monitor mixes from his Yamaha PM2800 monitor console. "I try to pay equal attention to everyone in the band," Trout says. "I would almost say I spend the least time with George."

If the opening act has no monitor or house engineer, Trout and Rogers will fill in. But a very relaxed, hands-off approach prevails if the support act does have engineers. "Everybody knows that an engineer can hear someone's mix and say, 'If only I could fix that one thing, it would be a great mix,'" Rogers says. "That's why I leave opening acts' mixers alone. That's their domain. If I feel there's something damaging happening, I'll say something. But a lot of these opening act engineers are surprised at how easy-going I am. Any knob you want to twist, twist it."

Rogers is now comfortable juggling his three jobs, although his situation is a recent development. "Until the first of this year, I had a system tech—Allen Miller. This guy was the best tech I ever had. I used to walk in [to soundcheck] and say, 'Sounds good, Allen,' and that was it. He and I would reach for knobs at the same time—literally reach for the same knob at the same time and sit there and laugh at each other. Now he's doing my job—production manager and mix engineer for Allen Jackson. When I lost him, I knew I'd never find anyone to do it the way I wanted, so I decided to do it myself. I called up Charles [Belcher, of Dallas Backup] and said, 'How 'bout I go back to work for you?' It's been great to be back in touch with my system again."

Lindsey Buckingham

"I HAD BEEN WANTING TO TRY SOMETHING larger for a while," explains guitarist/singer/songwriter Lindsey Buckingham. "Something that went beyond what people normally would try to do. On records, there are a lot of levels of orchestration that most people would opt to pare down onstage."

But rather than trim parts, Buckingham chose to use ten musicians, including four additional guitarists (two male, two female). "The challenge is to keep it from sounding like mush," he cautions. "On a lot of songs you have people waiting to come in for something very specific, and then dropping out again. A lot of people said that it wouldn't work, but this is great. All the parts can be realized by a band of this size, which never would have been done in a million years [when I was] in Fleetwood Mac.

"The other reason for having this many people," Buckingham continues, "is that you can double up on three- or four-part [vocal] harmonies. When you've got seven people singing at once, you get a lot of strength. And it's a concept that nobody's really doing, and that in itself appeals to me."

BY DAVID
(RUDY)
TRUBITT

Front-of-house duties fall to Rob Mailman, from Sound Image of San Marcos, Calif. (Mailman has been with the company since 1985; his last major tour was with the Indigo Girls.) "It's been working pretty well," Mailman explains, "but it's quite a chore keeping up with five guitar players. With all that material in the same bandwidth, there are a lot of separation and placement problems, especially when two people are playing the same part.

"Originally," he continues, "everybody was going direct, with no amplification onstage. It was a great place to start, but it wasn't working well for them, particularly on the Fleetwood Mac material that was more rock 'n' roll-oriented. We're using fairly small amps, but they pack a lot of punch. Even though we went with amps, everybody is still DI'd. On people who are playing leads, I mix the DI and mic. Lindsey, in particular, I blend the whole night.

"The DIs are all Countrymen," Mailman adds, "which are very standard and reliable, although not necessarily the best in the world. We use a stand-up bass [on two tunes], and on one of those, Lindsey uses a ukulele and one of the women plays a mandolin. With that in mind, I needed a good, reliable active DI."

In addition to the wall of guitars, the band includes three percussionists. Originally, no trap set was planned, but a basic kick/snare/hat set evolved in rehearsals. The percussion community's close proximity to guitar amps created the potential for leakage problems. "We baffle [with clear Plexiglas] right behind the guitar line," says Mailman, "because we have so many open percussion mics and open-back guitar amplifiers up there."

The tour is carrying a 24-box Phase Loc rig, Sound Image's active five-way JBL and TAD-loaded loudspeaker system. A modified BSS unit is used as the system crossover. Sound Image uses QSC amps

exclusively, although the company is engaged in the development of new cabinet, crossover and processing configurations. As a result, they are evaluating amps from other manufacturers, using their existing QSC amps as the benchmark.

"I haven't worked in most of these venues before," explains Mailman. "So when I walk in, I generally take a look around, see what's available to me in the house P.A. That, plus seating and sightlines, dictate how much [of my own] P.A. I'm going to bring in. I try to make the best call possible without getting too overbearing, but without leaving myself short. We do play at quite an appreciable SPL level. Lindsey's a little bit adamant— he really wants you to feel it."

At the gig (at Bimbo's 365 Club, in San Francisco), the club's system included six Meyer UPAs in left-center-right pairs, 650 subs and two small EAW cabinets installed as delay fills in the back of the room. Bimbo's house sound man, Kirk Schreio, took a vocal-only feed for this system. Mailman brought in one Phase Loc stack, comprising two high-mid and two bass cabinets, per side, although in larger

most problematic, as well as varying the most from room to room. 'Don't Look Down' is one of those. It fits together like a jigsaw, and its impact hinges on the level of things in relationship to each other, [such as] the vocals coming in loud enough. Certain things have to be really close to being right, at least in my mind, for it to come off."

"I work with cue cards all night long," Mailman adds, "because of all the different instrumentation. The set builds and falls twice. It starts out with Lindsey doing a couple of solo acoustic things. Then the band comes out and it builds through some Fleetwood stuff. After it gets really hot and heavy, it drops off again for another couple of acoustic things [before coming up for the finale]. Through all that there are a lot of fader moves going on."

The tour is carrying a Midas XL-3, although Mailman admits he has mixed feelings about the board. "On the last leg," he explains, "I started out with a PM-4000, which is a real nice, friendly board. As far as routing, user-friendliness and terminology, the XL-3 has shortcomings, although I've been able to work around [most of them]. I've had contact with Midas, and they're hopefully going to send me a modified master module [to address] the things that I wasn't able to get around." High on his request list was the ability to preview the main stereo mix in the phones with automatic solo override. Mailman also feels that "there's a lot of wasted real estate in the matrix," adding that he has found no use for it as currently implemented. "But sonically," he adds, "it's a pretty superior-sounding board, and I can live with most of the shortcomings, especially with a view [toward its continued evolution].

"Processing-wise," he continues, "I'm using typical stuff: REV-5, SPX900, the new Sony R-7, which is a real nice-sounding unit. I don't do a lot of gating or compressing. I use compression on Lindsey's

venues the ratio of high to low boxes is somewhat higher.

When it comes to mixing, "We are re-creating [the records] pretty close," Mailman says. "As far as the processing and ambience goes, I have a pretty free hand. A lot of times, [room] environments dictate how much you can do there. But as far as the placement of things in the mix, it's real close to the record, because [Lindsey's] very specific about where he wants little pieces placed and how it's knitted together."

Buckingham regularly spends some soundcheck time at the FOH. "We have a couple of tunes that seem to be our focal points," explains Buckingham, "ones that are so conceptual that they tend to be the vocal, the bass and the keys, but none of the backup vocals. I come from the school where the less processing, the better. It keeps things cleaner, and I don't really need it with this particular act."

At the Ramsa WRS-840 monitor desk is John Oster, another longtime Sound Image staffer. Oster runs ten mixes, one for each player. The front-line players get most of the instruments off the stage, relying primarily on wedges for their vocals. "Most of the stage sound is shaped around their own volume and where they are placed on stage," Oster explains. "When they're soundchecking, I'll stand in Lindsey's spot and listen. There's an incredible separation up there, especially in this large of a band. It can be hell—having seven vocals and that many mixes up there; it's a challenge, but it's a fun gig."

Most of the band uses Sound Image's latest wedge, a dual 12 with a TAD 2-inch design. Buckingham started with that wedge in rehearsals, but at the last moment switched to an older Sound Image single-15 wedge. "I can get the two 12s a lot louder," says Oster, "and they sound better, but the single 15 sounds more like a rock wedge, and that's what Lindsey wants to hear. So I'm running two cue wedges—one of each.

"I give Lindsey vocal, a little percussion, keys and a sizable amount of guitar," continues Oster, "because he likes to be surrounded up there. When he goes into a solo, I pump it up about a notch and a half. [On the other hand,] Lindsey also likes to hear the house, especially when he does his solo [acoustic] stuff. I pull his vocal way down in those numbers." Whatever the requirements, communication seems to be very open on this tour.

"You can talk frankly with him and work things out," says Oster. "He's probably the most reasonable artist I've ever done monitors for."

Sound at the gig was loud and clear, with an emphasis on *both*. Diverse musical arrangements were complemented by equally varied mixes, both in relative level placement and ambient treatment. Some of the sparser material, often mixed with extended depth of field, showed off the Sound Image system exceptionally well, which is not to say that the system was any less punchy on the louder tunes, but that stage level became more of a factor on those numbers.

Most enjoyable was the energy traded between Buckingham, the band and the audience. Buckingham summed it up nicely during the sold-out show when he told the audience that on this tour he was "probably having the best time I've ever had!" It showed.

Buckingham engineers— monitor mixer John Oster (left) and house engineer Rob Mailman.

Suzanne Vega

S<small>UZANNE</small> V<small>EGA</small> P<small>LAYED</small> T<small>HEATER-SIZED</small> venues across the U.S. in support of her *99.9 F°* album. The tour featured strong material and performances by Vega herself, a skilled band and crew with much individual and joint experience, and dynamic musical arrangements enhanced by moderate stage volumes. Carrying FOH gear and a full monitor rig from Scorpio Sound (West Bridgewater, MA), the tour picked up "stacks and racks" (main loudspeakers and amp/drive electronics racks) at each gig to complete their sound system.

At the house mixer (a Yamaha PM3000) is Geoff Keehn. "I've never been on a long tour with Suzanne, but I've worked with her a long time," says Keehn, who did some second engineering on her first two records and co-engineered *Days of Open Hand.* Keehn's previous gig was a year-long stint with Curtis Stigers. Also on that tour was Vega's monitor engineer, John Gallagher, as well as the drummer, bassist and guitar tech. "We work together well. Once you know somebody, it's easier," says Gallagher.

"It's like a little family," Keehn adds. "John's one of the best monitor engineers I've worked with. He makes the stage sound great. I was having a talk with the drummer just the other day and his remark was, 'It's not just volume—it's musical.'"

The four-piece band (electric guitar, bass, drums and keys) and Vega's vocal and acoustic guitar re-create (or outdo) the performances of material from her four

BY DAVID (RUDY) TRUBITT

records. Vega's *99.9 F°*, produced by Mitchell Froom (Crowded House, Richard Thompson), is something of a departure from Vega's previous efforts. Though her dry, intimate vocals remain a familiar landmark, occasional looped rhythm tracks and intense shifts in ambience give the new record a sound of its own. The question was, how would this translate in a live setting?

"Mitchell and I spoke before we went out on this tour," Keehn explains. "He said he pretty much wanted it to punch off the stage, so keep it very dry and not very processed. On the record, there are a lot of vocal effects: time delay, phasing, very tight doubling. You can try to re-create that kind of stuff in a live situation, depending on the [venue]."

Monitor engineer Gallagher describes Vega's vocal mic choices since 1986: "We're using a [Shure] Beta 58 right now. It has that high-end cut; it's very sibilant, and it's smooth in the low end. We used a Beyer M88 for a while, but the proximity [effect] of that mic [didn't suit] her—if she gets off it at all, it goes away. We tried an EV 757, which is perfect on certain singers. I call it the 'Steven Tyler mic': If you want to be screaming into it all night, it's fine. We used an AKG 535 on the last tour. It was okay. But in general, I don't like using condensers as a vocal mic. Sometimes cables start moving around and cracking and popping—you should be able to catch that at soundcheck, but I'd

Venue: **The Warfield Theater, San Francisco**
Sound Company: **Scorpio Sound**
House Mixer: **Geoff Keehn**
Monitor Mixer: **John Gallagher**

rather not worry about it at showtime. And I don't mind dropping a Beta 58; you know it's going to work."

In the house, her vocal runs through a Summit Tube limiter set for very mild compression. "For a vocal compressor I wouldn't ask for anything else; it's very smooth," says Keehn. "But this particular Summit is very hissy [for such a quiet show]." For the following European leg, Keehn requested a BSS DPR-901, a frequency-dependent, four-band dynamics processor. "It's a very flexible box," says Keehn. "Any [band] can be compression,

expansion, de-essing, whatever you like. I used it at the end of Curtis' tour. For example, when the singer backs off the mic, you can expand the low end, compress the top and try [to control the variation in proximity effect]."

"Suzanne sings very softly," continues Keehn. "That sets the volume of the show, depending on how far back upstage I can get her vocal mic from the P.A. Trapezoidal cabinets are much easier for us to use than square cabinets," due to what Keehn feels is their greater directivity. "With square cabinets, I'm finding [sound from] the

Vega's engineer Geoff Keehn (Yamaha PM3000 in background)

horn just wraps right around the back of the cabinet and goes right into the vocal mic." When wraparound is a problem, Gallagher positions his sidefills to try and block part of the path between P.A. and mic.

Vega's soft singing also complicates the mix. "The band isn't loud, but the vocal mic is picking up the entire mix," says Keehn. Rather than try to gate or ride the vocal when Vega goes off-mic, Keehn uses it to his advantage. "I'll start the soundcheck with the vocal mic open at the level I think it's going to be, and I'll start bringing things in. Sometimes if you just put up the kick drum and bass, you've got a great mix."

Fortunately, Vega's monitor mix does not unnecessarily complicate matters. Her forward position enables her to hear her vocal effects from the house, rather than needing them in the monitors, a fact Gallagher appreciates: "Effects in the monitors, especially in smaller places, are not always compatible with the effects being used in the house. Then it ends up being more of a mish-mash of sound than something coherent.

"She knows what she wants," Gallagher continues. "She's got very good ears,

which helps me. I've worked with other people who also knew what they wanted, but the way they say it is not always pleasant, let's put it that way!"

Gallagher runs seven to eight mixes, including stereo sidefills. Vega uses two or three wedges, depending on the size of the venue. (The low-profile Scorpio wedges are comprised of a single 12-inch woofer and a TAD 2-inch driver.) When three wedges are used, her vocal alone is run through the center with her acoustic guitars in the outer pair.

"Her guitars are good-sounding," says Gallagher. "I don't have to do anything radical to them. One has a pickup and the other has [an internally mounted condenser mic] and a pickup. I don't use the mic onstage, just the direct. She does everything from hard strumming to really soft finger-picking, and she plays with the level on her guitar a bit, so I kind of have to watch her."

The tour's Soundcraft 800B monitor desk lacks one feature Gallagher misses. "I'm used to faders for subtle changes," he explains, "as opposed to rotary controls, which are hard to find quickly. When a vocal is on the edge of feedback, it's more comfortable for me to ride the fader than keep my hands on a rotary pot. But it's a nice desk; the EQ is nice."

Although the stage has an open look, the movement of each player is constrained. "Everything's in the same position every day, measured from the vocal mic to the drum riser," Gallagher notes. "It helps me, because I don't have to mix things loudly. Normally, a drummer would have kick, snare and bass guitar right off the bat. But there's no bass in his wedge, because he's close enough to him that he doesn't need any. It's one of the quietest stages I've ever heard."

The low stage level offers additional drum-miking flexibility. "I close-mic just about everything—all the drum kit and so on—just to get some meat out of things," Keehn says. "But I've also got a pair of overhead AKG 414s, which come in extremely handy. I've gotten to the point where I take the entire kit except for the kick and put it on one VCA and the overheads on another. Mitchell and I had a talk about this at the beginning. His suggestion was to try squashing the overheads, which surprised me since I'd never done that before. But I tried [using BSS 402s], and it seems to work pretty well. It tightens it all up."

As for the P.A., "The Scorpio system is very compact and tidy," Keehn explains. "They've got everything down to multicore and Elcos from desk to effects and returns." Keehn also notes that the system makes "buzz-busting" easy, with ground lifts available at numerous points in the AC and signal chain.

"Getting stacks and rack every night makes for some interesting situations." continues Keehn. "There have been some nights it's been absolute hell, but other times, like today, it was quiet as a mouse." The Warfield's system consists of Meyer MSL-3s, 650 subs and Crest amps, supplemented by additional 650s and racks from Ultrasound.

As it happened, producer Froom was also present at the San Francisco show. He noted that clarity in musical arrangement is as important live as in the studio. He also explained that to help re-create some of the album's sounds, samples (recorded with appropriate effects) were drawn from the sessions. Some of the looped rhythm beds on tunes from *99.9 F°* used sounds manually triggered by the band, while others actually did loop. The intent was to use these rhythm tracks in such a way that the audience would not be aware of what

was live and what, if anything, wasn't.

Froom offered one other interesting anecdote. At one point during the sessions, what he describes as an Indian-made P.A. was brought in. It had a huge fiberglass horn, built-in delay and an obviously "unique" sound. For the tour, however, this unusual P.A. was replaced with a somewhat more portable bullhorn, used by Vega during "Blood Makes Noise."

Poi Dog Pondering

BY DAVID
(RUDY)
TRUBITT

POI DOG PONDERING'S FIRST U.S. TOUR was played on street corners for dinner and gas money. Since then, they've found their major-label deal, toured the club circuit and released three albums for Columbia. We asked Poi Dog's sound woman, Deanne Franklin, to describe club tour realities with a band looking to take the next step up.

"They're selling so well at smaller places without a new record out [the tour came before the release of their third album, *Volo Volo*] that it's only a matter of time before the places get bigger," Franklin says. "The first thing that we're going to spend a little money on is our own monitor engineer. I'm setting up all of my own stuff in the house, and now I have to go up and set up seven monitor mixes."

And just how much sound is the tour carrying? "What I carry are my toys—my own essentials," she says. "I need a minimum of four compressors—two dual dbx 166s, a REV7 and three SDE delays. I also carry a Yamaha REV50, which is a little guitar reverb. It fits in a briefcase, and if worst comes to worst, it's more programmable than a lot of reverbs you'll find in small clubs. I finally got a Furman line conditioner, because I blew up my REV7 on the last tour in Baton Rouge. That was a good $100 lesson!

"For the most part, I am depending on the house P.A.," Franklin continues. "I send out a rider requesting a 32-channel board, because Poi Dog is an eight-piece band where many people play more than one thing and everyone sings. Sometimes I need upward of 27 channels on the stage, and most of the places don't have a 32-channel board. Most places we play at would normally have two monitor mixes from the house, but we require seven monitor mixes. I always request six more compressors—I just want that control. It's really just finding out what we can afford and from whose pocket the money comes."

What does she look for when walking into an unfamiliar club? "The most important thing of all is having a competent and friendly house engineer," says Franklin. "I've found too many engineers who don't want to ask questions and never get anywhere. I know what I don't know, and I'm the first one to admit it." Franklin has a regular routine to tune an unfamiliar system. "The first thing I do," she says, "is flatten out everything that they already have. I like to ask the house engineer what they think, and I'll keep that in the back of my mind. I'll look at the boxes and what's in them. Sometimes you can blow something up because you're expecting a lot more to come out of the box. Then I'll plug in my CD player and almost always cut out certain amounts of highs that hurt. I'll try to get things as close as possible with the crossover, and then I'll go directly to the house EQ. I'll also check the loudest things at soundcheck to find out how far I can go before the club starts turning me down. I try to make it simple for them to tell me what they're doing. Otherwise, you'll find some guy in a back amp room somewhere with a secret knob taking your middle out! Sometimes they're

Chris Isaak, and he's my inspiration. Louie Beeson is a sound god!" She also works with a number of San Francisco bands, including the Limbomaniacs, Psychefunkapus and Sister Double Happiness.

"Poi Dog called me to go on a tour a year ago in May," says Franklin. "At that point, I was going to Europe with a heavy metal band called Gwar. Two weeks after I came back from that tour, Poi Dog was playing here at Slim's. Peter Keppler was doing their sound, but he was getting ready to go out with someone else and they needed somebody in two weeks. I've had a lot of fun this year. With Poi Dog, it's always an adventure. I'm hoping that [the new album] pays off, because all they want in the world is a monitor engineer and a tour bus."

"I'll check the loudest things at soundcheck to find out how far I can go before the club starts turning me down. I try to make it simple for them to tell me what they're doing. Otherwise, you'll find some guy in a back amp room somewhere with a secret knob taking your middle out!"
—Deanne Franklin

so worried that they'll just do it without telling you.

"When I started working for Poi Dog," she adds, "I thought, 'Ooh, lucky me, I get to do an acoustic band and I'll never lose my hearing!' But boom, on the very next tour, 'Well, we're not using acoustic guitars anymore, we're all electric. Not only that, but we're going to add a couple more keyboards.' Now I request 120 dB at the front of house, which means a P.A. that can get 120 dB cleanly. Out of the club systems I've been using, the EAW KF850s, EV manifolds (the MT series) and the Meyers are tops."

In addition to her tours with Poi Dog, Franklin also works at Slim's nightclub in San Francisco. "[The late] Louie Beeson was the production manager at Slim's," she says. "He did a multitude of people, including

k.d. lang

BY DAVID (RUDY) TRUBITT

"IT'S NOT ROCK, IT'S NOT COUNTRY—IT'S A bunch of things put together," says k.d. lang's house mixer and production manager, Grant McAree, who has been with lang for the last seven years. Generally, lang prefers playing smaller (2,000-seat) venues. "She doesn't want to play really big places," McAree continues. "She feels she can reach everybody at this level. This particular material [the *Ingénue* album] is moody and dark, and she wants that kind of focus. I have no complaints—I'm quite happy working in theaters. Also, we don't do more than three shows in a row, or five in a week. The more shows you do, like everybody else, the quality of the voice starts to go away. The fewer you can do, the better, but finances dictate you've got to do a certain number."

Sound equipment for lang's current tour is provided by Kian (Richmond, British Columbia). The system centers around a Gamble EX Series console, BSS drive gear and flown Meyer MSL-3 loudspeakers with 650 subs on deck. Meyer UPAs and UPA-1s are used both as stage monitors and balcony fill, depending on the specifics of the venue at hand. "Our basic theory is 'fly the box,'" says McAree. "She doesn't mind the boxes behind her. It can be a little bit of a problem at times, but basically they go up in the air." The tour's 12 monitor mixes are handled by Rob Hadfield, who has been with the organization for three tours.

"Before the tour started," McAree says, "we did some rehearsals in a small hall and then a week in a theater. This year everybody showed up with as much signal processing as I have up front. They have MIDI controllers to run it, so most of the processing is done by the band."

McAree describes some specifics regarding individual instruments: "If it's an acoustic guitar, most times it's a Takemine. You can have the most beautiful Gibson or Martin, but you'll spend months trying to get a pickup system that sounds as good as an off-the-block Takemine. It offers a lot of control for the monitor mixer and the house. The piano's got Helpenstill in it with a Schubert preamp. When you want to hear it, you just turn it up. You don't have to fight with it. The vibes have an Ayott pickup system in them for the same reason."

lang's performance is filled with precise mic-handling technique. "She takes care of a lot of [the level control]," McAree acknowledges. "She's singing through an AKG 535. She does have some limiting on her [a dbx 900 rack]. Not much effects on her vocal—just a little reverb and the odd in-time delay. The records sometimes have more processing, but it seems like more is less with k.d. People come to the show to hear her sing, so you can't get too zealous trying to hear every instrument because you'll find the reason people came is buried. It's a bit of a trick. But if it's being played, it should be heard."

McAree on Hearing Protection

A TOUR WITH WIDE DYNAMIC RANGE AND moderate overall level is a fairly low-risk gig as far as one's hearing is concerned.

"If it's being
played, it should
be heard."
—Grant McAree

lang, house mixer
McAree

However, most mixers work a variety of tours, and lang's McAree is no exception. "I recently worked 15 months with a Canadian artist called Collin James, a fairly loud rock/blues thing, opening for ZZ Top and doing our own shows. When that tour ended, I decided I'd take a bit of an ear break, and worked about 5 months with Bryan Adams as a P.A. tech for Jason Sound Industries." On that gig, McAree used earplugs regularly. "I use the roll-up foam ones—I kind of think it's healthier to dispose of whatever you put in your ears, rather than ad infinitum shoving [the same thing] in your ears."

Lou Reed

BY DAVID
(RUDY)
TRUBITT

"**I**T'S MOSTLY BEEN A THEATER TOUR, WITH A few selected sheds," says Lou Reed's house mixer, Bill Fertig. "He prefers to play to a more intimate audience. The lyrics are a big part of the show, so intelligibility is a factor. Hence, we don't play places with long reverb times."

Equipment for the U.S. leg of the tour was provided by See Factor (Long Island City, N.Y.), including a Crest amplifier-powered Meyer loudspeaker rig with additional DS-2 mid-bass cabinets. "We have 24 MSL-3s, eight DS-2s and four 650 sub-woofers," Fertig says. "This is the first time I've used the DS-2s." Depending on the situation, Fertig adds the DS-2s to various parts of the system. "When we played the [L.A.] Greek Theatre, there was a long-throw system with four MSL-3s, four DS-2s and two 650s per side, and a near-field system with full-range MSL-3s. We tend to work in zones. You have a choice of running the DS-2 down to its full range, or you can cross it over into the 650s. That's one of the reasons we only have the four 650s—they're not handling as much program. It's only been a couple of weeks, but I've been really happy with them."

The tour is using two different measurement techniques for setting up delay times for various parts of the P.A., depending on the venue. The first makes use of the BSS TCS-804 delay line and remote control. The remote control incorporates a beta version of new software from Signet Sound that implements the SignAlign Analysis signal alignment system.

"I delay the system referenced to the band's amp line, which is the loudest thing on the stage," Fertig says. "In measurement mode, the remote emits a signal that comes out of the last output of the delay line. That gets sent back down to [a stage loudspeaker] at the point I want to reference to. It calculates that delay time, then you call up another speaker, and it sets the proper delay time. Sometimes you don't want to reference everything to one point. If you're in a position where you can see [and hear several different sets of speakers], or you're upstairs, you just look for the next loudest source and reference to that. The whole process takes about 20 minutes. The remote is nice because you now have the controller and the mic in the same package, as opposed to moving the mic and going back and forth to the delay."

At selected gigs, the latest incarnation of Meyer's SIM system, SIM II, is used. The system's delay finder mode calculates propagation times from loudspeakers to microphones placed at strategic points throughout the venue. "Then," Fertig explains, "it listens to each part of the system and measures the response [at the various mic positions]. You match your parametric EQs to those curves. I have six channels of Meyer CP-10s for that. Then you go to a matching mode where you match the left side to the right side. If the left and right equalizations are not the same, your image is so weird that it doesn't really work. Lou wants the utmost sound quality, and he knows that it can be had by taking these

steps and using SIM. But because SIM is a fairly expensive process, it comes down to the importance of each gig to the artist. We SIM'ed London, New York and L.A."

Reed's choice of vocal mics is somewhat atypical—an AKG 460 with a CK-61 capsule. "It gives us a very revealing sound, as opposed to dynamic," Fertig says. "Condensers have little idiosyncracies regarding proximity effect and humidity, but we work around everything, and it has gotten us the best vocal sound that he's ever had. The stage level is pretty moderate, and the mic's flat response gives you a good amount of [feedback] control—it hasn't been a problem." Reed avoids the use of limiters on his vocal.

The Midas Pro-40 is the console of choice, but the tour carries stand-alone mic preamplification as well. "We have eight channels of Hardy M1 mic preamps," explains Fertig, "which we use on selected channels: [Reed's] two vocal and two guitar channels, and the other guitar player's two channels and the two bass channels. That gives us a studio-quality mic preamp, which is so

much more revealing than plugging into the Midas or any other console. Also, you have the option of sending a line-level signal down your 300-foot snake. You do have to trim it properly, but it lives up near the monitor desk so he can keep an eye on it. It has very elaborate metering, both peak and VU. It's a really classy piece of gear. The guitars use SM57s or 58s up close, with a PZM off-center in front of the cone, sitting back about four inches. It gives more of an airy type of sound. There's a lot of nice clean guitar sounds with delays and chorusing—there's not a lot of loud, thrashy guitars."

Speaking of an absence of loud guitars, just what are the overall levels for the show? "As low as the crowd will let me!" Fertig exclaims. "That's another reason to have the delay lines reference back to the amp lines. When you work at low levels, the stage level can be enough for small venues. Most of the show is at a very low level. It's almost like a poetry reading—he tells stories. We try to make it very intelligible and very comfortable for the audience."

"I delay the system referenced to the band's amp line, which is the loudest thing on the stage. When you work at low levels, the stage level can be enough for small venues."—Bill Fertig

TOUR PROFILES: CLUBS AND THEATERS

Tori Amos

BY DAVID
(RUDY)
TRUBITT

AMERICAN-BORN, BRITISH-MADE SINGER/ songwriter Tori Amos toured the U.S. in solo support of her *Little Earthquakes* album. The show has been playing clubs and small theaters, easily selling out most dates. It is a three-person tour: one artist, one tour manager and one soundman. "It's so simple, it's great," says mixer Ian Thorpe. "To go back to absolute basics, which for me is one woman and a piano…that's why I'm here."

Thorpe is a principal in W&T Ultra-sonics, a 31-year-old sound manufacturing and hire company in South Humberside, England. W&T was contracted to provide sound for a local show with Amos on the bill. Having heard her music by chance beforehand, Thorpe decided to mix the set himself. "I really enjoyed the show," he explains, "and Tori said, 'I like what you've done. Will you do my London shows?' So I went to a meeting for the London show, and this agent said 'Oh, are you Tori's soundman?' So I said, 'Yeah, I think so,' and he said, 'Well, you're going to be a busy man.' The album had just gone straight into the charts at Number 15!"

The tour carries only microphones, picking up everything else at each gig. "It's such an intense show," Thorpe continues. "The lyrics are everything, so it's got to be loud and clear. I carry a vocal mic—a Shure Beta 58. I needed a mic that would give me clarity and handle wide sound levels, because Tori can be as quiet as a mouse and then roar like a lion. Also, I need lots of level without feedback."

Thorpe does not use a limiter on her vocal, although he constantly rides the overall and reverb send levels. "Sometimes when she goes up high [and loud] I let her go," Thorpe explains, "and sometimes I pull her back a bit and add reverb to give it the bigness. When I advance the shows, I ask for a Yamaha SPX900 if possible, which I put my own program in. It isn't anything special, just two seconds of reverb, 30 milliseconds of delay, and I take the highs up and down according to the room."

Amos sits sideways on the piano bench, facing the audience, with wedge monitors behind and to her right. "She rides that sustain pedal," he adds. "I try and get an overall level for the piano and leave it at that. Her style has to be allowed to go as big as it wants, and there's no way I'm going to try and [ride the gain on] something like that. She naturally plays that way with just a little help from me when I feel it's right. It's a unique experience."

She likes her monitors loud, according to Thorpe. Careful placement keeps the monitor sound from bouncing off the raised piano lid into the piano mics. Thorpe says of the piano miking, "It's my own fairly unique combination. For the bottom end I use a Shure PZM mic, an SM91, taped to the lid. I've got an SM7 for the mid of the piano and an AKG 451 for the highs. The combination of the three gives me a reasonable sound, although obviously that's dictated by the sound of the piano." As far as consoles, "I spec Soundcraft or Amek/TAC," Thorpe adds.

Amos, engineer Ian Thorpe

"Soundcraft is such an international desk that you're likely to get one anywhere in the world.

"This is the quietest show you'll ever hear," he concludes. "When I say a pin drop, I mean it. I have to sit and not move at the desk in case the chair creaks. The intensity of the lyrics and performance has been described as mesmerizing, and that's why it's so quiet."

Rock In Rio II

BILLED AS "NINE DAYS OF MUSIC AND PEACE," Rio de Janeiro's mega-event seemed to deliberately echo the billing of the 1969 Woodstock Festival ("Three Days of Peace and Music"). Rock In Rio II was staged in Rio's Maracana Stadium by Brazilian promoter Roberto Medina and his Artplan advertising agency, at a cost of $20 million. It offered Brazilian concertgoers a rare chance to see international rock and pop headliners such as Prince, George Michael, INXS, Guns N' Roses, a-ha and New Kids on the Block. Crowds exceeding 100,000 per day attended the event.

While Rock In Rio I (January 1985) was televised only to viewers in Brazil, Rock In Rio II was broadcast to approximately 50 countries around the world. MTV excerpted portions of the event, and multitrack recordings were made of the proceedings.

BY
MIKE
STANDE

The well-attended, eclectic festival offered a sampling of many musical styles, including reggae (Jimmy Cliff), heavy metal (Judas Priest, Queensryche and Megadeth), hard rock (Billy Idol), dance funk (Deee-Lite), classic rock (Santana and Joe Cocker), pop (Debbie Gibson) and rap (Run-D.M.C.). Other international participants included Faith No More, Information Society, Colin Hay and Lisa Stansfield. The festival also showcased a diverse selection of Brazilian artists, from thrash-metal artists Sepultura to popular singer/lambada dancer Elba Ramalho and the jazz-influenced Moraes & Pepeu.

Showco Inc. of Dallas was contracted to provide sound reinforcement. The company sent a 12-person crew under the direction of Mike "Dr. Funk" Ponczek, who was house sound mixer and Showco crew chief for Paul McCartney's world tour when it touched down at this same stadium in the spring of 1990. "In planning for Rock In Rio II, we were fortunate that we had already put the same type of Prism stadium-format system into this venue for McCartney," Ponczek notes. "We knew what to expect—the weather, the labor force, the crowds, the building architecture. It gave us an edge in deciding how to approach this festival."

The Site

Maracana Stadium, located in suburban Rio, is a huge, oval-shaped concrete bowl enclosing a grassy field. It is the site of epic soccer matches, and is equipped with ten-foot-deep concrete moats to control unruly crowds. A soccer stadium's greatest asset is its playing field; for Rock In Rio II, that field would be sacrificed. In fact, $200,000 was included in the event budget to replace the ruined field with new sod after the end of the festival.

In the Southern Hemisphere, January means summer. But summer in Rio can mean hot and humid days or torrential downpours with high winds. To allow a million or more people to walk about on the potentially muddy playing field, labor crews covered the grass with wooden platforms, providing a hard surface that made the daily trash cleanup go more quickly. Trenches were cut in the sod to enable snake cables, communication and electrical

lines to run underneath the wooden deck between the stage and the sound and lighting scaffolding towers.

Advance Planning

The Showco staff began planning early to ship four large sea-cargo containers full of audio gear on the 6,000-mile trip. Nearly a month before the first show, these containers, each almost the size of a semitrailer unit, were carefully packed, inventoried and sealed for the ocean voyage.

The sound system equipment list was extensive: 60 power amplifier racks, over 150 microphones, 32 direct boxes, 70 stage monitor wedges, 16 Clear-Com beltpacks, 21 chain-motor hoists, six Harrison mixing desks and three auxiliary Yamaha consoles, 16 digital reverbs, 266 main system loudspeaker enclosures and subwoofers and more than 1,600 feet of 48-pair multicore snake cable made up just a portion of the 50-ton cargo load. "We knew that we didn't want to spend time looking locally for something we might need in a pinch," Ponczek explains. "We took whatever we might need down there with us."

"We got as much information as far in advance from as many of the artists in the show as possible," adds Showco staff engineer David "Gunque" Selg, who, together with Mike Ponczek and crew chief Leon Hopkins, worked for weeks in advance of the festival. "We like to provide as many of the tools for a particular band's sound team as we can. If they say they want an AKG D-12 on the kick drum, that's what we give them. Or a Sennheiser 421. Or whatever. We want them to have the items they need to do the best job they can. Many of these bands are our clients, like INXS and George Michael. But many of them aren't. Even though this is a festival situation, where you have to hit the ground running, we try to give them every possible advantage. That's just our philosophy."

Maracana Stadium, with the stage and house mix positions

143

Harrison consoles in the three-tiered house mix position

Notebooks were compiled with daily schedules that included all stage plots and mic input charts. Computer-generated system wiring diagrams, job-assignment flow-charts and cargo-container load plans were drawn up. The sound system team was carefully chosen, consisting of Randy Bryant, Jeff Cohen, Mark Harvey, Leon Hopkins, Paul Kalenak, Robert Kosloskie, Andy Moore, Mike Ponczek, Jim Putnam, David Scheirman, "Gunque" Selg and Randy Williams.

Sound System Format

For Rock In Rio II, Showco supplied a 12-column Prism system for each side, arranged in identical left/right arrays. The boxes were hung six deep from custom aluminum hanging bars. Each array was supported by six two-ton chain motors. Special Aeroquip locking braces with metal

supports were used to anchor the Prism arrays firmly to the scaffolding structure for the duration of the event. A total of 32 subwoofer enclosures per side were grouped in double-tiered stacks below the main Prism arrays. The total distance from the ground to the top of the array was 76 feet.

An "elevator bay" was provided beside each array position, so that the Showco crew could use a chain-motor hoist mounted on a rolling headblock to get speakers and cable bundles up to the higher scaffolding levels.

"We've gotten things worked out to a quick and reliable system for putting this rig into a stadium," offers Showco staff engineer Leon "Bone" Hopkins, who was in charge of the P.A. drive system and overall system maintenance. "We get a good curved wrap on the overall system, so the left and right arrays are each giving us a realistic 165-degree horizontal coverage angle, yet the rig has a relatively small footprint—just about six meters wide [about 20 feet] as viewed from the front."

Showco's half-size Prism enclosures were used for delay fill arrays. These were located 30 feet above the sound and lighting control positions, approximately 180 feet out from the front edge of the stage. Midrange and high-frequency program information was fed to these auxiliary systems, effectively moving the image of the show's sound closer to the rear audience seating areas.

Mix Positions

Despite advance efforts by the production staff to convince the event promoters to place the mixing station in the middle of the audience area, it was constructed off-center, directly in line with the house-right speaker array. The lighting tower was positioned opposite this, in front of the house-left array. Television cameras were positioned on platforms above both sound and lighting control areas, with spotlights on even higher decks. A radio broadcast booth was constructed directly above the sound mixing area. Steel scaffolding faced with plywood was used for crowd control as well as offering some privacy to the mix position, which was equipped with a 3/4-inch plywood roof, refrigerator, portable toilet and a hammock or two. Roll-down plastic siding offered protection from the frequent rainstorms.

On the sound platform, up to three main consoles, each with a 20- or 32-channel extender, were lined up in a row, with the rear board group slightly elevated. Typically, the front guest console was preset during a morning soundcheck for the final headline act of each day's show. The upper console was usually patched and preset for the next-to-last major act(s) during afternoon soundchecks. The center console functioned as the "showmaster" desk, offering control of other inputs such as an announce mic, audio-visual playback feeds, and cassette, DAT and compact disc units for playback. The upper rear console sometimes functioned as a "scramble" desk for up to five acts per show—those on the program that did not soundcheck during the day.

Two 300-foot lengths of 48-pair Mogami input snake cable were run from the stage to the front-of-house position. Military-grade, hermaphroditic sliding aluminum connector sleeves were used for system cable links, due to their waterproof and gasproof characteristics. The A and B snake lines were switched to the appropriate boards during set changes.

Showtime!

Each console position was treated as a self-contained mixing station, complete with channel-insertable signal processing devices, including noise gates and compressors from dbx and Drawmer, and an effects rack that contained reverb and delay devices. These included Lexicon 224XLs, PCM70s and PCM42s, Yamaha REV5s and SPX90-IIs, Roland SDE-3000s, Eventide H3000 and 949 Harmonizers, and an AMS RMX 16 stereo digital reverberator and DMX 15 delay/pitch changer.

The Harrison HM-5, specially built by the manufacturer for Showco, is a 32-input mainframe with eight assignable VCA groups and mute groups, eight stereo audio subgroups, 16 auxiliary sends and

Stage sets for Billy Idol (top), Prince.

position. The consoles were typically staffed for about 22 hours straight—from 7:00 a.m. until 5:00 a.m. the following morning—as the team did each day's system check, prepared for the primary headliner's early soundcheck and worked on through the day and night. Crowds usually arrived at about 3:00 p.m., with showtime at 6:00.

Numerous visiting engineers arrived to mix various bands during the course of the festival. For Brazilian sound mixers, the promoter provided a sound engineer/translator (Franklin Garrido) to work with the front-of-house crew, whose efforts were much appreciated. Major Brazilian acts took the opportunity for a soundcheck on the day that system setup was complete.

Stage Monitors and Input Format

Onstage, Showco's festival sound strategy centered around an A/B monitor mix position setup. A Harrison SM-5, with an auxiliary Yamaha 1642 desk, was set up on the stage-left deck, with an identical console position directly above it on a scaffolding and plywood shelf. Depending on the day's activities, one console could be preset and left for the final headliner, or upstairs/downstairs flip-flops could take place. In some instances, arriving tour groups (such as Prince, INXS and George Michael) carried their own monitor mixing gear, which was placed on a rolling riser adjacent to the downstairs Showco position.

Randy Bryant, Robert Kosloskie, Paul Kalenak and "Gunque" Selg ramrodded the monitor mix area. Mark Harvey acted as "patchmaster," coordinating all mic charts and input lists for use by the sound reinforcement, broadcast and recording crews. Showco supplied Brooke-Siren active splitter systems to ensure mic signal integrity.

Andy Moore, Jim Putnam and Randy Williams kept stockpiles of mic stands, subsnakes and monitor wedges handy for

16 auxiliary returns. Harrison SM-5s were used as extender panels, offering a total of 64 inputs per console location. Showco also used short-frame, 20-channel HM-5 extender panels. Each console sat on a wheeled table-rack loaded with full patch bay facilities and the console power supply.

The Showco Prism digital control system was used to drive the main system. Located in a rack at the house position along with Showco-customized Industrial Research T.E.Q. graphic equalizers and a Klark-Teknik DN60 real-time analyzer, the electronics drive package presented a visual overview of system performance. A backup drive rack was located onstage.

Ponczek, Scheirman and Cohen took rotating turns of duty at the house mix use in the three different staging areas. Upstage center became the preparation area for rolling risers and band gear used by the Brazilian bands. Offstage left and right areas were used to preset and wire large rolling risers for drum sets, keyboard and percussion positions and other equipment used by headline acts.

A preliminary plan to use massive rolling risers on steel tracks broke down at the last minute. Sound crew, stage hands and production managers alike were kept scrambling to make the best use of limited space, since acts such as Billy Idol, Prince and a-ha brought in major set pieces that had to be assembled and left in place.

A wide variety of monitors were supplied. Drummers received full-range wedges on each side with Showco's B-1 subwoofer beneath them; as many as 16 or 20 wedges were strung along the front edge of the stage for larger, louder shows such as Guns N' Roses.

Showco also supplied a massive flying sidefill system, with six Prism enclosures suspended on each side of the stage from custom adjustable steel hanging frames flown about 20 feet above the stage deck. Low-frequency cabinets were available on rolling dollies for stage left and right. An A/B switching network allowed the sidefills to be changed over instantly from one monitor mix position to the other. This switcher also controlled feeds to the five downstage edge monitor zones.

System Power Requirements

Electrical power generation for Rock In Rio II was provided by Showpower of Santa Ana, Calif. Self-contained generator plants with oversized fuel tanks were shipped to the site in sea cargo containers.

Showco relied on power amplifiers from Crown International. PSA-2s and Macro-Tech 1200s typically were mounted in modular, rolling amp racks that received rugged power feeds directly from meter-equipped, three-phase AC power panels located beside the amplifiers. These units were connected with 2/0 gauge cable to four of Showco's "disco" power distribution panels, which were linked via 4/0 cable to a pair of 300 KVA transformers, providing 800 amps per leg (one for each side of the P.A.).

Showtime

After final technical preparation two days before the show, the sound crew came in early the following day for soundchecks with Prince and Joe Cocker. The first performance day included these artists and Colin Hay as the featured international stars; Brazilian act Gal Costa opened the festival. For the next ten days, the crew worked long hours, with only a single day's break in the action.

While the crowds varied from night to night based on the different headline attractions (New Kids On The Block drawing a different audience than, say, Guns N' Roses and Judas Priest), their enthusiasm never waned. As one New York Times observer reported, "An enthusiastic audience of 100,000 people ready to dance, sing, shout, wave their arms or light matches on cue was dazzled by…laser light…giant video images…[and] a sound system with remarkable punch and sonic detail."

For the twelve sound crew members, success was indicated by the runway lights of Rio's airport receding in the background as their jumbo 747 lifted off. "A project like this one works only because we like doing what we do," Ponczek noted. "If you try to figure out your pay scale by the number of hours worked, or expect all of the conditions to be perfect, you'll be disappointed. But in our industry, an event like this is a marathon race. Just knowing that you, your crew and sound system not only finished the race, which is winning in itself, but also came in first—that's what makes it worthwhile. We're just doing our job the best that we can, and we're glad to be here."

Telluride Bluegrass Festival

BY
KAREN
MITCHELL

"TELLURIDE IS HARDER THAN MOST FESTIVALS," admits Mark R. Miceli, system engineer for the 19th annual Telluride Bluegrass Festival, held in Telluride's Town Park. "We have acoustic acts, strings, then full-blown rock 'n' roll sets. There's a lot of diversity." So much, in fact, that this year's festival offerings, playing to an audience of 10,000, included the no-nonsense Virginia bluegrass strains of Ralph Stanley & The Clinch Mountain Boys, a late-night Blue Rodeo set, Emmylou Harris, Peter Rowan, Poi Dog Pondering, Shawn Colvin and Delbert McClinton, not to mention the saffron-robed Drepung Monks, a group of nine Tibetan monks who can each hold three notes simultaneously.

Telluride is a southwestern Colorado town some 8,745 feet above sea level. While it's a spectacular setting for music, the high-alpine, semi-arid climate can wreak havoc with sound. "I modeled Telluride for Stage Sound," says Miceli, who came to Colorado just after doing the Mariachi Festival in Tucson. "I used [Renkus-Heinz's acoustical simulation program] EASE. This is the first time I've ever modeled a festival." The software enabled him to place speaker towers, check coverage and see where the dead spots would occur.

The flip side of the modeling coin is measurement at the site. "I use a TEF analyzer [see glossary]," Miceli says. "That's the only way to measure [small time delays between audio sources at different distances] within a microsecond. We time-align everything back to the stage instead of the tower. With the multiple delays, we can cover the whole seating area and keep the sound pressure level just around 100 dB. Otherwise, the people in the front have their ears bleeding. And this is a bluegrass festival." The main system provided by Tucson's Stage Sound included 30 Meyer MSL-3 cabinets with 650 subs and USM-1 monitors, a Yamaha PM3000, Crest amps, outboard equipment by Lexicon and Yamaha and microphones by AKG, Neumann and Shure.

One of the founders of the Telluride Bluegrass Festival is Kooster McAllister, who is with Record Plant Remote, NYC. "Even if they hadn't brought the remote truck out, I'd be here as chief engineer," says McAllister, who was recording at Telluride for a two-CD live set. "It's always a challenge to do acoustic, with all of its nuances. And in Telluride, you're flying by the seat of your pants—there are never any soundchecks. We hold off on the multi-track for the first couple of songs."

McAllister records everything in Dolby SR using Meyer HD-1 monitors, a Trident console, Lexicon 300s and 200s, Eventide H3000s and various compressors and limiters. "I use Neumann KM84s for guitar and mandolin, Shure SM98s for drum kits and Shure SM91s for kick drum," he says. "For vocals I use Shure Beta 58s, and I like AKG 414s for overheads. Audience mics are AKG 451s with CK8 short shots, Shure SM81s and two PZM Crown mics."

Richard Battaglia, tour manager and sound engineer for Bela Fleck and the Flecktones, says that the band carries its

The Nashville Bluegrass Band on the Telluride stage; festival system engineer Mark Miceli

own personal equipment geared to festivals. Gear includes what he calls "the usual compressors," including dbx and a BBE 822. "Here, festival check equals line check," says Battaglia, who has also worked with the New Grass Revival. "But there is enough time to set up; there's no pressure."

Battaglia also designs and builds preamps for Chard Stuff, his 6-year-old, Nashville-based company. Among his customers are Bernie Leadon, Sam Bush, Jerry Douglas and, of course, Bela Fleck. "They're designed for acoustic musicians," Battaglia says. "We do limited production. The preamp allows the musician to make a blend [between the pickup and mic in the instrument] and send out one signal."

Kathy Wolter has been a monitor engineer for Emmylou Harris for the last two years and has worked in the business for eight. "This is a little harder because we only get a half-hour set change," she says. "But if the crew is together, we can do it. I get different gear at every venue, but I carry Clair Brothers 12AM monitors. This way, Emmylou hears it the same each time."

The unpredictable climate in Telluride, where a summer afternoon temperature in the 70s can plummet 30-40 degrees when the sun goes down, also affects performers. "I actually avoid some outdoor shows because they're sonically difficult," says singer/ songwriter Leo Kottke. "When the sun goes down, that's a nightmare. The sound shifts second by second, and it's a squirrelly mix that can go haywire."

Among other sonic difficulties, the speed of sound varies slightly with temperature. This can cause problems with a distributed delay-tower system, since the delay times set during the day become inaccurate as temperatures fall. There are other, less esoteric problems as well: "The Telluride weather causes problems in getting the instruments tuned up," says Maple Byrne, Emmylou Harris's production manager. "Here I tune them about ten to 12 times, twice as much as for indoor shows. But it's the last one that counts."

"It's always a challenge to do acoustic, with all of its nuances. And in Telluride, you're flying by the seat of your pants."
—Kooster McAllister

New Orleans Jazz & Heritage Festival

BY
HOWARD
MANDEL

AS A VERMILION SUN SETS ON THE FINAL hour of the New Orleans Jazz & Heritage Festival, Dr. John, backed by some of the finest session players in town, croaks syncopated "rhumboogie" from his piano to some 15,000 revelers. Way across 33 acres of the Fair Grounds Race Track infield, the Neville Brothers—a family so extended it's better described as a tribe—pump African-American rhythms and stevedore harmonies to another 20,000 celebrants from a second stage. Forty yards away, the Zion Harmonizers sing the most fervent gospel this side of the River Jordan. And a listener who shortcuts through the Louisiana craft and food booths, darting among lightly clad tourists and locals of various ages and degrees of sobriety, can still catch the last few measures of acts such as jazz pianist Ellis Marsalis, Cajun traditionalists Beausoleil, the National Dance Troupe of Senegal or the Olympia Brass Band.

Every year the crowds descend on the Fair Grounds Race Track on the last weekend of April and first weekend of May to enjoy literally hundreds of performers, ranging from thumb-pianists to big bands. This year's headliners included B.B. King, Linda Ronstadt and Aaron Neville, Peabo Bryson, Toots and The Maytals, Little Feat, Freddie Hubbard, the Mighty Clouds of Joy, Bo Diddley, John Prine, Ashford & Simpson, Daniel Lanois, Branford Marsalis, Al Hirt, Harry Connick Jr. and Boz Scaggs.

At rare points on the field one can hear a band in each ear. But very seldom do the sounds of the 14 stages encroach on each other. There's hardly ever bleed-through, and even less distortion. The New Orleans Jazz & Heritage Festival provides the biggest of challenges in live sound mixing and one of the very best jobs, according to the man who has it.

"I like to think of my mix as a 33-acre console with 14 inputs, playing to an audience of 75,000 people on our final Sunday, or 300,000 people over the ten-day stretch," says John "Klondike" Koehler, audio director of the jazz fest for the past seven years. "I try to provide good ambient mixing between stages so people get audio invitations to go to a specific site, and once they get there they're not distracted by the neighbors."

Koehler admits—no, boasts—that it's a feat to tune the noon-to-dusk, simultaneous presentations of rock 'n' roll stars, R&B legends, blues veterans, gospel choirs, zydeco groups, ragtime orchestras, Caribbean troupes, African griots, regional folklorists and children's acts so that all of their musics remain clear and don't compete for the attention of the audience. Each has distinct sound system requirements, preferences and stage styles. Among Koehler's tasks is sorting out sound companies from across the U.S., who bid for jobs, to work in the open-air venues and tents of the internationally acclaimed fest.

"We send out specifications to about 50 companies and about 30 respond," explains Koehler, whose Klondike Sound Company is based in Wendell, Maine. "From that we pick ten. The competition is keen 'cause we've got a world-class festival

with world-class talent, and that makes for a very good opportunity to showcase systems to many artists the companies would like to work with.

"Companies who bid are asked to submit equipment lists and draw a sketch of their speaker design, showing how they're going to stack and splay to meet a certain acoustical spec," Koehler explains, touring the unusually empty Fair Grounds on a day between the fest's two weekends.

"We give sound companies an audience area—say 200 feet wide by 400 deep, with an SPL rating of about 85 at the rear of the crowd—and ask them to come up with a plan to meet the needs of everyone in that area without being painfully loud down front," he continues. "There are centerfill and sidefill suggestions. In the tents we specify 220 degrees of coverage from downstage center. Speakers have to be flown on trees or tresses of some type, and we specify the number of inputs, monitor mixes, patchable gates and compressors

and types of effects based on the kinds of acts we've seen at the particular stage."

The Fair Grounds Race Track is comprised of 14 separate stages. "We have two stages configured for national acts, with audiences of up to 20,000 people," says Koehler. "Those are 32-input stages with onstage mixes of 24 or 32 by 8 with drumfill and sidefill. Then there are three other stages configured for audiences of 2,000 to 5,000; those are 24-input stages with onstage mixing as well.

"Then there are four aluminum frame tents with onstage mixing, although many of the contractors bring their own. That includes the gospel tent, the jazz tent, the Economy Hall Dixieland tent and Lagniappe, which means 'something extra' in New Orleans vernacular. The Music Heritage tent features piano solos and lectures, and finally there are three performance areas with very small systems."

Rather than thinking in terms of equipment tonnage, Koehler and Don Sydney,

the Fair Grounds online producer, rate the job's vastness by the number of people working sound.

"There's something like 44 technicians for all the stages combined. That's sound crews, not including the 72 stage managers and stage hands I hire," says Sydney. "It's about 125 people after you count everybody else involved in music production."

Koehler adds, "It's between 60 and 70 performances each day of the six days of the fair. The nighttime concerts are another story, but over two weekends between 360 and 420 distinct concerts are produced, without soundchecks but with extremely fast set changes. We take pride that you can often set your watch to the start times of each act. In fact, we were ready to start Santana, with 64 inputs and 12 mixes onstage, five minutes early. With careful programming and a lot of advance work and attention to detail, we can execute on that level."

When the fest's in full swing, the Fair Grounds is a swirling circus of sensations and a maze designed, among other purposes, to baffle sound.

"I have a lot of ways of aiming stages: putting up blocks in the form of beer trucks, Ozone water trucks, Portalets, sound company semis; the tents themselves help baffle as well," Koehler says. "But it's the actual aiming of the stages and the focusing of the systems into particular patterns that allow us to keep sounds tight."

The Fair Grounds, fronting on Gentilly Boulevard, is in a middle-class residential neighborhood that's jammed with parked cars and city tow trucks on fest days. "We try to aim the stages whenever possible into audience areas that are backed by a parking lot or a neighborhood," Koehler says, "rather than more stages. Stages that are aimed at each other have to be a certain distance apart, so that the 85 dB at the edge of one audience area doesn't overlap with the stage they're facing.

"We mix in mono, generally," he continues. "There are a few stereo systems; if artists rely on stereo effects, we'll try to accommodate them. But we're into good pattern control, very good fidelity and focusing the systems carefully. We have a prevailing wind direction I always try to work with; occasionally it comes from the other direction and the plan has to be changed.

"I can give you a little cameo on each system," Koehler offers, wheeling his vehicle to the eastern end of the long field. One side of this area rises toward the racetrack's close turn; it's bound on the other by a paved walkway.

"Stage 1 belongs to Quickbeam, from Albuquerque, N.M., for the fourth year," he continues. "When there's an opportunity to make musical history, like Bonnie Raitt coming to sing with Jimmy Buffett or Allen Toussaint or John Hiatt, they have the extra inputs available, and she's on at the snap of your fingers.

"Our house mixes are all done from fixed positions 85 to 100 feet out from the stacks," Koehler explains, pointing to a rickety covered platform in the grass, "usually on-axis with one stack and sometimes in the center. Each sound company is given a sound pressure level meter with an assigned speed limit—they're told not to mix beyond that level. At the larger stages it's around 105; in the smaller ones, sometimes in the tents like Economy Hall, it's 85 or 90. This keeps the levels appropriate to the types of music being played, and also helps me control leakage between sites.

"Stage 2," he says, rounding a fenced-off pond and crossing the infield's entrance path, "is being run this year by Propaganda Productions Ltd.," from Harahan, La. "Last year Propaganda was a new company, at stage 4. They walked their audience area a lot, to see if they could possibly accommodate the crowd better by twisting the axis of a box. I try to impress on the sound companies to mix to the size of their audience, not to the acreage they've been given. If the crowd shrinks, their output level should also come back. That creates a little more intimacy and helps eliminate leakage. Propaganda's been very sensitive to that.

"Our choices are based on a firm's festival experience, not necessarily with us—their price, quality of their equipment and integrity of their design. That is, how well

they feel they can tackle this, and whether their speaker array fits the geometry of the site. We're not interested in companies that have million-dollar inventories; we're interested in people who have the best interests of the festival at heart. They need to have a strong sense of altruism. They'll have to work extra hours, be prepared for surprises, be able to adapt to rapidly changing weather conditions and stage plots, and be able to *work with us*."

Koehler emphasizes, "It's a custom-built festival, and it gets tuned up as the day goes on. A lot of things change, not just weather or crowd size or a few inputs. We're showcasing the musical quality that earned an artist the privilege of appearing at this festival. This is a music festival, not a hardware convention."

He pulls up at the gospel tent, run by Sound Services of Little Rock, Ark. "We like to play all the tents on their long wall, to have the most number of front row seats and the shortest throw to the furthest person. But due to the topography of the ground here, we had to put the stage at the far end. We're fortunate to have a sound company whose cabinets are adaptable to a long-throw, rather than an in-the-half-round, medium-throw situation.

TOUR PROFILES: FESTIVALS

**"We mix in mono, generally. There are a few stereo systems; if artists rely on stereo effects, we'll try to accommodate them. But we're into good pattern control, very good fidelity and focusing the systems carefully."
—John "Klondike" Koehler**

"Gospel is difficult music to mix. You've got 70- to 100-voice choirs, plus rhythm sections and solo vocalists down front. They parade one choir on as the next one's going off—there's absolutely no time between them. And it's hard to get a good choir sound and a good band sound in the same mix. We're using PCMs over the choir risers, and Sound Services has a warm, all-cone system that doesn't give the choirs that blaring, compression-driver-on-a-horn quality that can ruin a gospel performance.

"Stage 3, where we've scheduled Santana, Roy Orbison and Robert Cray, is the biggest stage," Koehler continues. "We've got about 500 feet of throw here to the rear of house left, and it's approximately 300 feet wide. This is the first stage we've had to power by a generator, because of the amps' requirements. That's an Agreco Hush-powered generator out there, which is 200 amps a leg, three-phase, a good 50 percent of which is used on average by the sound system. This company is Bernard Brown Inc., out of Dallas. Bernard's been around the fest for five years or more.

"Here's the jazz tent, where the cutting edge is: the Marsalises, Harry Connick Jr., Charles Lloyd. Sound Chek Music, from Metairie, just outside of New Orleans, has been with us about five years.

"Bernard Productions, from Avondale, La., is handling the Lagniappe tent. And the last one is stage 4, run by Gemini Concert Systems in West Monroe, La.

"The bigger bands tend to bring in their own house engineers and often monitor engineers, too. But that's only about 10 percent of the acts in the fest, so our guys have the major responsibility to get into the groove—and quickly!

"I guess I got prepared for this job by being exposed to lots of different types of music, working outdoors with audio, and understanding the behavior of sound waves," Koehler continues. "In the 12 years I've worked here, I've gained a deeper appreciation for the music. And I hope I've sharpened my ability to coach the sound companies into making the whole thing happen as a macro mix.

"The only problems we've ever had were due to rain. When a stage gets wet we shut it down, then we go through major calisthenics to get it dry and back up on the air as soon as possible. Our chief electrician, Eddie Lambert, and his crew are phenomenal at keeping the Fair Grounds safe with an enormous electrical installation and distribution system.

"Ken Kennard does most of the scaffolding and the roofs; he's an incredible rigger and manages to keep us dry as long as the rain goes straight down and not sideways. Garnett Harden, who's head of the construction crew, does all the board roads, planking on the stage, ramps backstage, panels to put consoles on—he's our 'hit-and-run, one-man carpentry team.' These guys are simply indispensable.

"It's a proving ground for a lot of sound companies. It's a boot camp for most of us because it's the first big fest of the season. You know, there aren't many bigger, more complicated festivals than this one," concludes Koehler.

His pride is justified, and the proof of his success is that the festival's enormous sonic complications aren't obvious to audiences. And the Fair Grounds crowd keeps swelling.

Both Atlantic and Flying Fish Records have released live albums from the New Orleans Jazz & Heritage Festival; in 1988 Ken Ehrlich Productions created *Best of the Fest*, a television version hosted by Herbie Hancock. But nothing compares to a spring weekend in New Orleans: the fabulously costumed performers, the spicy aromas and flavors, the pulsating collage of sounds you mix for yourself at the Fair Grounds. For lovers of American popular music, one exposure to the macro mix at the Fair Grounds is reason enough to come back.

Montreux Jazz Festival

**BY
DAVID
SCHWARTZ**

SUMMER MUSIC FESTIVALS IN WESTERN Europe are nearly as common as county fairs in the States. In Switzerland alone, large musicfests seem to fill every valley and population center during the month of July. Among the most enduring of these events, as well as the most musically varied and technically ambitious, is the Montreux Jazz Festival on the eastern edge of Lake Geneva.

This 16-day, three-stage event, which frequently runs well into the wee morning hours, is the ongoing brainchild of one-time aspiring chef, and more recently WEA International managing director, Claude Nobs. The fiftysomething impresario, who in 1964 booked the Rolling Stones into Montreux for their first performance outside of Great Britain, has sought to bring the best music to the Montreux Festival with a fervor reflected in his lifelong compulsion for jazz and record collecting (more than 25,000 LPs).

This year's festival was co-produced by Quincy Jones and was given a new name: the Montreux Jazz & World Music Festival. Headliners covered the gamut of the world's record charts, with each evening loosely held together by a musical theme.

Western Night grouped Emmylou Harris, Glen Frey and Mark O'Connor; Blues Night featured Buddy Guy, the Blues Brothers band and Eddie Floyd; Gospel Night teamed Andre Crouch, Gladys Knight and Tremaine Hawkins with the Atlanta Super Choir. Rock acts Simply Red, Eric Clapton and Ringo & Friends each carried their own evenings and usu-

ally finished before midnight, unlike the more typical 2 a.m. rave-up jams of the multi-artist groupings. And there were even jazz performances here and there from artists such as local favorite Rachel Farrel, Randy Crawford and the VSOP-ish quintet of Herbie Hancock, Wayne Shorter, Tony Williams, Ron Carter and Wallace Roney Jr.

Performing artists at this festival are treated to one of the world's most enthusiastic audiences, partly due to the intimacy of the 2,500-seat headliner room at Montreux's Casino (immortalized in Deep Purple's "Smoke on the Water" after burning down in 1971 during a Frank Zappa concert). The audience also benefits from a tremendous technical effort to optimize sound, lighting and video support. Described by crew members as a high-tech summer camp, the MJF is a fortress of production capabilities in remote recording, digital multitrack in-house recording facilities, high-definition video recording, live radio and television broadcast, three-camera archiving and state-of-the-art live sound reinforcement, all coordinated with Swiss precision.

It takes four weeks for the festival support staff to set up, run the show and move out. Hyperson Sonorization, Switzerland's local Meyer Sound dealer, provides the sound equipment to augment the house system in cooperation with Best Audio, a French company. A British production crew headed by Fraser Kennedy has been coordinating the technical aspects of the event for a number of years,

The Montreux stage

with chief mixer Chris Ridgeway running the sound booth and mixing all artists who do not bring their own mixer.

Providing sound to the main performing room is no small chore, as the room is shaped more or less like a three-leaf clover with the stage at the top of the stem. In order to provide even coverage to the audience, the house sound is oriented as three separate stereo systems, each feeding a section of the cloverleaf.

"The extreme upstage positions were filled in with MSL-3s," says Meyer Sound's Mark Johnson, "and this year we wanted to include DS-2 loudspeakers for that mid-bass chest thump. If we were going to hang them individually like we did in previous years, it would have gotten very unwieldy. So we were able to get Andrew Martin to supply his ATM flying rigs, which made it easy to get the clusters of three together

and suspended from one point. We had six hanging points, one stage right rear for a left channel, two points stage right front for right channel to the right audience area and left channel to the front of the house, and the reverse on the other side. Actually, we also used some UPAs for front fill because of the size and positioning of the main system. So that really made for four stereo systems to the house. We added little UPM systems on delays in mono to cover overflow areas and the Gallery, which was the balcony area."

The main house console used by most artists is a 40-channel Midas XL-3, and the signal from the board goes into what Johnson calls a "scratchpad EQ, which consisted of a [Meyer] CP-10 parametric and a Klark-Teknik graphic." The system's performance is monitored with Meyer's Source Independent Measurement (SIM) system, which compares the output of the console with that of the loudspeakers, allowing the system to be tuned with the music as the test signal, even when the audience is present.

"We also had one more CP-10 combined with a BSS 820 digital delay for each stereo channel of the system, because we delayed everything back to the stage," he continues. "During our original SIMing of the system, we determined the position of the loudest acoustic source onstage. We wanted to know without the benefit of a P.A. what was going to generate the loudest noise: probably a drum kit. So in that small room, if you have a drum that may have as much acoustic output as the P.A., you want the two sound sources time-coherent, which necessitated a delay of 20 milliseconds or so on all of the main reinforcement systems.

"This type of delay system is a practice that started being used on theatrical productions, and is now becoming more common in popular music," Johnson adds. "It's quite a nice effect. I likened the resulting sound to sitting in the living room listening to your hi-fi. But it was really powerful, obviously, with a total of ten MSL-3s and six DS-2s.

"As far as signal processing," Johnson says, "with 16 days of shows and sometimes four different artists per night, Chris wanted to have lots of processors to satisfy the variety of mixers who would be passing through the sound booth. The limiting/gating rack had some Drawmer gates, some dbx compressors and some BSS gates. The reverb rack had the standard Lexicon 480, a REV 5, PCM-70, a couple

Festival chief mixer Chris Ridgeway

of SPX90s, and everything came to a patch bay. The main goal was to make the whole thing as easy to adapt to as possible so that a mixer could walk in and there wouldn't be any surprises."

Getting a major arena artist such as Eric Clapton to play such a small venue has a lot to do with the ease of getting in and out of the show with a minimum of setup and the confidence that the sound and other support services will showcase the artist nicely. Little amenities, such as presenting band members with audiophile-quality cassettes of their performance as they leave, also make this event a class act.

Poised lakeside in one of the world's truly beautiful settings, the Montreux Festival is a high-priority tour stop for many international artists. Their obvious pleasure in appearing is a fitting complement to the adoring audience that stands there cheering for encores until 3 a.m., year after year.

Monsters In Moscow

"WE WERE ON TOUR IN EUROPE WITH THE Monsters of Rock—Queensryche, Metallica, AC/DC, The Black Crowes and occasionally Motley Crue," says dB Sound president Harry Witz. But before the tour reached its final stop, the wheels were set in motion to add one more date to the nine-week tour. Monsters production manager Jake Berry explains, "Management rang me up and said, 'What do you think about doing Moscow after the last show in Barcelona?' We didn't think it was a very good idea. A couple of days later they came back and said they really wanted to do it. Time-Warner was promoting it—it was a free show [for the audience] but they'd pay the expenses. So we said yes, it was feasible, provided that we took our own production and hopefully got a lot of help from the Russian military. I don't know whether we were wise or foolish, but we said, 'What the hell, let's go do it.' It was on."

BY DAVID (RUDY) TRUBITT

The search began for a venue capable of holding a crowd of up to a million. "We looked at an enormous airfield outside Moscow," Berry says. "Imagine trying to play a show at JFK or LAX. It was not quite that big, but the grass runway was over a mile long." Then, according to Berry, came the red tape. "We were going to play the airfield, then the square, then we didn't have permission to play the square, then we had permission to play the airfield, then we didn't. It went on and on."

In the meantime, plans had to be made. "We figured out a rough plan to try to cover up to a million people," says Witz, "which was quite a bit larger than what we'd been doing. There were limits to how much gear we could send and how much it was going to cost. We decided to put up seven delay towers (which would get their feeds via broadcast, rather than hard-wiring). We had 42 blocks onstage, plus four blocks on the center delay, and every other delay was six more blocks. [A block consisted of two Electro-Voice MT-4Hs, two MT-4Ls and three Crest 8001 amps.] We had a total of 80 blocks with 730,000 watts."

Planning for contingencies meant bringing everything themselves. Besides extra items like three daylight video screens, the tour carried its own food, catering, communications (a briefcase-sized satellite phone), work lights, barricades and plywood. Extra sound gear and generators were provided by SSE Hire (London), which did the Monsters tour in tandem with dB Sound, Rocksound (Hanover, Germany) and ALT (Estonia).

The next question was transportation. "The plan was to send two Russian Antanov 142 cargo planes to Barcelona," says Witz. "What ended up happening was that there was only one available, and it had to shuttle a couple of times. The first flight got 17 semis worth of gear onto it—that's how big the plane is. The second flight got six semis onto it."

"We loaded them in the Barcelona airport," says AC/DC-Metallica monitor engineer Paul Owen. "We drove four trucks on the front, loaded the rest of it and flew to

the gig. But because of the Russian customs, we had to take it off a case at a time, open it, and then take the case to the gig."

The crew arrived at the field with the first planeload of gear at 7 a.m. the day before the show. "We started setting up the delay towers, with little or no help from the Russians," says Witz. "If there was a forklift, one person drove it. When that person took a break, that forklift stopped working. Our crew started doing the work ourselves. One by one, we took cabinets out to the field. We put motors up and ran generators at each tower to hoist cabinets onto the decks. It was a lengthy process."

"During the middle of the day," Witz continues, "we got some Russian marines, who reluctantly helped us dig up some dirt to link sets of towers together for redundancy in case of a transmitter failure. By the time we got into the evening, we had not yet seen the main parts of the P.A.

system. We had cabinets, but we didn't have motor control, AC distro and none of the front of house. It got to be 8 p.m. and we were starting to get worried, because the [second] plane should have been back by then." It turned out that a truck wheel had broken in flight, and it took all night to remove the truck and clear customs. "The next truck we saw was at 5 o'clock on the morning of the show," says Witz. "We had been working since 7 a.m., coming up on 24 hours, when we finally got the gear, and didn't have any labor."

The traveling sound crew for the tour numbered ten, and representatives from the cooperating sound companies bolstered that number to 16. They proceeded to set up the system, accompanied by *a cappella* renditions of Metallica and AC/DC songs by a crowd whose numbers were approaching 100,000. The entire system was ready at noon, two hours before

159

Pantera's set

showtime, despite some frightening moments. Witz explains: "The Russian military showed up and proceeded to dump about 25,000 to 50,000 troops onto the field, who then formed a human barricade across the front, an inner loop of people that stretched from either side of the mix tower back to the stage, and another loop another 50 yards beyond the mix tower in a big square. There were sections of people separated by military. I can only personally speculate that they're used to controlling crowds that have a violent or hostile intent, not simply kids that are very excited about a show. The military are kids too, and they were standing face to face with people who were pushing and getting shoved—before you knew it there were clubs swinging.

"People were being kicked and beaten and carried off by the military. The crowd reacted violently by throwing bottles, and soon there were guys with helmets and crash shields out there. It was dangerous,

scary and chaotic. Then the military came up onto the mix riser so they could get a better vantage point, but they just drew fire [bottles tossed at the mix platform]. It was like sitting behind the target in a batting cage. Finally we got the military guys off the riser and had somebody translate [to the crowd] that we came here to put on a show for them and asked for their cooperation. From that point on, you could walk through the crowd with a pass, and it was like Moses parting the sea. We were able to get the whole thing off without a hitch."

Once the show was underway, it was almost business as usual, according to monitor mixer Paul Owen. "It was a straight format, because we'd been out for nine weeks doing the same bands every day (the gig included a Russian band followed by Pantera, The Black Crowes, Metallica and AC/DC). The overall thing was just another day for us. But it was a real weird vibe—you looked onto a field and saw so many thousand kids and then a huge, three-deep row of soldiers, another so many thousand kids and another row of soldiers. The delay towers looked like matchboxes in the distance, and past that you saw a convoy of trucks taking more troops around the other side, and troops beating kids for no reason—for just coming over the barrier. It was very strange."

It was also very large. "The field was huge," says Berry. "You could put a million and a half people in there and not notice. You know how big the Monsters of Rock stage was—it was like a fingernail in the middle of nowhere." Witz agrees: "From the mix tower, there were people as far as I could see. I don't know the official count, but there were between 500,000 and 750,000 people there. In retrospect, we might have tightened up our mix towers so that everybody got something a little more dense, but we were totally capable of covering a million people at heavy rock volume."

Then it was over. The crowds emptied out while the skies opened up. A rainstorm drenched everything, making the load-out and customs inspection that much more of an adventure. Once again, every case was inspected, loaded onto trucks and sealed. Part of the P.A. was heading to Australia with AC/DC, part to Oakland for A Day On The Green, with the rest returning to the companies who provided the extra equipment.

And how did the whole experience look after two weeks of hindsight? "Were we crazy to go?" asks Berry. "Yes. Would we go back again? Two days after the show you'd have gotten a negative response from everyone. But now? Yeah. Now we'd go. But it was a unique experience in more ways than one."

"I don't know whether we were wise or foolish, but we said 'What the hell, let's go do it.'" —production manager Jake Berry

Glossary

alignment

When using different speakers to reproduce segments of the frequency spectrum, it is important that the sounds from these individual components reach the listener at the same time. For example, even very short delays between sounds generated by a woofer and tweeter create audible anomalies, sometimes referred to as "time smearing." Careful physical positioning of devices within a loudspeaker enclosure, as well as precision delays and crossover networks, eliminates this potential problem; this process is often referred to as "alignment." (See *phase cancellation*.)

array

An array is a group of loudspeakers arranged to cover a wider arc than would be possible with a single cabinet. The term implies (but does not guarantee) that the cabinets are designed to be used in groups and will provide even coverage with a minimum of anomalies in areas of overlapping coverage. (See *phase cancellation*.)

cardioid microphone

A microphone with a directional pickup pattern that is most sensitive to sounds coming from the front and sides, while rejecting sounds coming from the rear. The pickup pattern is roughly heart-shaped when viewed from above, hence the name "cardioid."

center fill

Loudspeakers which are used to provide direct sound for audience members directly in front of the stage, who otherwise would be somewhat out of the coverage area of the main P.A. Also called *front fill*.

clipping

A distortion condition in which the top of a waveform is cut off ("clipped"). Usually caused when a signal overloads a stage of the device being driven.

cluster

A suspended group of loudspeakers. The term sometimes implies a speech-oriented system, but can also apply to theatrical and musical applications. (See *array*.)

compression driver

A specialized mid- or high-frequency speaker consisting of a small diaphragm and voice coil coupled to a large magnet structure. The unit is mounted to a horn, which acoustically matches the impedance of the driver to the impedance of the air and shapes the signal. Compression drivers tend to be expensive due to the precision tolerances required in their manufacture, but they deliver many times more sound pressure per watt of input power than traditional direct-radiating cone speakers. (See *horn*.)

compressor

A device that smoothes the level of an input signal by regulating its dynamic range. A compressor prevents the signal from rapidly exceeding or falling below a selected amplitude threshold. Beyond the threshold, the ratio of the signal's input level to output level (e.g., 2:1, 4:1 and so on) can be user-selected. Compression commonly is used to keep mic levels within an acceptable range. (See *limiter*.)

condenser microphone

A microphone that picks up sounds via an electrically charged, metallized diaphragm, which is separated from a conductive back plate by a thin layer of air. Sound waves striking the diaphragm cause a minuscule voltage change, which is increased by a tiny amplifier circuit within the mic body. Since power is required by both the microphone capsule and the amplifier, condenser microphones must have a power source, which can be a battery inside the mic body or "phantom" power from a mixing console or external power supply.

controller

In sound reinforcement, usually refers to an electronic device designed to operate with a specific loudspeaker enclosure to smooth and extend frequency response and protect the drivers from excessive power levels. The term *processor* is also used for devices of this sort.

crossover

A dividing network that splits a full-range signal into two or more frequency groups and routes them to feed the various components (e.g., woofers and tweeters) in a speaker system. Passive crossovers usually are built inside speaker cabinets, where they divide an amplifier's output signal for routing to different speaker combinations. Most professional sound systems use active crossovers, which divide a line-level output signal from a mixer or other sound source and route the resulting signals to individual amplifiers that drive different speaker components. (See *drive rack*.)

crossover slope

Audio filters (used in crossovers and equalizers) are often described by the rate at which sounds outside the selected band are attenuated. This "slope" is measures in decibels of attenuation per octave (an octave representing a doubling of frequency). A typical crossover slope is 12 or 24 dB/octave, although DSP-based digital crossovers offer much steeper slopes, such as 96 dB/octave. Note that the steepness of slopes on either side of a specific crossover band need not be the same. This is referred to as "asymmetrical crossover slopes." (See *digital signal processing*.)

cutoff frequency

The frequency point above or below which a filter strongly attenuates a signal. (Usually, the signal's output level at the cutoff frequency is 3 dB below its input level.) In a lowpass filter, a high cutoff frequency allows most of a sound through and generally produces a bright sound, while a low cutoff frequency blocks most of the sound and produces a muted or plain sound. (See *lowpass filter, highpass filter*.)

dB

Abbreviation for "decibel." See *decibel*.

dBm

A term expressing an electrical power level, referenced to 1 milliwatt (i.e., 0 dBm = 1 mW). Originally, dBm was used to express the power dissipated in telephone applications with 600-ohm impedances, but it is not necessarily referenced to a particular impedance.

dBu

A means of expressing voltage, referenced so that 0 dBu equals 0.775 volts, regardless of impedance. One mW of power is dissipated if 0.775 volts is applied to a 600-ohm load, so when the load impedance is 600 ohms, 0 dBu = 0 dBm.

dBV

A means of expressing voltage, referenced so that 0 dBV equals 1 volt RMS, regardless of impedance.

dBv

Synonymous with dBu but rarely used due to potential confusion with dBV. See *dBu*.

decibel (dB)

A unit of measure used to logarithmically express ratios of change in power or signal levels. Equal to one-tenth of a Bel (named for Alexander Graham Bell).

DI

Stands for "direct injection." Such devices, commonly referred to as "direct boxes", take an unbalanced signal (typically 1/4" phone connector) from an electronic instrument, such as an electric bass or an acoustic instrument with a pickup, and produce a low-impedance, balanced output signal, typically a 3-pin XLR connector.

digital signal processing (DSP)

A technique using computer technology to analyze and manipulate sound or other waveforms.

drive rack

A generic term referring to the audio equipment between a mixing console and power amplifiers, typically including crossovers, graphic equalizers, protection limiters and line amplifiers.

dynamic microphone

A transducer that relies on the law of induction, with an output proportional to the velocity of a moving element within a magnetic field. The most common type is the moving-coil microphone, which picks up sounds when sound waves strike a diaphragm attached to a coil of wire. When the coil moves within the magnetic structure of the microphone, it creates an output voltage. The process is exactly the reverse of the way a speaker operates. Moving-coil dynamic microphones tend to be extremely rugged, making them well-suited for most sound reinforcement applications. The other common type of dynamic microphone is the ribbon mic (see *ribbon mic*).

dynamic range

A ratio (expressed in decibels) of the difference between the softest and the loudest sounds that can be produced, reproduced or captured by a musical instrument or audio device.

dynamics processing

Audio equipment designed to automatically manipulate the amplitude of its output, based on the changing level of the signal at its input. Equipment in this category includes compressor/limiters, expanders and gates.

equalization

A circuit that allows the frequency-selective manipulation of a signal's amplitude. The simplest equalizers are shelving types, offering the ability to cut or boost gain above or below a given frequency. Circuits that allow tonal shaping in multiple frequency bands include graphic and parametric equalizers. Abbreviated "EQ." (See *graphic equalizer, parametric equalizer*.)

feedback

A condition where the output of a circuit recycles through its input. Acoustic feedback is a whine or howl that occurs in live audio situations when an amplified sound reenters a sound system through the same microphone (or pickup) that reproduced the original source, creating a loop. Feedback also can be used in signal processing; for example, part of a signal routed through a digital delay can be fed back into the delay to create a more complex effect. This is also called "regeneration."

filter

A device that attenuates or removes certain elements or data from an audio waveform. (See *lowpass filter, highpass filter*.)

FOH

An abbreviation for "front of house," referring to the audience's portion of a room and the location of the main mixing position.

frequency

The number of times a periodic waveform cycles or repeats over a period of time. See *hertz*.

front fill

See *center fill*.

gain

A ratio expressing the difference between the input and output power, level or current in a circuit.

gate

A device that opens or closes a pathway by stopping signals that fall below a user-defined level. Audio gates often are used to salvage noisy tape tracks and silence "dirty" sound systems: The gate stays closed—blocking residual low-level noise—until the audio signal's level exceeds a user-determined threshold; then the gate opens, allowing the sound to be heard. Gates also can be used to create effects, such as gated reverb. (See *dynamics processing*.)

gobo

A surface positioned to control the spread of sound. Originally developed for studio use, gobos are not uncommon in live sound. They are made from clear Plexiglas and are sometimes positioned around drum sets. (See *leakage*.)

graphic equalizer

A frequency-shaping device with multiple filter bands, typically operating at a fixed frequency and bandwidth.

ground loop

A condition occurring when several ground pathways exist between two devices, resulting in hum and increased noise.

headroom

The margin of safety (usually expressed in decibels) between nominal operating levels and a signal-overload condition.

hertz

A unit of measure of the frequency of a vibrating object, such as a guitar string, speaker cone or electrical signal. Equivalent to cycles per second, it is named for Heinrich Hertz and abbreviated "Hz."

high-pack

A cabinet containing high and midrange loudspeakers. Many sound reinforcement loudspeaker systems are designed as two cabinets, with identical external dimensions, one containing high and mids, the other lows. (See *low-pack*.)

highpass filter

A circuit designed to attenuate, or cut, frequencies that fall below some designated point, while allowing higher frequencies to pass unaffected.

horn

A device used to control the spread of sound from a transducer. This spread is often measured in terms of degrees, in both horizontal and vertical axes. Most commonly used with compression drivers, horns are manufactured to precise tolerances to accurately control sound. Some cone transducer loudspeakers also use horn loading as part of their enclosure design, to control the direction in which midrange (and sometimes lower) frequencies are radiated.

hypercardioid

A variation of the cardioid microphone pickup pattern. A hypercardioid microphone is most sensitive at the front and sides, while rejecting sounds entering 120° to the rear.

impedance

Measured in ohms, this is a way of expressing a circuit's opposition (resistance and reactance) to a signal or current attempting to pass through. The practical difference between impedance and resistance is that impedance changes as a function of frequency.

leakage

Leakage refers to other sounds from a stage which can be heard "leaking" into microphones which would ideally only pick up a single instrument. Loud guitars being picked up by a vocal mic is a common example of leakage.

limiter

A device that severely restricts the upper dynamic range of a signal, regulating the rate of increase of an input signal's amplitude to keep it from exceeding a predetermined threshold. Limiters are closely related to compressors but apply much higher compression ratios, usually in excess of 20:1.

long-throw

Refers to loudspeakers designed with narrowly focused coverage patterns, especially in high and midrange frequencies. Concentrating the available acoustic energy of a cabinet in a tight arc allows higher sound pressure levels to be achieved at longer distances. Cabinets which "throw" sound for longer distances are typically placed at the top of arrays and aimed at the far end of the audience. Cabinets of this type are sometimes referred to as *high-Q* enclosures.

low-pack

A cabinet containing bass-frequency loudspeakers. Many loudspeaker systems are designed as two cabinets, often with identical external dimensions, with one containing high and mids, the other lows. (See *high-pack*.)

lowpass filter

A circuit designed to attenuate frequencies that occur above some designated point while allowing lower frequencies to pass unaffected.

mute

A control that interrupts ("mutes") the flow of a signal. For example, a console with muting would allow the engineer to silence a noisy guitar track during a quiet introduction and activate it just before the guitar part begins. Some mixers offer the ability to store various combinations of channel muting, called mute groups. A few consoles can recall mute groups under automation control, often in response to MIDI or SMPTE time code.

omnidirectional microphone

A microphone that is equally sensitive to sounds coming from all directions. These mics have limited usefulness in sound reinforcement, as they tend to pick up extraneous sounds. (See *leakage*.)

parametric equalizer

A circuit designed for frequency-selective attenuation or boosting of a signal's amplitude, with independent controls for gain, center frequency and bandwidth (including continuously adjustable Q). A quasi-parametric EQ may provide full frequency and gain adjustment, but only two or three Q settings. Sweepable EQs have an adjustable (sweepable) center frequency, but operate on a fixed bandwidth. (See *Q, equalization*.)

phantom power

A method of powering condenser microphones by sending DC current (typically 9 to 52 volts) over the same mic cable that carries the audio signal. "Phantom" is derived from the fact that there is no visible power cord and the voltage is not perceptible in the audio path.

phase

The relative measurement of a period of time referenced to the start point of a cycle of a periodic waveform. In one complete period, a wave's polarity fluctuates 360° (180° positive and 180° negative). Absolute phase is a reference point in time within one cycle: Halfway through one period, the waveform's phase is 180°; at one-quarter of the waveform, the phase is 90°. Relative phase is an instantaneous ("snapshot") measure of the difference in time between two acoustic or electronic waveforms of the same shape and frequency. For example, if one waveform is one-quarter of the way through its cycle (90°, at its peak positive value) and the other is three-quarters of the way through its cycle (270°, at its greatest negative value), they are 180° out of phase with respect to each other. The two signals are "in phase" if their amplitudes are identical at the same point in their cycles.

phase cancellation

An attenuation of signal components resulting when out-of-phase waveforms are combined. When two waveforms are mixed, their harmonics are added. If the signals are out of phase with each other, the amplitudes of the harmonic components differ at various times (as determined by the phase relationship). If the added harmonics have the same polarity, the signal is reinforced at those frequencies. If harmonics with positive values are added to harmonics with negative values, the signal is attenuated (canceled) at those frequencies.

phase shift

A slight time difference between two similar waveforms, which puts them out of phase with respect to each other.

pink noise

A test signal composed of random noise that has been shaped to provide equal intensities of sound in each octave band. Pink noise is used for test signals because its spectral balance closely compensates for the frequency sensitivity of the human ear.

proximity effect

A boost in the low-frequency response of a directional microphone that occurs when the sound source is relatively close to the microphone. The phenomenon begins when the source is about two feet away from the mic capsule and becomes more noticeable as the subject gets closer to the mic. A singer can use the proximity effect as a means of adding fullness to a voice; however, the effect can also emphasize low-frequency noises such as breath sounds and popping consonants ("p" and "b" sounds).

Q

In filters, the ratio of a bandpass or band-reject filter's center frequency to its bandwidth. Thus, assuming a constant center frequency, Q is inversely proportional to bandwidth (i.e., higher Q values indicate a narrower bandwidth). For this reason, the term often is used to denote bandwidth. (See *parametric equalizer.*)

reverberation

The decaying residual signal that remains after a sound occurs, created by multiple reflections as the original sound wave bounces off walls and other barriers within a room or other acoustical environment. Modern effects processors use digital signal processing (DSP) techniques to simulate reverberant acoustical spaces.

ribbon microphone

A type of dynamic microphone that uses a thin metal ribbon placed between the poles of a magnet. Most ribbon mics are bidirectional, meaning they pick up sounds equally well from either side of the mic. (See *dynamic microphone*)

RMS

Abbreviation for Root-Mean-Square, a formula for describing the level of a signal. RMS is derived by squaring all the instantaneous voltages along a waveform, averaging the squared values and taking the square root of that number. When used to describe power amplifiers, RMS power (in watts) is considered a more useful measure of power output than "program" or "peak" power. (A power amp's performance depends on the nature of the input signal. "Peak" power ratings don't account for this, whereas RMS ratings, because they are derived from multiple points in a sine wave, more closely reflect the actual energy content of the input signal.) RMS also is used to measure input sensitivity (in volts) in a preamp or line amplifier.

roll-off filter

A circuit that attenuates a signal that is above (lowpass filter) or below (highpass filter) a specified frequency. For example, microphones frequently have a bass roll-off filter to remove wind noise and/or excessive breath pops. (See *lowpass filter, highpass filter.*)

shed

A partially enclosed outdoor amphitheater.

sidefills

Loudspeaker cabinets positioned on or above the sides of the stage, directed at the performers. They are typically used in conjunction with wedge monitors.

signal-to-noise (S/N) ratio

A ratio (in decibels) that expresses the difference between the level of a signal at a reference point in a circuit and the level of electrical noise at the same point.

solo

A feature on a mixing console that automatically routes one or more selected channels to the headphones without disturbing the main audio mix, allowing the engineer to check console channels while the concert is in progress. In-place solo is a function that permits the user to hear individual channels, but in the correct stereo perspective as defined by that channel's pan control.

SPL

Abbreviation for "sound pressure level," a means of expressing sound levels. Frequently used as a comparative measure of speaker efficiency or maximum system output.

subwoofers

Loudspeaker enclosures designed specifically to reproduce the lowest portion of the audible spectrum.

supercardioid microphone

A variation of the cardioid microphone that is most sensitive at the front, while rejecting sounds entering 150° to the rear.

TEF

TEF stands for Time Energy Frequency. The TEF analyzer, made by Techron, is a device which can make sound system measurements while largely ignoring the effects of the surrounding acoustical space. Additionally, a room's acoustical artifacts, such as predominant early reflections, can be accurately measured.

watt

A unit of measure of electrical power dissipation, formally defined as one joule (a unit of energy) per second, which is equal to the power absorbed by one ohm of resistance when one ampere of current is in the circuit. Electrical power, measured in watts, can derived in three ways: the voltage squared divided by the resistance (V^2/R), the current squared times the resistance (I^2R) or the product of the voltage and the current (VI). Named for James Watt, inventor of the steam engine and the speed governor.

white noise

A test signal comprised of random noise, providing constant energy at all frequencies (similar to the sound heard when an FM radio is set between stations).

Selected Sound
Reinforcement Companies

A-1 Audio Inc.
6322 DeLongpre Ave.
Hollywood, CA 90028-8191
(213) 465-1101

ATM Group
20960 Brant Ave.
Carson, CA 90810
(213) 639-8282

Audio Analysts U.S.A. Inc.
3286 N. El Paso St.
Colorado Springs, CO 80907
(719) 632-8855

Bernhard Brown Inc.
11311 Indian Trail
Dallas, TX 75229
(214) 241-4334

Burns Audio
10937 Pendleton St.
Sun Valley, CA 91352
(818) 768-2370

Carey Sound
216 N. Church St.
Greensboro, NC 27401
(919) 379-1943

Clair Brothers Audio Systems
P.O. Box 396
Lititz, PA 17543
(717) 665-4000

Concert Sound Consultants
P.O. Box 831
Julian, CA 92036
(619) 765-2220

Dallas Backup Inc.
12569 Perimeter Dr.
Dallas, TX 75228
(214) 686-4488

dB Sound Inc.
1219 Rand Rd.
Des Plaines, IL 60016-3402
(708) 299-0357

Delicate Productions Inc.
1390 Flynn Rd., Ste. A
Camarillo, CA 93012
(805) 388-1800

Eighth Day Sound
1305 W. 80th
Cleveland, OH 44102
(216) 961-2900

Electrotec Productions Inc.
6735 Eton Ave.
Canoga Park, CA 91303
(818) 888-8687

LD Systems Inc.
467 W. 38th St.
Houston, TX 77018
(713) 695-9400

Maryland Sound Industries
4900 Wetheredsville Rd.
Baltimore, MD 21207
(410) 448-1400

MD Systems
128 Space Park South Dr.
Nashvillle, TN 37211
(800) 637-6257

Morgan Sound Inc.
2004 196th St. SW, Ste. 2
Lynnwood, WA 98036-7004
(206) 771-7257

Pro Media
3563 San Pablo Dam Rd.
El Sobrante, CA 94803
(510) 222-0307

ProMix
111 Cedar St.
New Rochelle, NY 10801
(914) 633-3233

Proshow USA
6675 185th Ave. NE, Ste. 250
Redmond, WA 98052-5038
(206) 861-4484

Quickbeam Systems Inc.
3716 High St. NE
Albuquerque, NM 87107
(505) 345-9230

Rat Sound
11800 Sheldon St., Unit D
Sun Valley, CA 91352
(818) 504-2930

Schubert Systems Group
7325 Hinds Ave.
N. Hollywood, CA 91605
(818) 503-1234

Scorpio Sound Systems Inc.
56 Manley St.
West Bridgewater, MA 02379
(508) 584-0080

See Factor Industry Inc.
37-11 30th St.
Long Island City, NY 11101
(718) 784-4200

Showco Inc.
201 Regal Row
Dallas, TX 75247
(214) 630-1188

Sound Image
258 La Moree Rd.
San Marcos, CA 92069
(800) 962-9422

Sound on Stage
290 Industrial Way
Brisbane, CA 94005
(415) 468-2990

Sun Sound Audio Inc.
518 Pleasant St.
Northampton, MA 01060
(413) 586-3465

United Sound Associates Inc.
2112 W. Nob Hill Blvd.
Yakima, WA 98902
(509) 452-8686